For John
with l...
Frankie
January 1989

PLANNING AND POWER IN IRAN

Ebtehaj in the early 1960s

PLANNING AND POWER IN IRAN
EBTEHAJ AND ECONOMIC DEVELOPMENT UNDER THE SHAH

FRANCES BOSTOCK
AND
GEOFFREY JONES
London School of Economics

FRANK CASS

First published 1989 in Great Britain by
FRANK CASS AND COMPANY LIMITED
Gainsborough House, 11 Gainsborough Road,
London E11 1RS, England

and in the United States of America by
FRANK CASS AND COMPANY LIMITED
c/o Biblio Distribution Centre
81 Adams Drive, P.O. Box 327, Totowa, N.J. 07511

Copyright © 1989 Frances Bostock and Geoffrey Jones

British Library Cataloguing in Publication Data

Bostock, Frances
  Planning and power in Iran : Ebtehaj and
  economic development under the Shah.
  1. Iran. Economic planning. Political
  aspect, 1900–1979
  I. Title   II. Jones, Geoffrey
  388.955
  ISBN 0-7146-3338-0

Library of Congress Cataloging-in-Publication Data

Bostock, Frances.
  Planning and power in Iran : Ebtehaj and economic development
under the Shah / Frances Bostock and Geoffrey Jones.
    p.   cm.
  Bibliography: p
  Includes index.
  ISBN 0-7146-3338-0
  1. Iran—Economic conditions—1945–   2. Central planning—Iran.
3. Iran—History—Mohammad Reza Pahlavi, 1941–1979. 4. Iran–
–Politics and government—1941–1979. 5. Ebtehaj, A.H. (Abol
Hassan), 1899–   . I. Jones, Geoffrey.   II. Title.
  HC475.B67 1988
  330.955'053—dc19   88-23716
                                                                  CIP

All rights reserved. No part of this publication may be reproduced, stored in a retrieval system, or transmitted in any form, or by any means, electronic, mechanical, photocopying, recording, or otherwise, without the prior permission of Frank Cass and Company Limited.

Printed and bound in Great Britain by
A. Wheaton & Co. Ltd, Exeter

CONTENTS

List of Illustrations	vi
Foreword by Eugene Black	vii
Preface	ix
Introduction	1

PART ONE
Revolt Against the Old Order 1900–1936

Chapter 1:	Pride and Prejudice	11

PART TWO
Nationalism and Internationalism 1937–1953

Chapter 2:	The First Technocrat	27
Chapter 3:	Putting Iran on the Map	50
Chapter 4:	Challenging the British Bank	70

PART THREE
Planning Iran's Future

Chapter 5:	'Expectations Unlimited, Resources Limited'	87
Chapter 6:	Ebtehaj's Alternative Government?	111

PART FOUR
The Clash of Values

Chapter 7:	'More European than Iranian'?	147
Chapter 8:	The Private Citizen	169

PART FIVE
Planning and Power

Chapter 9:	Ebtehaj in Perspective	191
References		199
Bibliography		225
Index		233

LIST OF ILLUSTRATIONS

Mohammad Reza Shah and Abol Hassan Ebtehaj	*jacket*
Ebtehaj in the early 1960s	*frontispiece*
1. The Ebtehaj family in the early 1900s	10
2. The young Ebtehaj	21
3. Visit of Mohammad Reza Shah and Queen Fawzieh to the Bank Melli	36
4. Heads of delegations at Bretton Woods, 1944	60
5. Ebtehaj and Hossein Ala, 1955	83
6. The Shah with members of the government and Ebtehaj in 1957	110
7. Ebtehaj inspecting potential harbour sites in the Persian Gulf 1956/7	114
8. Ebtehaj on the train to Khuzestan, late 1950s	134
9. The Dez Dam	139
10. Ebtehaj being visited in the police hospital by his wife, Azar, in early 1962	164
11. Abol Hassan and Azar Ebtehaj in 1988	186

FOREWORD

This book is sure to become a major text for those seeking an understanding of the circumstances which led up to the Islamic Revolution in Iran at the end of the 1970s. It also contains powerful insights on the fateful course of relations between the West and Iran. However, and above all, it is a penetrating study of the life and times of one of the most significant Iranians in the post-second world war period: a man who, in different circumstances, might conceivably have saved the Shah his throne.

As president of the World Bank when Abol Hassan Ebtehaj was head of the Plan Organization in the 1950s, I had no hesitation in lending him the Bank's full support. Ebtehaj was, I believed, an outstanding pioneer of Third World development – a nationalist utterly committed to the promotion of his country's interests, but also a man prepared to work with international agencies to achieve this goal. His appointment to and management of the Plan Organization were of fundamental importance for the Bank in its dealings with Iran.

On a personal level, I have always held Abol Hassan Ebtehaj in high esteem, and my working relations with him were of the finest. It seems to me wholly characteristic of the man that he was prepared to talk openly and honestly to two independent historians, and I am delighted that his valuable services to his country have now been recorded.

Eugene Black   Southampton, New York
                                              June, 1988

PREFACE

This study of planning and development in Iran before the Islamic Revolution of 1979 has been written in full collaboration with the leading character portrayed, Abol Hassan Ebtehaj. He has given extensive interviews to the authors, and provided written memoranda on a wide variety of subjects. These materials will be made available for public consultation. The book is not an apologia for Mr Ebtehaj. We insisted, and he completely agreed, that we were to retain freedom of interpretation. Our book has benefited enormously from his collaboration, but the judgements expressed in it are our own.

The writing of modern Iranian history presents considerable difficulties in the wake of the Islamic Revolution. It proved impossible to undertake research on primary sources within Iran. We have consulted published Persian language sources, although the leading Iranian economists and historians have tended to publish in English over recent decades. More importantly, we have made extensive use of 'oral history' to compensate for deficiencies in primary Iranian documentation. This book rests heavily on interviews, not only with Mr Ebtehaj but also with other Iranian (as well as western) figures. The problems of faulty memories, retrospective justifications and so forth are well-known. Oral history is highly fallible when it comes to establishing dates. Nevertheless, we believe that interviews can provide unique insights into motivations and policies of the past, as well as illustrating the atmosphere of a particular period. In using interview material, we have frequently given substantial quotations which should enable readers to judge for themselves the weight to be given to the opinions expressed. We have not cited oral history quotations where written evidence suggests that the information is erroneous or misleading.

In interviewing Mr Ebtehaj, we were fortunate to be able to draw on the services of a professional oral historian, Christopher Cook, who conducted wide-ranging initial interviews with Mr Ebtehaj. We also drew extensively on the interview given by Dr Khodadad Farmanfarmaian to Habib Ladjevardi as part of the Iranian Oral History Project undertaken by Harvard University's Center for

Middle Eastern Studies in 1982. We are extremely grateful to Dr Farmanfarmaian for allowing us access to his copy of the transcript, and permission to quote from it.

We used a variety of archival sources in the West in writing this book. There are grave dangers in seeing Iran through foreign eyes but – as with the use of oral history – we believe the benefits outweigh the costs. We would like to thank the Hongkong Bank Group and the Bank of England for permission to use and cite their historical records. The British Public Record Office yielded much important information, and we would like to thank the Controller of H.M. Stationery Office for permission to quote previously unpublished crown copyright material. Many of our most valuable sources were found in the United States. The use of the Freedom of Information Act yielded a fruitful crop of documents about events in Iran in the 1950s and 1960s, many of which have not – at the time of writing – been made available in the National Archives in Washington. Unfortunately some of the documents released under the Act were not stamped with any file or access code, and this will make the checking of these when the Iranian files are eventually opened to scholars in the National Archives very difficult. The External Relations Department of the International Monetary Fund, Washington, kindly supplied us with the group photograph of heads of delegations at Bretton Woods; it has proved impossible, however, to trace the copyright. We are grateful to the Estate of the late Roloff Beny, and to the National Archives of Canada, for permission to reproduce Beny's photograph of the Dez Dam.

No special rules have been followed for transliteration of Persian words, except those of current common usage, general phonetics and, so far as possible, consistency: names, in particular, have been transcribed, where appropriate, according to the practice of the people concerned, and in the case of certain institutions – for example, the Bank Melli and Bank Rahni – anglicised. Diacriticals have been omitted.

As already implied, our greatest debt in writing this book is to Abol Hassan Ebtehaj himself. He greeted the initial suggestion with enthusiasm, made himself available for interview whenever necessary, was endlessly interested in all the information elicited from archival sources whether this reflected well or badly on him, allowed us access to his library and papers, and provided us with as much help as he could in our efforts to cross-check information. The contribution of Dr Azar Ebtehaj was also considerable. She not only agreed to be interviewed, but helped us to find suitable

PREFACE

photographs for inclusion.

Our special thanks are due to Alireza Arouzi, who is helping Mr Ebtehaj to write his memoirs in Persian, for his help and advice generally and with Persian language sources; Dr Khodadad Farmanfarmaian, who not only allowed us access to his Harvard interview but also talked to us at length; Dr Cyrus Ghani, who was a mine of information and suggestions; and Dr John Gurney and Professor Fred Halliday, who read the manuscript and made a number of useful comments.

We talked to and corresponded with a number of people who knew Abol Hassan Ebtehaj at various stages of his career. We should like to thank the following in particular for their help – Peter Avery, Aqa Khan Bakhtiar, Eugene Black, Dr Eprime Eshag, Dr Weldon Gibson, Manouchehr Kazemi, Jan Kruthoffer, Habib Ladjevardi, Dr Reza Moghaddam, Hector Prud'homme, Mehdi Samii, Robert Schott, Peter Wodtke, Sir Denis Wright, Colonel Gratian Yatsevitch.

Finally, our grateful thanks are due to our respective families for their unfailing encouragement and support at all times.

Frances Bostock	London
Geoffrey Jones	November 1987

INTRODUCTION

This book is a study of the origins of development planning in Iran, focusing on the career of a remarkable twentieth-century Iranian, Abol Hassan Ebtehaj. As Governor of Iran's Bank Melli – effectively the central bank – between 1942 and 1950, and head of the country's Plan Organisation between 1954 and 1959, he pioneered planning in his country, and, indeed, in the Third World. As a leading public figure, he was close to the Shah for two critical decades in the 1940s and 1950s, and a central influence on economic decision-making. And in a regime in which corruption appeared to be endemic, he became, as the *New York Times* observed in 1962, 'a symbol of incorruptibility'.[1]

Ebtehaj's life spans a period of enormous political, social and economic change within Iran. When he was born at the end of the nineteenth century Iran was a poor, backward and almost entirely isolated state. It was primarily an agricultural country, with more than three quarters of its population of some ten million consisting of nomadic tribes or existing in poor villages. Industrial activity was very limited. There were hardly any roads and the first proper railway was not to be constructed until the 1930s. The administration of government was rudimentary in the extreme. Tax and revenue collection was 'farmed' to the highest bidder. The country was subject to constant interference from the imperial powers, Russia and Britain, and seemed at times on the verge of disintegration.[2]

In the 1920s Iran began to change under the influence of Reza Khan, a former army colonel who staged a coup in 1921 and declared himself first shah of the Pahlavi dynasty in 1925. After re-asserting the authority of the central government, Reza Shah launched campaigns to modernise, industrialise and secularise his country. Reza Shah's son, Mohammad Reza Shah, continued these general policies. For a period in the 1960s and early 1970s, Iran was hailed in some western quarters as the Japan of the Middle East, as economic growth rates soared and an affluent – and very secular – middle-class emerged. However, the Revolution at the end of the 1970s, and subsequent establishment of the Islamic Republic, set Iran on another course.

Iran's recent history has been marked by apparently puzzling paradoxes. The process of intense westernisation which the country underwent under Reza Shah was accompanied by an equally intense xenophobia, expressed in terms of suspicion and resentment of foreigners and foreign influence. Westernisation and modernisation were accompanied, simultaneously and relatedly, by a fierce assertion of national spirit.[3] Iran's two major twentieth-century revolutions provided similar ambivalences. The Constitutional Revolution of 1905–9 saw the triumph, albeit shortlived, of a modern intelligentsia, inspired by such western notions as nationalism, liberalism and socialism, who drew up a predominantly secular constitution and hoped to model their society in the image of contemporary Europe. The 1979 Revolution, on the other hand, brought to power a traditional clergy inspired by the golden age of Islam, who drew up a thoroughly clerical constitution and denounced all western influence. Yet, ironically, the considerable socio-economic transformation undergone by Iran between these revolutions had served to swell the ranks of the intelligentsia and industrial proletariat and reduce the ranks of such traditional classes as the clergy.[4]

While the Constitutional Revolution had looked towards Europe for its inspiration, the 1979 Revolution turned its back on 'western' influences and ideals in favour of the precepts of Fundamentalist Islam. Iran was not unique in this sense. The establishment of an Islamic republic after the Revolution was part of a trend which saw the rise and spread of Fundamentalist Islam throughout the Middle East, and parts of Africa and Asia. Where Iran was unique, perhaps, was in the complete *volte face* this represented, and the speed and success with which it was implemented. Furthermore, the implicit contradictions of Iran's 1979 Revolution gave it a distinctive character in comparison with other Third World rebellions and coups of the 1970s for it took place in the context of rapid capitalist growth and political independence rather than in the more archaic conditions of revolt against old colonial regimes or pre-capitalist monarchies.[5] But the real novelty of Iran's Revolution lay in the paradox that it was both 'reactionary' – in its leadership and ideology – and 'modern' – in being the result of a massive urban protest movement. It was the first Third World revolution to take place exclusively in the cities, using such tactics as the mass demonstration and the political general strike more normally associated with

INTRODUCTION

conflict in the developed world. Yet it was also the first 'to be unequivocally religious, and so deeply hostile to ideas of progress'.[6]

Not only therefore has the twentieth century been one of dramatic change for Iran, but the process has been neither smooth nor painless. As well as such major social and political upheavals as the Constitutional and Islamic Revolutions and Reza Shah's modernisation programme, the country has long remained subject to foreign interference in its affairs – most dramatically during the First and Second World Wars and in the overthrow of Mossadeq (the Iranian Prime Minister responsible for carrying out the nationalisation of British oil interests in the early 1950s), but perhaps most insidiously in the pervasive Americanisation of the 1960s and 1970s. This, together with its often chaotic internal situation, helps to explain why Iran's periods of economic growth have alternated with periods of grave economic difficulty.

Few Asian, African or Latin American countries this century have found the path of economic and social development an easy one. Yet Iran's difficulties have been particularly acute for a country so blessed with natural resources. The discovery of oil in 1908, the first such discovery in the Middle East, presented Iran with unique opportunities. While many developing countries have had to battle against scarce resources and rapidly increasing populations, Iran has had no such difficulties. Although never sufficient for perceived needs, Iran's oil revenues poured into the coffers of government at a rate which many a developing country might have envied, expanding from £600,000 per annum in 1920 to £16 million in 1950 and £464 million in 1970.[7] At the same time population growth, which was under 1 per cent before the 1920s, was still under 3 per cent in 1970; there was no pressing shortage of arable land; there were other exploitable mineral resources apart from oil; and, although water was short, the rainfall of the country's two great mountain ranges – the Zagros in the west and the Alborz in the north – offered plenty of opportunity for expanding the supply.

Constraints on economic development in Iran focused not so much on scarcity of revenue and natural resources as on a variety of other factors – exogenous and endogenous. The country's geopolitical situation led after the Constitutional Revolution, during the World Wars, and in 1953, to political and military intervention in its affairs by the Great Powers, and in the 1960s and 1970s, when Iran became an integral part of American regional strategy in the Persian Gulf area, to a degree of western encouragement of military aggrandisement, which distorted the process of development.

Internally, the degree of Iran's backwardness relative to its financial resources — as characterised by such factors as illiteracy, low productivity of agriculture, inadequate communications, absence of institutional infrastructure, and a weak modern industrial sector — provided major constraints on economic development. There were other problems also. The nature of the state under the two Pahlavi shahs — Reza Shah's autocracy in the 1930s, and the increasingly dictatorial tendencies of Mohammad Reza Shah from the 1960s — interfered with the process of development. So also did the clash of values which existed between western notions of modernisation, development and planning, and a society which reflected, despite twentieth-century attempts at secularisation, the often quietist, oppositional and anti-structuralist nature of Twelver Shiism, the state religion of Iran. It was an individualistic society in which personal relations, personal influence and personal advantage were all important; a society which inclined towards authoritarianism on the one hand and conspiracy and schism on the other.[8]

Despite Iran's enormous natural endowment for development, therefore, there were equally great, and distinct, obstacles in its path. However, as oil revenues grew, greater political stability was established, and the need to bolster national independence became an overwhelming preoccupation, the country's central problem was increasingly seen as how it could best use its resources to promote economic development in a rational fashion which would bring benefits to all. It was a problem which became not only Ebtehaj's principal concern, but the focus of his crusading zeal.

The significance of Ebtehaj's career in twentieth-century Iranian history is threefold. First, he was a great nationalist. From the time of his appointment as Governor of the 'central' bank, the Bank Melli, Ebtehaj worked to reduce the influence of foreign business within Iran, to gain credibility for his country in international financial circles, and generally to raise its status in the world. He headed, for example, Iran's delegation to the International Monetary Conference at Bretton Woods in 1944. Ebtehaj offered an alternative model of nationalism to that of many twentieth-century Iranians, as symbolised most vividly perhaps by Mossadeq. For Ebtehaj was never simply anti-foreign: rather he sought to use foreigners for the benefit of Iran. Within some circles in Iran this attitude earned him — quite unjustly — a reputation as a foreign 'stooge'. At the same time, outside Iran, while ironically he was regarded by some as a rabid nationalist, he gained the respect of

INTRODUCTION

many who tended to criticise his countrymen in general. A British Foreign Office official described him in 1951 as 'by far the strongest and ablest of all Persians and perhaps indeed the ablest Government official in the Middle East'.[9] In the United States his reputation stood, if anything, even higher, and the State Department, like the Foreign Office, looked upon him as 'possibly the ablest banker and administrative executive in the Middle East'.[10]

Second, Ebtehaj was a builder of institutions. As inter-war Iran embarked on rapid modernisation under Reza Shah, competent administrators were in desperately short supply. Iran, like many Third World countries, faced a critical problem of how to construct an effective bureaucracy and institutional framework which could implement government policies. Ebtehaj in the 1940s and 1950s played a decisive role in creating the efficient institutions which were a vital prerequisite for sustained development. He was Iran's first technocrat.

Third, but most importantly, Ebtehaj was the pioneer of the idea of planned economic development in Iran. During the late 1930s, confronted by the inconsistencies and inefficiencies in the implementation of Reza Shah's industrialisation programme, Ebtehaj began to argue the case for a more rational approach to economic development. As Governor of the Bank Melli, he was the moving force behind the establishment of a planning organisation. Between 1954 and 1959, Ebtehaj ran the Plan Organisation, and launched – among many other projects – a massive regional development programme in Khuzestan province.

Ebtehaj's role here has been neglected by posterity. A recent study of Iran's economic planning system by Hossein Razavi and Firouz Vakil typically contains no mention of his name.[11] In part this neglect arises because of a widespread assumption that 'real' planning in Iran only began in the 1960s. According to Razavi and Vakil, the Third Development Plan launched in 1962 – three years after Ebtehaj left the Plan Organisation – 'was the first effort in the direction of comprehensive planning'.[12] 'Despite the initiation of planned development in the early post-Second World War period', a journalist writing in 1978 commented, 'the emergence of strategic objectives has been a recent phenomenon. Growth until the Fourth Five Year Plan was piecemeal.'[13] While not disputing that Iranian planning became more comprehensive and sophisticated over the years, we will argue that the 'Ebtehaj period' of planning has a significance far beyond that of a historical footnote.

If Ebtehaj as an individual has been forgotten by historians, the professional technocrats and planners of whom he was a forerunner have received considerable criticism for pursuing policies which led to the Islamic Revolution. This book is not yet another attempt to explain the causes of that Revolution. There is, however, a powerful strand of interpretation which needs to be considered because it argues that it was Mohammad Reza Shah's rush for modernisation and westernisation, implemented by his apolitical technocrats, which was responsible for the tensions which underlay the Revolution.[14] Ebtehaj is an obvious candidate for consideration as a pioneer westerniser and moderniser, and there has been, in this context, more explicit criticism of the specific policies favoured by Ebtehaj as 'yet another example of the by now almost bankrupt development strategy of the 1950s and 1960s with its undue emphasis upon maximal growth, industrialisation and foreign technical assistance at the expense of better income distribution, more balanced growth and greater self-reliance'.[15]

Throughout his career Ebtehaj was always a controversial figure. While some accused him of being a foreign 'stooge', the British bank in Iran, which he vigorously challenged in the late 1940s, was among others who believed that he was consumed by blind hatred of foreigners. His absolute conviction that he was right was regarded by detractors as a sign of personal ambition and an overwhelming egotism. Ebtehaj's honesty, and his determination that Iran's resources should be used rationally to promote development, led him into conflict with the political system he nominally served. The inevitable result, perhaps, was his forced resignation from the Plan Organisation in 1959, and his arrest and imprisonment in Iran two years later, soon after having delivered a paper in the United States implicitly criticising the 'corruption, graft [and] suppression of freedom' in his country.[16]

This book will ask three central questions about Ebtehaj's career. To begin with, where did his ideas and motivations come from? Ebtehaj was a man who made things happen, a man who created wealth for his country. But he did so in a way which was distinctly unusual for his time and place. In part his story bears comparison with the great entrepreneurs of the West, and yet his life has also to be set against the wider canvas of Iran's – and indeed the Third World's – struggle for development. Why does Ebtehaj stand out and apart from the beliefs and conventions of so many of his fellow Iranians?

Second, why was Ebtehaj able to achieve so much? Although the plans of the 1950s may seem primitive by later standards, it will be

INTRODUCTION

argued that they were nevertheless a major achievement given the many and varied obstacles they faced. To some extent Ebtehaj's achievements can be explained by the very distinctiveness which set him apart in Iran, but it will also be necessary to explore his relations with the Shah and the nature of decision making in the Pahlavi regime.

Finally, the question arises as to why Ebtehaj ultimately failed – for, after his dismissal from the Plan Organisation, Iran's vast oil revenues were increasingly diverted to support ever more wasteful schemes of military and imperial grandeur, and planning became subordinated to power. The issues here are complex. On some interpretations Ebtehaj was an individual aberration, out of tune with his time and place. Commentators, for example, have sometimes suggested that the whole notion of planned economic development was doomed in Iran's 'anti-planning' culture.[17] From the perspective of the free market policies fashionable in the late 1980s, on the other hand, the entire concept of development planning might be seen as inappropriate and likely to fail in the end. Or did Ebtehaj present, perhaps, a viable alternative to the course eventually taken by the Shah; an alternative which might possibly have prevented the Revolution?

Ebtehaj himself had no doubts about where the policies and practices pursued after his resignation would lead. He was appalled by the corruption and waste of the Shah's regime, and by the strong and continuous support given to the Shah by successive American governments who saw him as a bulwark against Communism. From his prison cell in 1961 he warned the United States' State Department that

> The situation in Iran today is explosive. This statement is not intended to impress or scare anybody. It is a naked reality. Let me go down on record as the man who gave the warning even though it may not be heeded.
>
> When the explosion comes the reaction against the US and the West will be unavoidable and uncontrollable. It will be equally damaging to Iran.
>
> I firmly believe this danger *can be avoided*. The present regime could not survive but for US financial, military, moral and political support, it has no other alternative to turn to. The US can remedy the past mistakes by dissociating itself from all the evils and in this way by gaining the sympathy and friendship of the *people* of Iran. This would not only be in the interest of the US. It is the surest and perhaps the only way to save Iran.[18]

Eighteen years later, the Islamic Revolution, and the subsequent capture of the American hostages, demonstrated just how prescient his diagnosis was.

This examination of the life and times of Abol Hassan Ebtehaj will, it is hoped, offer new insights into the origins of development planning in Iran by restoring the period of the late 1940s and 1950s to the debates about the effectiveness and strategies of Iranian planning. In the process the problems of modernisation and economic growth in that country will be explored – and important new evidence shed on what went wrong with the Pahlavi regime. More fundamentally, this is the story of a man who offered twentieth-century Iran an alternative – an alternative which has, for the moment, been spurned, but might yet provide a guideline for the future.

PART ONE
REVOLT AGAINST THE OLD ORDER
1900–1936

1. The Ebtehaj family in the early 1900s

1

PRIDE AND PREJUDICE

Where did Ebtehaj get the ideas and outlook which differentiated him so starkly from most of his Iranian contemporaries? The answer to such a question for any great political figure or entrepreneur is never easy, lying as it does in the complex interaction between family and cultural background and external circumstances. This chapter attempts to understand how Ebtehaj's views and character evolved by looking at his family background, and his first career as an employee of a British-owned bank in Iran. By 1936, when he left the British bank, he had still to make a great mark on his country's affairs, yet many of the skills and ideas which were to flourish in subsequent years were already in place.

Abol Hassan Ebtehaj was born in Rasht in northern Iran on 29 November 1899, the second child of Ebrahim, Ebtehaj ol-Molk, and his wife, Fatemeh Khanoum. The couple had five other children, two more sons and three daughters. Abol Hassan's father was a professional functionary and his mother belonged to a middle-ranked landowning family.

The young Ebtehaj grew up against a background of political and economic chaos. Iran was one of the handful of Asian countries – alongside Japan, China and Thailand – which had avoided occupation by the great European imperial powers during the nineteenth century. Yet by the time of Ebtehaj's birth the country's internal condition was desperately fragile. In May 1896 Naser al-Din Shah, Iran's ruler since 1848, had been assassinated by a Muslim fanatic. Thereafter the Qajar dynasty sank into decline. Mozaffar al-Din Shah, who succeeded his father, was more interested in religion, cats and his own failing health than in government and diplomacy. During his reign Iran's political system came close to collapse, and the country acquired its first foreign debt, although debt per capita remained tiny compared with such similar countries as Egypt. The last two Qajar shahs, Mohammad Ali Shah and Ahmad Shah, were even more ineffectual.

The Qajar shahs had seized power over a fragmented Iran in the 1790s. During the nineteenth century they had succeeded in restoring a measure of internal peace to the country, and had constructed the framework of a centralised state. But the shahs lacked both an effective standing army to enforce their decrees, and an adequate bureaucracy to collect taxes. They resorted to selling – or 'farming' – functions and jobs, a practice which led inevitably to corruption and inefficiency at every level of public life. There had been several attempts at reform under Naser al-Din Shah, but with little success, and when he died the state's finances were in chaos, and the administration was both venal and ramshackle.

The implications for Iran's national sovereignty were serious. Iran was uncomfortably placed between Russia, which during the nineteenth century had steadily expanded southwards in central Asia, and British India. The country found itself in the front line of Anglo-Russian diplomatic tension in the late nineteenth and early twentieth centuries.[1] In 1907 an Anglo-Russian Convention divided Iran into 'spheres of influence', with a Russian zone in the north, a British zone in the south-east, and a neutral zone in between. Business and politics were, as so often, mixed. The Great Powers encouraged their nationals to establish business enterprises in Iran, and especially to secure 'concessions' at knockdown prices from the impoverished shahs. In 1872 Baron Julius de Reuter, founder of Reuters News Agency, had been granted a concession which gave him enormous powers over Iran's resources.[2] Although this venture collapsed, other concessions were more fruitful. In particular, an oil concession given to William Knox D'Arcy in 1901 was to result in the birth of Iran's oil industry.

During the late nineteenth century there were signs of growing discontent in Iran at foreign political and economic encroachment. When a monopoly over the marketing and sale of tobacco was granted to a British concessionaire in 1890, a mass protest forced Naser al-Din Shah to cancel the concession.[3] Mozaffar al-Din Shah's policies caused further dissension. He positively courted unpopularity by negotiating large loans from the Russian government in 1900 and 1902, and from Britain in 1903, the proceeds of which were frittered away on the extravagances of court life and European trips rather than used for much-needed reforms of the administration. External events fuelled the groundswell of discontent against the Qajars. Russia's defeat by Japan in 1905 encouraged those who resented foreign intervention in Iran's affairs, while the Russian revolution of 1905 provided a powerful stimulus to liberals who dreamt of replacing Qajar despotism with democracy. At first, during 1905, agitation for reform centred on the need for a House of Justice, codification of the law, and other measures necessary for dealing with the manifest decay and disorder in the country's affairs. It was not long before this developed into demands for an elected assembly, or *Majles*. In July 1906 there was a massive public demonstration in Tehran when 14,000 people took sanctuary – or *bast* – in the grounds of the British Legation. In October elections for an assembly took place and on 30 December, Mozaffar al-Din Shah, himself terminally ill, signed a decree granting Iran a constitution.[4] The essentially western and secular ideas of nationalism, liberalism and socialism which were enshrined in the constitution had a profound effect on the new generation of young Iranians who grew up in their shadow.

Abol Hassan Ebtehaj was one such. But his own family background, and particularly the character of his father, had an equal influence. The Ebtehaj family were middle-class and comfortably off. Rasht was the capital of Gilan, one of Iran's richest agricultural provinces. It was the centre of Iran's ancient silk industry, and also a fertile rice and tobacco growing region. Ebtehaj ol-Molk had for many years been in charge of the Anzali customs under Fathallah Akbar Khan who, until the advent of the Belgian customs administration, had farmed the Gilan customs. Although not himself a landowner, Ebtehaj ol-Molk managed the estates of Fathallah Akbar Khan, who was Gilan's wealthiest landowner. A prominent constitutionalist, and subsequently an active politician – he held several cabinet positions, was Prime Minister for a short time in 1920, and held the title Sepahdar Azam – Fathallah Akbar Khan spent most of his time in Tehran, and, like many of Iran's great landowners, he had little interest in his estates and knew almost nothing about agriculture. Through his wife, Ebtehaj ol-Molk had also acquired family estates of his own to manage. Fatemeh Khanoum was joint heiress, with her sister, of her father's property, and inherited enough land to maintain her husband and family in reasonable style.

Ebtehaj ol-Molk was a remarkable man. Born in central Iran, he was a *mostoufi*, a member of a group well known for their knowledge of accountancy and for their written and literary skills. He was an expert in the ancient and increasingly rare form of accountancy notation known as *siaq*. Ebtehaj senior had a reputation throughout Gilan as an honest man, and this proved to be both a source of pride and a strong influence on the young Ebtehaj. But while his judgement was highly respected and his reputation was beyond reproach, he did not make himself popular. His standards of morality were high, and he could be harsh and uncompromising in his treatment of those who failed to measure up. His son followed in his footsteps. The pride, self-confidence, stubborn character and independence of mind which were to be such hallmarks of Abol Hassan's life and career were a direct inheritance from Ebtehaj ol-Molk, as was the moral rectitude which was to make him so impatient of the failings of his fellow countrymen. The young man admired his father greatly, and although he saw little of him once he started his formal education, he gained in childhood a lasting impression of his father's upright character and strong regard for the truth.

Both Abol Hassan and his elder brother Gholam Hossein were educated abroad, first in Paris and then in Beirut. While it was not unusual in the late nineteenth and early twentieth centuries for sons of aristocratic Persian families to be educated overseas – usually in France since French tended to be the second language of the Court and of intellectuals – it was uncommon for a middle-class functionary like Ebtehaj ol-Molk to elect to educate two of his sons in this way. He was, however, fully aware of the benefits of such an education, and his wife's estates made it financially possible for him to follow his inclination. Abol Hassan was just eleven years old, and his elder brother Gholam Hossein nearly fourteen, when, in early 1911, they were sent to Paris to attend the Lycée Montaigne near the Luxembourg Gardens. Although they were at first understandably homesick and miserable – not only because of being parted from their family, but also because neither could speak a word of French – it was not long before the two boys were happily settled, and the language barrier was rapidly overcome. In the event, Abol Hassan and Gholam Hossein were in Paris for only two years. Their father heard about the English-language Syrian-Protestant College in Beirut, and, in 1913, sent his sons there to finish their schooling. They had, once again, to learn a new foreign tongue, but both boys were adept linguists. The fluent French and English Abol Hassan learnt as a schoolboy in Paris and Beirut were to stand him in good stead in the years ahead.

The Ebtehaj brothers were at home in Rasht, enjoying their long summer vacation, when the First World War broke out in August 1914. Despite their long years of rivalry in Iran, Britain and Russia were now allies in a common struggle against Germany and the Ottoman Empire, a struggle, moreover, which encompassed the Middle East. The War prevented the Ebtehaj boys from returning to Beirut. Gholam Hossein was in any case of an age to leave school. Abol Hassan was not and at first he was enrolled at the American School in Rasht. In 1915, however, he was sent to Tehran to finish his education. Additional Russian troops had landed at Anzali, Gilan's port on the Caspian Sea, in May, to reinforce those already in occupation, and with a pro-German government in power in Tehran, the province became a potential theatre of war, occupied by the Russians and under threat from possible German or Ottoman invasion. Ebtehaj ol-Molk decided that his young son would be better off away from Rasht. He arranged for Abol Hassan to have private tuition in Tehran, and to live *en pension* with two American ladies, with whom he remained until 1918.

Young Ebtehaj's upbringing and education had been more than a little eclectic, and this probably helped to explain his early interest in books, world affairs, and, especially, accountancy. He inherited a fascination for, and facility with, figures that had led to his father teaching him the *siaq* notation. As a quite young child he continually practised these skills, playing the game of keeping the accounts of the household servants and acting as banker for them. While still a schoolboy, he ordered for himself a set of the *Encyclopaedia Britannica*, complete with bookcase, reading this and any other books he could lay his hands on avidly. During the War, aged a mere 16 or 17 years, he started to correspond with the English newspaper, *The Morning Post*, supplying the editor with items of topical interest from Tehran for publication. He was also a regular contributor at this time to a leading Tehran newspaper, *Iran*, writing a short column entitled '*Aya Midanid*' ('Do You Know?'), the content of which ranged from comment on people and events to news of recent inventions and discoveries. He kept abreast of world affairs by reading the English newspapers, as well as magazines such as the *Illustrated London News*, and by displaying an intense interest in what was going on. Nearly sixty years later, for instance, he could still recollect his enormous excitement at hearing from his violin professor news of the October Revolution in Russia – 'I was in the street in Tehran on a bicycle when he stopped me, this professor, . . . and he gave me news of the revolution . . . and I was so thrilled . . . so excited.'[5]

Given Ebtehaj's independent mind and consuming curiosity, it would be surprising if he had not been affected by the intellectual atmosphere of Tehran at the time, and the Bolshevik Revolution in 1917 gave a considerable boost to Iran's young nationalists. In 1914 their own constitutional movement had appeared to be moribund, and many of the intellectuals were in exile or had gone to ground. The second elected *Majles* had been dissolved at the end of 1911 as a result of Russian pressure, and successive governments since then had been dominated by Russian and British intervention. Ironically, however, the outbreak of the First World War breathed new life into the radicals and nationalists. General elections were held for a new assembly, and the third *Majles* provided a public platform for them. The *Majles* resisted British and Russian pressure to declare war against Germany and the Ottoman Empire. In Gilan a nationalist guerrilla movement came into being and started to harass the Russians. Called the Committee of Islamic Unity, but popularly known as the *Jangalis* (literally, 'jungle dwellers'), the movement was under the leadership of a Rashti, Mirza Kuchek Khan. Meanwhile, intellectual opinion in Tehran was also formed by such influential periodicals as the weekly, *Kaveh*, published in Germany by a group of radical exiles, which focused on the need for national independence and internal reforms. It printed articles not only on such subjects as the history of the constitutional movement in Iran, but also the need to follow the western experience of separating religion from politics and introducing scientific rational knowledge into public education.[6] These were just the sort of ideas to appeal to the young Ebtehaj, and influence the development of his own brand of nationalism.

Ebtehaj returned to Rasht in 1918, having completed his formal education and in search of a job. The latter was no easy task. Northern Iran was in a state of ferment as a result of the overthrow of the Tsar and the subsequent Bolshevik revolution. Russia appeared to have turned away from the struggle for power in Iran, leaving Britain as the focus of Iranian nationalist resentment. Moreover, the disintegration and evacuation of the Russian forces who had dominated Iran's northern provinces for a decade had left a potentially dangerous vacuum. At the beginning of 1918 a small British military mission, under the leadership of Major General L.C. Dunsterville, was sent to Iran to do something about the situation. Dunsterville's ultimate destination was Baku and his task was to organise resistance in Transcaucasia against the possibility of a German and Ottoman attack on India. For some months his expeditionary force was held up in Gilan by the *Jangalis*, who were not only rapidly achieving fame as the 'Robin Hoods of the Caspian Marches'[7] but were also being used by both German and Ottoman agents and the Bolsheviks to stir up trouble in the region. However, by mid-1918, and with the aid of White Russian partisans, Dunsterville succeeded in overcoming *Jangali* resistance and occupying Rasht.

Dunsterville's expeditionary force, nicknamed 'Dunsterforce', made Rasht its base for the Transcaucasian adventure – a circumstance which proved particularly useful for the Ebtehaj family. They were able to rent one of their two interconnecting houses to Dunsterforce as its headquarters, and living in close proximity with the British soldiers gave both Gholam Hossein and Abol Hassan the opportunity of working for them as interpreters. Gholam Hossein's facility with the Russian language as well as English made him especially useful, and he was employed by Dunsterforce from the start. Abol Hassan was very envious, and was determined to learn Russian himself as soon as possible. Meanwhile he used to visit the British military police regularly and eventually they offered him a job at what seemed to him a princely salary – 700 *krans* a month (about £25).[8] He accepted immediately. As soon as he had acquired a reasonable facility with the Russian language, however, he joined Dunsterforce as interpreter to a detachment which had been detailed to go to Bandar-e Gaz, a small south-east Caspian port in the province of Gorgan. He spent about six months with them there, living with an Armenian family and polishing up his Russian. On his return to Rasht, he was offered what he thought of as his first proper job on his own, as assistant to the newly appointed governor of Anzali. However, the situation in Gilan was too volatile to permit of any permanent employment, and in 1919 he returned to Rasht.

By the time Germany and the Ottoman Empire collapsed in the autumn of 1918, British forces were established throughout Iran, and were also based in the south Caucasus where they were supporting the anti-Bolshevik local governments. The authority of the Tehran government was minimal, and the considerable provincial unrest and disorder throughout Iran was kept in check only by the presence of the British military. In the north the situation was particularly bad. Famine and disease were rampant as a result of the ravages of invasion and counter-invasion, and during 1919 the Bolsheviks attempted to profit from the disorder by encouraging the *Jangalis* in Gilan to become a separatist movement, demanding administrative autonomy. A provincial Communist party was formed.

The Ebtehaj family were thoroughly alarmed by the turn of events in Gilan; the escalating troubles with the *Jangalis* and the rumours of a Bolshevik advance convinced them of the necessity of maintaining as low a profile as possible. As soon as Abol Hassan returned to Rasht it was decided that the whole family should leave town for a safe refuge in the country. They fled on foot to one of Fatemeh Khanoum's estates, to a small village near Shaft in which Ebtehaj ol-Molk had built a small bungalow. It proved to be a disastrous move. Their presence in the neighbourhood of Shaft became known to the local *Jangali* rebels, and one night armed men came to the house to find Ebtehaj ol-Molk. They alleged that he was wanted for questioning and took him away. A few days later, the family heard that he had been murdered. The irony was that his death was as much a matter of personal vengeance in settlement of an old score as a political assassination. Moreover, it resulted from Ebtehaj ol-Molk's loyalty to his employer, Sepahdar Azam, and assiduous attention to his affairs. His murderer had been a villager on one of Sepahdar Azam's estates and had owed Sepahdar Azam a considerable sum of money. He had defaulted on his debt, which had brought him to the attention of Ebtehaj ol-Molk, and had been handled with the latter's customary severity in such cases. Subsequently the debtor had joined the *Jangalis* and become a leader of the group which operated in the area of Shaft.[9]

Fatemeh Khanoum and her family fled back to Rasht. They were still there in May 1920 when they heard that the Bolsheviks were in Anzali and were advancing towards Rasht. Fatemeh was filled with concern for her two eldest sons. Because the family was believed to be Anglophile, the two elder boys were already in some danger. Indeed, the *Jangalis* were known to be looking for Gholam Hossein, and Fatemeh had had to hide him when the house was searched. She urged both boys to flee. They left immediately for Tehran, on foot and empty-handed, escorted by one servant. They were not, however, the only refugees. The road was filled with people escaping the Bolshevik advance. They had taken no food with them, and went hungry as all the teahouses on the Qazvin road had been closed and evacuated. Fortunately, halfway between Rasht and Qazvin they managed to hire mules to take them over the mountains to Qazvin, and from there the journey to Tehran did not take long.

With many others, the Ebtehaj boys arrived in Tehran as penniless refugees. They were luckier than most, however, because their father's erstwhile employer, Sepahdar Azam, was Prime Minister and offered them both work in government. Gholam Hossein was given a job in the Prime Minister's own office, while Abol Hassan was sent to the Ministry of War. Gholam Hossein soon settled into his new career, but Abol Hassan remained only as long as it took him to organise his own life. Not only did he find nothing specific to do in his job at the Ministry, but he thoroughly disliked the idea of being a civil servant and thus, in the context of Iran, in some sense beholden. Also, though he loved politics in general, he had little time or respect for politicians. Banking, he thought, would be more in his line, so he turned his attention towards the Imperial Bank of Persia. With the help of a recommendation from a friend already in the Bank, he applied for a job, was interviewed, sat the obligatory entrance examination, and in December 1920 started work. His salary was 300 *krans* a month (about £8), considerably less than he had earned as an interpreter in Rasht.

The Imperial Bank of Persia was one of three British-owned businesses which dominated the modern economy of Iran in the early twentieth century. Destined to become the most important of these enterprises was the Anglo-Persian Oil Company, ancestor of today's British Petroleum, which originated in the oil concession granted to D'Arcy in 1901. D'Arcy had found oil in south-west Iran in 1908. Four years later the first cargo of crude oil was exported. By 1920 oil production had risen to about one and a half million tons annually, and over a thousand Iranians were employed by Anglo-Persian.[10] A second, and highly influential, British venture was the Indo-European Telegraph Company, established by the British Siemens Company in 1868 to complete the telegraphic link between Europe and India and build on operations begun in Iran under the auspices of the Indo-European Telegraph Department in 1863, which managed the internal telegraph network for the Iranian government.[11] Finally, there was the Imperial Bank (Bank-e Shahanshahi), established in 1889 under a monopoly concession from the Shah which made it state bank of Iran with the sole right to issue paper currency. It was popularly known throughout Iran as the *Bank-e Shahi*, the Royal Bank. The institution was wholly British-owned and managed, but its entire business was in Iran apart from tiny offices in Iraq, Bombay and London.[12]

The British enterprises in Iran offered the only real employment possibility for a young Iranian who wished to make a professional career for himself outside politics and the civil service. There was no national Iranian bank nor any similar institution for him to enter and opportunities in local industry were almost non-existent. Business and professional life was dominated by the bazaar, with all the traditionalism which that implied. Ebtehaj counted himself lucky, therefore, to have been accepted by the Imperial Bank. It was considered to be highly prestigious to work for the *Bank-e Shahi*, and it was also a logical career choice for him in view of the talent for accountancy and facility with figures which he had inherited from his father. Moreover, in the prevailing conditions of the early 1920s it offered a security of employment few other institutions in Iran could match. There was, however, one great drawback for a proud, ambitious, self-confident and nationalistically-inclined young Iranian like Ebtehaj. In the Bank, as in all other British institutions in the East at the time, there was a limit to how far his career could progress.

In 1920 the Imperial Bank was, to all intents and purposes, the only modern banking institution in Iran, and there was to be little serious competition before the end of the decade. The Bank's only pre-war competitor, the Russian bank, had been moribund for some time, and in 1921 its assets were finally handed over to Iran by the Soviet government. The Imperial Bank had branches all over the country, making it, perhaps, the only truly national institution in Iran in the early 1920s. It was a central bank and a commercial bank rolled into one. Like all banks it took deposits, made loans, dealt in foreign exchange, and financed trade and commerce. However, the Bank also issued bank notes and controlled their circulation; imported silver for minting into coins; and acted as the government's banker. To complicate matters further, the Imperial Bank co-operated closely with the British Foreign Office as well. Although its links with the British government were not as close as those of the Anglo-Persian Oil Company, in which the British government had taken a 51 per cent equity stake in 1914,[13] during the War, the Bank had handled the British government's extensive financial requirements in Iran, both political and military, often at the expense of the requirements of local trade and commerce.[14]

The young Ebtehaj initially found himself in the lowly position of a junior clerk in the Bank's Exchange Department, but within two weeks he had moved to the Superintendent's Department, and a few months later he was transferred to Rasht to help re-open the Bank's branch there. The Rasht branch had been closed in 1920 because of the activities of the *Jangalis* and the Red Army, and it remained closed until Iranian government troops defeated the *Jangalis* and re-occupied the town at the end of June 1921. Soon after, one of the Bank's young British officers was sent to re-open the branch, and Ebtehaj went with him. Much of Ebtehaj's grasp of the essentials of banking emanated from the time he spent at the Rasht branch as he had to turn his hand to any and every aspect of the Bank's business. He was soon keeping the branch's general ledger,

2. The young Ebtehaj

and providing the second signature on bills despite the Bank's official policy of permitting only British officers to 'sign' for it.[15]

Ebtehaj was promoted to the post of Assistant Chief Interpreter at the end of 1924, and re-joined the Chief Office in Tehran. By this time he was reading everything he could lay his hands on about the banking business. He ordered books from England on a variety of relevant subjects – books which he had heard of or seen advertised in the newspapers and magazines he read – and built up a library on accountancy, banking, economics, and English law. In the meantime, his career progressed. Soon after his promotion to Assistant Chief Interpreter, he spent a six-month period acting for the Chief Interpreter. By the end of 1929, he had been promoted to the position of Assistant to the Chief Inspector and his salary had risen to 2500 *krans* a month (about £43).[16]

The Chief Inspector was one of the highest executive posts in the Bank, and Ebtehaj's promotion to the position of Assistant to this senior British manager made him one of the most senior of the Bank's local staff. Ebtehaj marked his elevation by getting married to Maryam Nabavi, daughter of Taghi Nabavi, Muazzez al-Dawleh. Taghi Nabavi was in the Iranian foreign service. His daughter had grown up in India when Nabavi was consul general there, and had also lived for some time in the Caucasus. She was well-travelled, well-educated, and, like her new husband, spoke fluent Russian, French and English.

Ebtehaj's career progression in the Imperial Bank in the 1920s coincided with radical changes in Iran's political system following the rise to power of Reza Khan and the establishment in 1925 of the Pahlavi dynasty. The new Shah's ambitious programme of social, cultural and economic reforms, aimed at the modernisation of Iran, led to assaults on the power of the Islamic clergy, the foundation of western-style educational institutions, and the unveiling of women. During the 1930s a programme of state-led industrialisation was launched.[17]

It was not surprising that Reza Shah, as he became known, would soon turn his attention to the anomalous position of a British-owned and managed bank acting as Iran's state bank, especially given the fact of the Imperial Bank's past close association with the British Foreign Office. In 1928 the government established a new national bank, the Bank Melli Iran, which was intended both to replace the Imperial Bank as state bank and to challenge its commercial business. A concerted attack was launched on the Imperial Bank's note-issuing privilege, which it was forced to surrender in 1931.[18] The

Imperial Bank responded to the new political situation with neither grace nor good sense. Its directors in London were old, highly conservative, and burdened with an image of Iran as it had been before the First World War.[19] Although Reza Shah's industrialisation programme was marred by inefficiency and corruption, the Bank's dogged determination to resist every aspect of government policy was excessive, narrow-minded and ultimately self-defeating.

It fell to Ebtehaj to defend the Imperial Bank's position in negotiations with the government. He had no contact with Reza Shah himself, but his social standing was such as to allow easy and friendly access to Reza Shah's key men, such as Abdol Hossein Teimurtash, his close confidant and Minister of Court, and Ali Akbar Davar, Minister of Justice.[20] Ebtehaj was rarely given a specific brief, merely asked to go and talk with ministers to try to find a way through specific difficulties as they arose. On more than one occasion, the Bank's chief executive, who lived in Tehran and was known as the Chief Manager, commented in private correspondence with his London office that Ebtehaj's services were 'invaluable' – 'I can state with certainty that he does credit to the Bank, and is of great value to us, particularly as he is "persona grata" in the high circles ... Also ... he is honest and has never been found wanting.'[21]

Ebtehaj was given financial rewards for his services. His salary continued to increase steadily – if not as fast as he would have liked given that he was by now a married man with a certain position to maintain. By 1932 he was earning 4000 *rials* a month. Together with an additional entertainment allowance, his total remuneration was equal to that of a British manager in the Bank. Yet Ebtehaj grew steadily more dissatisfied with his lot. He wanted management status in the Bank on a par with the British staff. He wanted recognition of what he himself knew to be the case – that he was as good management material as, if not better than, any of his British colleagues. The Bank, predictably, did not agree. The Board saw its bank as a British institution run by British people: race and culture, rather than talent, were the decisive factors.

Ebtehaj, therefore, found himself participating in high level negotiations with his own government on behalf of a foreign institution whose employment policies limited him to an inferior status. The Bank seemed backward even when compared with other British businesses in Iran. The Anglo-Persian Oil Company, for example, began to improve its employment policies after the cancellation and subsequent renewal of its concession in 1932–3.[22] Ebtehaj had a close friend in Anglo-Persian, Mustapha Fateh, who had acquired the status and privileges he himself so desperately wanted, and he kept asking why the Bank could not take a leaf out of the Oil Company's book. The Board's answer was typically bleak: the status of the Bank's staff was a matter for settlement by the Board whose views were not influenced by the policy of other corporations established in Iran.[23] Ebtehaj found the Bank's attitude to its local staff more and more galling, especially as it clung to very visible symbols of Iranian inferiority such as separate washrooms for Europeans and Iranians.[24] The clash between Ebtehaj's pride and the Bank's prejudice moved towards its inevitable climax. After having repeated requests for management status rejected, on 1 July 1936 Ebtehaj handed in his resignation. Over the following months there was an ill-tempered dispute between him and the Bank over the size of the leaving gratuity to be granted to him.

Ebtehaj's early life exercised a major influence on the development of his personality and intellect. From his father had come, in addition to the obvious genetic inheritance of a forceful personality, a high regard for numeracy and an even higher concern for unswerving rectitude. His cosmopolitan education had strengthened and broadened his naturally enquiring mind and, by giving him a knowledge of foreign languages, had extended his vision beyond Iran. And despite his ultimate frustration with the Imperial Bank, Ebtehaj had gained much from his sixteen years in its employ. He had acquired banking skills to reinforce his earlier knowledge of accountancy. He had perfected his English. He had developed high level contacts with the Shah's ministers. But the blocking of his career had also sharpened his nationalism. Why should a British bank not promote Iranians when it derived almost all its earnings from Iran? It was only a short step to questioning the right of a British bank to operate at all in Iran. The Imperial Bank had not heard the last of Ebtehaj. Meanwhile, he was about to begin a new career.

PART TWO

NATIONALISM AND INTERNATIONALISM 1937–1953

2

THE FIRST TECHNOCRAT

Ebtehaj's resignation from the Imperial Bank in 1936 was a turning point in his career. At the age of 36, when many people are already settling down to an established and comfortable life, he had abandoned his secure niche with the respected Imperial Bank. His new job was in the altogether more volatile arena of government service. It was to be an arena in which he soon displayed a powerful and much needed talent for building institutions.

Never a foolhardy man, Ebtehaj had done his best to minimise some of the risks involved in his move. Before resigning from the Bank he had secured a firm job offer from Iran's Finance Minister, Ali Akbar Davar. Ebtehaj had in earlier years negotiated with Davar, in the latter's previous incarnation as Justice Minister, on behalf of the Imperial Bank, and a close friendship had developed between the two men. Davar was eager to attract bright young Iranians to his Ministry, and Ebtehaj readily responded to his overtures. However, Ebtehaj insisted that the Shah was made aware of his appointment. He had no wish to be dismissed by the autocratic Reza Shah, and it was quite conceivable that the Shah might object to a long-time employee of the British bank entering government service. The Shah did indeed query Ebtehaj's reliability, but he was reassured by Davar's pledge that he was 'a most patriotic Iranian'.[1]

A rapid series of promotions soon justified Ebtehaj's decision to abandon the Imperial Bank. He was initially appointed Controller of state-owned companies, attached to the Agricultural Bank. In 1938 he became Vice-Governor of the Bank Melli, and two years later he became Chairman and Managing Director of the Bank Rahni, the State Mortgage Bank. In all these positions Ebtehaj extended his responsibilities beyond those of his nominal job description. As Controller of state-owned companies, for example, he advised on government's foreign exchange policies. Finally, in December 1942, he was appointed Governor of the Bank Melli: a mere six years after leaving the British bank he was in a position to dictate policy and terms to the institution which had turned a deaf ear to his requests for equal opportunity and treatment.

The attributes and skills Ebtehaj brought to his new career were in very short supply. Iran had few men of his calibre in government service at a time when the country was trying to cope with the effects of the rapid modernisation and industrialisation launched by Reza Shah. The lack of competent administrators was painfully demonstrated by the confusion, inefficiency, and corruption which surrounded government actions in the 1930s. Iran was not unique in this respect. It naturally takes time for any country embarking on economic modernisation to construct an effective bureaucracy and institutional framework which can implement government policies. However, Iran's poor educational facilities meant that there was a particularly acute shortage of able administrators. Ebtehaj's experience, competence and honesty were rare commodities. During his 14 years with the Ministry of Finance and as Governor of the Bank Melli, Ebtehaj played a decisive role in creating the efficient institutions which were a vital prerequisite for sustained modernisation in Iran. In the process, he staked his claim, even before his period as head of the Plan Organisation in the 1950s, to be Iran's first technocrat.

In some ways Ebtehaj could not have picked a worse time to join the government, for by the mid-1930s the stresses and strains of Reza Shah's modernisation programme were beginning to tell on the country. There had been, it is true, achievements. The country's armed forces had been reorganised and expanded. Communications had been improved. A Trans-Iranian railway was finally under construction, financed entirely by Iranian capital. Standards of public health had improved and hospitals had been built. Iran's first university, at Tehran, had been founded. But many of the gains were at best only skin deep, and had largely been accomplished as a result of widely-resented government regimentation. Reza Shah's increasingly autocratic behaviour and self-aggrandisement made him hugely unpopular and, by 1936, it was already apparent that government policies were creating as many problems as they solved.[2] Reza Shah could, and did, dictate, but he had no magic wand which could remove the formidable obstacles in the way of modernising what was essentially still a medieval country.

Moreover, in 1941, Reza Shah's success in bolstering Iran's national sovereignty was abruptly reversed when Iran was invaded and occupied by the country's old imperial predators, Britain and

Russia. During the 1930s Reza Shah had sought to free his country from the traditional domination of Russia and Britain by recruiting aid and expertise from other countries, especially Nazi Germany. The outbreak of the War thus found German influence strong in Iran, and although Reza Shah took refuge in a policy of declared neutrality, this did not allay Allied apprehensions of a German presence at the centre of their important Middle East position, especially after Germany had invaded the Soviet Union. In August 1941 British and Soviet troops invaded Iran and marched on Tehran, and on 16 September, the Shah was forced to abdicate in favour of his 21-year-old son, Mohammad Reza, who promised the British authorities that he would carry out all the reforms considered necessary by them, and observe the Iranian constitution.[3] Tehran was briefly occupied by Allied forces, and then, for the second time in the century, the country was divided into three zones – with the Soviet forces occupying most of the north, the British the south, while Tehran and some other towns constituted the 'neutral' zone. British, Russian and, from 1942, American troops remained in the country for five years, the Soviets only being ejected in April 1946 after a formidable diplomatic tussle.

Reza Shah's abdication had a traumatic effect. Tehran initially lost control over much of Iran, and the country sank yet again into political disarray, social disorder and economic hardship.[4] The more positive economic achievements of his reign seemed lost as tribalism reasserted itself, and brigandage increased. Taking advantage of Britain's insistence on constitutional government, and the fact that there was a new, young and inexperienced ruler, the *Majles* was able to assert its parliamentary authority, becoming the new focus of Iran's political system. But the lack of a viable party system, and the presence of a variety of conflicting interest groups within the *Majles*, made it impossible for the *Majles* or government to function effectively.[5] More than ever, ministers shuffled from post to post and in and out of government 'in a sort of perpetual musical chairs of personal politics'.[6] Cabinet government was weak because influential vested interests within the *Majles* had no wish to see any return of a strong restrictive government; for while the economic chaos brought about by war and the Allied occupation had caused widespread suffering and hardship, it had also provided lucrative opportunity for profiteers and black market operators, some of whom were members of the *Majles* or had *Majles* connections.[7] Nevertheless, there was a marked liberalisation in many areas of Iranian life. By 1942, the trade unions, banned by Reza

Shah in 1927, had re-formed; opposition leaders were released from prison; there was a resurgence in the vigour and freedom of the Iranian press; and many of the late regime's economic controls had been relaxed.[8]

It was against this shifting background of autocracy, war, occupation and political instability that Ebtehaj's career in government blossomed. In his first post, as Controller of state-owned companies, he began his work of improving Iran's ramshackle economic bureaucracy. As part of his industrialisation drive, Reza Shah had created state-owned companies in a number of sectors, but these were notoriously inefficient and poorly managed. Ebtehaj's task was to introduce some control over these ventures on behalf of the Ministry of Finance. No specific department existed when Ebtehaj took on the job — his staff consisted of himself and one typist — so he had to start from scratch and create a viable administrative structure. His immediate need was for a team of good accountants, and it seemed quite natural to approach people whose worth was tried and tested and whom he had known for years — in short, his former colleagues at the Imperial Bank. Six or seven of them took up his offer of a job and joined him. Predictably, his tactics infuriated the Imperial Bank. Its Chief Manager complained to Davar that Ebtehaj was stealing all the Bank's best men, and Davar felt constrained to ask Ebtehaj to stop provoking the Bank. In deference to Davar, he employed no more ex-employees of the British bank, but those who had answered his original call for help were not abandoned when he moved to the Bank Melli in 1938 — they moved with him.[9]

Ebtehaj and his team seem to have performed their duties well. Despite the fact that his mentor, Davar, committed suicide in February 1937, less than a year after appointing Ebtehaj, and that Davar's successor was a man for whom Ebtehaj had little liking or respect, he was retained in his post. And during this period his name began to be known in government circles, for Ebtehaj was always ready to make his views known on a number of contentious issues, writing freely and openly to various government ministers, for instance, to express his doubts about the haphazard way in which Reza Shah's industrialisation policies were being implemented.

Meanwhile Ebtehaj had acquired a new mentor in Davar's place — the veteran politician, Hossein Ala, who had been Iran's Minister in London, and whose future appointments would include the governorship of the Bank Melli, Court Minister, Ambassador to Washington and Prime Minister. Ebtehaj first met Ala early in

THE FIRST TECHNOCRAT

1937, when Ala came to tell him that he had been appointed Minister of Commerce and that Ebtehaj's department in the Agricultural Bank would henceforth come under his Ministry.[10] He had, he said, made his acceptance of the appointment conditional on Ebtehaj being willing to work with him. Ebtehaj could not have been happier. He had long admired Ala's reputation and the way he conducted his business. From the time his department came under Ala's jurisdiction, Ebtehaj saw him daily, and in Ala he found someone with 'the same feeling' as himself, 'the same way of thinking, the same method of work'.[11] Ebtehaj shared his views on what was going wrong with the industrialisation programme with Ala, and explained to him his conviction that it was vital to have an economic coordinating body. Ala persuaded Reza Shah to establish an Economic Council in April 1937 to undertake this role but, as explained in Chapter 5, this was dissolved a year later.[12]

With no immediate prospect of being able to implement his ideas on planning, Ebtehaj saw little point in remaining in a job in which he was unable to attack the fundamental problems. With Ala's blessing he accepted the suggestion of his old friend General Amir Khosrovi, Governor of the Bank Melli, that he should be appointed a Vice-Governor of that Bank.[13] Two years later, early in 1940, Khosrovi was appointed Minister of Finance, and his deputy, Mohammad Ali Farzin, replaced him. This was a blow for Ebtehaj. Not only had he no respect for the new Governor's ability – Farzin, in his opinion, knew less than nothing about banking (a view shared by officials in the British Legation) – but also Farzin was pro-German, convinced, like Reza Shah himself, that Germany would win the war, while Ebtehaj, for his part, was convinced of the necessity of an Allied victory and sure that Britain would in the end carry the day. Fortunately he did not have to suffer working under Farzin too long. Hearing of the almost total lack of communication between the two men, Khosrovi asked Ebtehaj if he would care to take on the direction of the newly formed State Mortgage Bank, Bank Rahni Iran.[14]

The Bank Rahni was still a very new creation when Ebtehaj became its second President and Chairman in early 1940. A state mortgage institution had been in existence since 1926. In 1931 it had been taken under the wing of the Bank Melli, and in 1938 it finally graduated to full independence as the Mortgage Bank of Iran, with a capital of 200 million *rials* (£2.5 million), half of which came from the Bank Melli and half from the Ministry of Finance.[15] At first the Bank's business largely consisted of helping people to re-build on the constricted space remaining after buildings had been pulled down to allow for Reza Shah's street-widening campaign in Tehran. But its real object was to provide loans for people either to buy or to build their own homes. Under Ebtehaj, loans were only granted to people who did not already own a house: moreover, they were made on easy terms in the context of Tehran, for a 25-year period at the relatively low fixed rate of interest of about 6 per cent – a good deal lower than the rates ruling in the bazaar which were in the region of 24 per cent. Ebtehaj was quick to rise to the challenge of his new job, and enthusiastically propounded the principles and benefits of the mortgage system to all who would listen. He was particularly anxious that civil servants, and similar levels of salaried employees, should understand that they were eligible for mortgages, since they were poorly paid and needed the kind of help the Mortgage Bank could give.[16]

The two and a half years Ebtehaj spent with the Mortgage Bank were instructive and valuable; they provided him with an opportunity to put into practice many of his controversial theories as to how an institution should be run, and were thus a valuable preparation for his next job – the much more demanding governorship of the Bank Melli. Ebtehaj was appointed Governor of the Bank Melli in December 1942, in succession to his friend and mentor, Hossein Ala, who had held the position since September 1941. His appointment had been brewing for some time and came as no surprise, according to the American Ambassador, since it was well known 'that Ala was anxious to leave the Bank and have Ebtehadj [sic] who was more or less his protégé succeed him'.[17] But it was the sponsorship of Iran's new, 'strong' Prime Minister, Ahmad Qavam, which proved the deciding factor: he named Ebtehaj as Governor.

Reza Shah had created the Bank Melli in 1928, fulfilling at last a nationalist aspiration voiced by Iran's constitutional reformers in 1906. In the early twentieth century, Iran, like most other countries, had no central bank. Central banking functions were performed, if at all, by commercial banks: in Iran's case, the Imperial Bank of Persia undertook these tasks. The Federal Reserve System in the United States was only established in 1913. After the First World War it became fashionable to create central banks. An International Economic Conference held in Brussels in 1920 had urged all countries to create their own institutions – primarily as a means of achieving international monetary cooperation. During the 1920s, a series of Latin American countries obeyed this call, and in the next decade other nations, including Canada and New Zealand, followed suit. The foundation of the Bank Melli, therefore, had been part of a world-wide trend, although this had not prevented the Imperial Bank from deeply resenting the loss of its privileged position.

The Bank Melli had rapidly succumbed to the chronic lack of professional — and honest — administrators in Iran. Initially it had been taken for granted that the Bank would be managed by Americans. An American Mission headed by Dr Arthur Millspaugh was in Iran between 1922 and 1927, attempting to reform the country's chaotic financial administration.[18] However, Millspaugh lost favour with Reza Shah towards the end of his Mission, and a German management for the new bank was decided upon. In 1928, a German, Dr Kurt Lindenblatt, formerly of the National Bank of Bulgaria, was appointed as chief executive. He was to prove an unhappy choice. When the Bank opened for business in September 1928, it had a tiny capital, no experience, and a management team which within four years was under official investigation for irregular practices. Yet its brief was to help finance the country's trade, agriculture and industry at a time when Iran was going through a serious foreign exchange crisis, a huge industrialisation programme was underway internally, and there was a growing world depression.[19] In addition, the Bank Melli had to fight the competition of the well-established Imperial Bank of Persia.

Public confidence in the Bank Melli was severely shaken by corruption and incompetence. By the end of 1931, there were already rumours that the Bank Melli's lending policies were ill-advised to say the least, and when it was disclosed that its loss for the year ending March 1932 was 8.7 million rials (£900,000), Reza Shah ordered a full-scale enquiry into the Bank's affairs. In June 1932, Lindenblatt left the country — purportedly to see his doctor — and in September his deputy, Vogel, fled to Beirut where he committed suicide while in detention. On Lindenblatt's eventual return to Iran to answer the charges against him, there were allegations that Reza Shah's Court Minister, Teimurtash, had been involved in various questionable deals and speculations with the Bank Melli. Lindenblatt was dismissed, and left Iran. Teimurtash was imprisoned in January 1933, tried and convicted in March, and died in October: the general belief was that the scandals uncovered at the Bank Melli had provided a convenient vehicle for trumped-up charges against him because he had been getting too powerful, and that Reza Shah had had him liquidated.[20]

Bank Melli's reputation recovered during the mid-1930s. Lindenblatt's eventual successor was an Iranian whom Reza Shah had been grooming for the position – an old colleague, General Amir Khosrovi. Reza Shah gave Khosrovi charge of the Army Bank in 1931, and then sent him off to France to learn about banking – a not altogether successful venture since he spoke very little French. Khosrovi's regime was good for the Bank Melli in the post-Lindenblatt years since he was a strict disciplinarian, and ran the Bank like a military barracks. Under him, and then Hossein Ala, the Bank's branch network expanded enormously, and other state financial institutions were nurtured.[21] However, Khosrovi was no born banker, and Ala's term of office was always by way of being a temporary stand-in until a more permanent appointment could be made, so that the principles on which the Bank was managed were no different to any other department of government – favour and patronage were rife, salaries were low, and accountancy practices were lax. Furthermore, the Ministry of Finance habitually took the lead in questions of money supply, foreign exchange and so on, rather than the National Bank. Under Ebtehaj, there were to be fundamental changes.

Ebtehaj's immediate concern was to establish the Bank as an autonomous institution, independent of government or any other control. This was no easy task in a political system which worked on the basis of personal relationships, influence and patronage, and in which such positions as governorships of state banks and directorships of state companies seemed primarily to be used as political rewards.[22] Indeed, Ebtehaj's own career since leaving the Imperial Bank had benefited from the patronage of such men as Davar, Khosrovi, Ala, and, ultimately in the case of the governorship of the Bank Melli, the Prime Minister, Ahmad Qavam. And Ebtehaj, no less than anyone else in his milieu, profited from the contacts built up through élite social networks. Indeed, it was this patronage from on high which helps to explain how Ebtehaj was able to rise so quickly in government service: the Iranian political system rarely rewarded merit alone.

Yet Ebtehaj was highly unusual, in the Iranian political context, in his refusal to compromise his independence of action once appointed by deferring to the wishes of anyone, whether they be friend or patron or even the Shah himself. The point is well illustrated on a private and public level by his attitude to three loan requests by Ahmad Qavam when he was Prime Minister in 1946. Twice Qavam asked Ebtehaj to bend the rules and make him a private loan without the usual security: on both occasions Ebtehaj refused – no one, he explained, was exempt from the Bank Melli's procedural rules. The same attitude prevailed when Qavam, at a time when government was in considerable financial difficulties but no *Majles* was sitting, officially requested a loan from the Bank Melli. Again Ebtehaj refused: loans to government without *Majles* ratification were outside the constitutional authority of the Bank. Yet his relationship with Qavam, and admiration for him, remained unimpaired. Similarly, although frequently accused by British and American officials of being a protégé of Mohammad Reza Shah's twin sister, Princess Ashraf, Ebtehaj refused to bend the foreign exchange regulations when she was in India, and remit her rupees to pay her debts, despite being asked to do so by the Finance Minister, and indeed by the Shah himself. Moreover, when another prominent Iranian notable, Amir Hossein Ilkhan Bakhtiari, also an unsuccessful petitioner for a loan, asked the Shah to intercede on his behalf, the Shah apparently told him that having failed to persuade Ebtehaj to grant a loan to his own sister, such intercession would be useless.[23]

Ebtehaj could not long have sustained his independent status at the Bank Melli, or, later, the Plan Organisation, without a power base, particularly once his policies began to arouse the public outrage and widespread discontent in official government circles which characterised most of his term at the head of both organisations. He found this vital support – the ultimate in patronage – in his relationship with the young Mohammad Reza Shah, who was still in his early twenties when Ebtehaj was appointed to the Bank Melli. The Shah had had nothing to do with Ebtehaj's initial appointment. Ebtehaj did not meet him until he asked for an audience a week after he became Governor of the Bank. However, there was an immediate rapport between the two – as Ebtehaj later recollected, 'I liked him and I think he liked me and we got to be very close to each other.' After that first meeting, Ebtehaj saw the Shah on a regular official basis once a week – 'never asking him what to do, but reporting to him what I was doing'.[24] The close relationship which developed between the two was the subject of considerable comment and curiosity, and it was even thought likely that Ebtehaj had some sort of hold over the young Shah. The pro-British Sayyid Zia al-Din Tabatabai, co-leader with Reza Shah of the 1921 coup, described the Shah's 'fear of Ibtihaj' [sic], which 'he was sure ... was due to some Court secret possessed by him'.[25] Years later, Mozaffar Firouz, a close collaborator at one time of Sayyid Zia's, indicated to Ebtehaj's wife that Ebtehaj was believed to have helped Reza Shah

3. Visit of Mohammad Reza Shah and Queen Fawzieh to the Bank Melli

THE FIRST TECHNOCRAT

to move his assets from Iran to England.[26] The truth was, according to Ebtehaj himself, considerably simpler:

> I was not ambitious in the sense of seeking advancement. Except for the IBI [Imperial Bank] I never sought a job in my life. Every position I held in all my life was offered to me, and with the exception of IMF, I accepted the job on my conditions and only if I was reasonably sure that I would be successful.... I was not dishonest; I was not a lackey or a stooge. I always tried to be fair in my treatment of people and of problems, and never showed nepotism. I was not afraid to lose my job although I always depended on my salary for a living. And the Shah was aware of these facts.[27]

The fact that Ebtehaj had the ear of the Shah and that this helped him to stay in office was commented on by many contemporary observers. The Commercial Secretary of the British Embassy in 1945, for instance, remarked that 'but for the backing of the Shah he would have little or no prospect of being renewed in his appointment as governor'.[28] The United States Embassy held the same opinion.[29] In 1948, a former Minister of Finance observed that Ebtehaj would long ago have been removed from office were it not for the Shah's insistence on keeping him at his post.[30] There were times when Ebtehaj lost even the Shah's support – notably when he was dismissed from the Bank Melli in 1950, and again in 1959 when he resigned from the Plan Organisation – but given the constantly shifting pattern of Iranian politics and the general instability of the ten-year period between 1941 and 1953, when 144 people filled roughly 400 cabinet positions in 26 different cabinets, the Shah's support for him seemed remarkably consistent. Furthermore, it seems that the Shah went so far as to offer Ebtehaj the Prime Ministership on at least two occasions, in 1944 and again in early 1950, as well as trying to persuade him to become Minister of Finance.[31] True to form, Ebtehaj turned down all such offers, remaining absolutely consistent in his categoric refusal to enter the political arena directly. The wisdom of such an attitude will be discussed later.

At the Bank Melli, as earlier at the Bank Rahni, Ebtehaj strove to create an institution of independence, integrity and competence. Dr Millspaugh, who returned to Iran in 1943 as Financial Administrator, recollected that Ebtehaj had 'impressed me as a vigorous administrator, a good technical banker, and an honest, courageous man'.[32] This opinion was shared by the foreign diplomats and financial experts with whom Ebtehaj came into contact, although most of them would also have agreed with Millspaugh's observations on 'his nervousness, his incredibly hot temper, his inclination to ride rough-shod over opposition, and his dictatorial propensities'.[33] They were the characteristics of an impatient man who knew what he wanted to achieve and had neither the time nor the inclination to suffer fools either gladly or in any way whatever.

Ebtehaj's reforming zeal had been much in evidence at the Bank Rahni. The way in which the mortgage system worked meant that the Bank's employees were exposed to the usual Iranian practice of gifts offered for favours given, since each property had to be evaluated before a mortgage loan was made. Ebtehaj insisted that the Bank's team of property evaluators, upon whose skill and judgement the amount of both the loan and the Bank's security depended, should take their responsibilities seriously and adhere to a strict code of conduct. The acceptance of presents and gratuities was forbidden. Staff who violated this rule were instantly dismissed. Moreover, Ebtehaj had no compunction about treating customers who disregarded his rules to a furious tirade about the way their actions were encouraging his staff into dishonesty. But although the standards of discipline and rectitude he expected of his staff were high, he was prepared, on his side, to reward them suitably, by providing them with good salaries and terms of service. While he could not himself conceive 'of an honourable man, a man of self respect and self confidence' accepting any sort of bribe, he had long argued that honesty could hardly be expected of an employee who did not receive a living wage. Ebtehaj was determined that his bank employees should earn enough to live on. And salaries were not his only concern. One of the first things he did at the Bank Rahni was to open a bakery for the staff and their dependents – subsidised bread was an important benefit at a time when wheat was in very short supply because of the War and the Russian occupation of the important wheat-growing province of Azerbaijan in the northwest.[34]

By the time Ebtehaj joined the Bank Melli as Governor, he knew the changes he wanted to make. He wasted no time in indicating to his staff how he intended to proceed:

> The day I took over Bank Melli, Iran, I addressed all the members of the staff in Tehran in the large banking hall of the chief office.
>
> ... I informed my colleagues that I proposed to open a new

account between them and myself starting as from that day. I asked them to forget the past and proposed that the new relationship between them and myself should be in the form of a banking account with a debit side and a credit side.

On the credit side, I pledged myself to use every means at my disposal to make it possible for every member of staff and their families to have a minimum decent standard of living without having to look to other sources than their salaries and assured the staff that no authority outside the bank could bring pressure to bear either for or against any member of the staff. I added that the bank was not a Government agency offering a service to the public which they had no option but to accept, whether they were satisfied with the service or not . . . No persons or private institutions had any obligation whatsoever to use our services for their banking needs if they were not entirely satisfied with these services. . . . No law or Government decision could compel people to place their money and their confidence in a bank they could not trust and whose services they did not find satisfactory. I said I demanded from them absolute integrity and honesty, accuracy and attention and courtesy to the customers.

. . . it was my hope that we would all try to set an example of how we all behaved vis-a-vis our clients . . . always remembering that we were their servants and not their masters.[35]

These principles were put into action at the highest level. Before accepting his appointment, Ebtehaj had made it quite clear to Prime Minister Qavam that he intended to run the Bank his way and would brook no interference on matters of management or policy from the Bank's High Council — the equivalent of the board of directors — a group of elderly and eminent politicians. Qavam, in turn, indicated the position to the High Council and made it clear that Ebtehaj had his full backing. As a result, in the eight years Ebtehaj was Governor of the Bank, he had little or no trouble with the Council. As well as insisting on freedom of action, he also demanded — and after a tussle received — a salary commensurate with the responsibilities of his job: he asked for 10,000 *rials* a month (or some £70) more than he had been earning at the Bank Rahni. The increase put him in the top rank of government employees: he was paid more than other public servants and most politicians, although not as much as Millspaugh and the senior members of his mission were to receive.

Ebtehaj fulfilled his side of the bargain he had made with his staff. The salaries they earned were high in comparison with other organisations: 5 per cent of the Bank's net profits annually was set aside for distribution to the staff (excluding himself) as a bonus at the discretion of the management, and generous pension and retirement fund arrangements were established. Of more immediate importance perhaps in wartime, when wholesale shortages existed and inflation was rife, Ebtehaj introduced a system whereby all categories of employees were given rations of such basic food items as rice, tea, sugar, and cooking fat. The amount of these was irrespective of rank and position, and related only to the size of a staff member's family, so that a doorkeeper with a wife and five children received seven rations while a senior executive with a wife and no children received just two, plus one for his servant. The rations were all exactly the same so far as quality and quantity were concerned, and were purchased in bulk by the Bank at appropriate centres of production across the country and at wholesale prices. In addition, the Bank's subsidised staff restaurant was reorganised: the same menu was introduced for everyone from the Governor to the floor sweeper, and two levels of price were instituted. Those whose salaries were above a certain figure paid 12 *rials* (just over 9 pence) for a meal, while those whose salaries were below paid 8 *rials* (a little more than 6 pence). The Bank's health care service and hospital became renowned for their excellence. And in time a swimming pool was built for the staff, and a *zoorkhaneh* (gymnasium for the performance of ancient Persian calisthenics with traditional apparatus): the Bank security guards, for example, were required to attend the *zoorkhaneh* three times a week, with notable results.

A new recruitment policy was established to ensure that applicants for positions in the Bank, who were always in excess of the Bank's requirements, had a strictly equal chance: all applicants took the necessary tests, those who passed were registered under the date of their acceptance of their test result and they were invited to join the Bank as soon as their name came to the top of the list. One interesting and controversial innovation had already been introduced by Ebtehaj into the Bank Rahni's recruitment procedure. When he took over that Bank in 1940, he discovered that all applicants for a job at the Bank had to specify their religion. This practice was immediately done away with – a move which caused quite a commotion since all applicants for government jobs were required to give the information. When he joined the Bank Melli, he did the same again –

THE FIRST TECHNOCRAT

My philosophy was that what the institution expected from its staff was integrity, loyalty and efficiency and that religion was a matter purely personal which did not concern anyone other than the individual concerned.

Once recruited, staff were treated strictly but fairly:

I wasn't unkind but I didn't go out of my way to please my colleagues .... I demanded discipline, I demanded honesty, and any departures from these principles were punished, and severely punished.[36]

Any overt political affiliation was regarded as such a departure since the Bank had to be seen by the public to be strictly independent and apolitical, and when, in 1946, a bankers' union was set up by some of the staff who were known to have been members of the Tudeh Party (Iran's communist party), Ebtehaj reacted strongly. Ironically, the union was neither politically inspired nor aimed at undermining the Bank's senior management. It was merely formed as a means of a channelling through to management and the governing body the views and complaints of those junior staff members who had no direct access. Ebtehaj, however, took the whole business as a personal affront and challenge to his authority. He called a meeting of the Tehran staff (who numbered about 1500), and explained that there was no need for a union — he himself would sort out any grievances. He was prepared to go so far as to appoint their chief spokesman as their representative. He could not, however, permit the existence of the union and he demanded its disbandment. One of the three principal promoters of the union — Eprime Eshag, a graduate of the London School of Economics, described by Ebtehaj as a brilliant young intellectual — leapt onto the platform to address the assembled staff, which, after a scuffle and the withdrawal of Ebtehaj and his entourage, he was able to do. The following day, Ebtehaj summoned the ringleaders and, despite the events of the previous day, informed them that all would be forgiven and forgotten if they agreed to disband the union. They refused; whereupon they were given the opportunity of accepting as 'punishment' transfer to some such remote branch of the Bank as Zahedan, on the Baluchistan border, or of leaving the Bank's service. Eshag chose the latter course. His two colleagues accepted temporary banishment. One, Mehdi Samii, actually went to Zahedan. It was, as it turned out, less of a punishment than a valuable learning experience, for as assistant manager, and for much of the time acting manager, of a busy commercial branch he learnt much about the business of banking – indeed, in his own view, his time in Zahedan transformed him from an accountant into an experienced banker. Nor did his 'exile' last long; after some six months, he returned to Tehran, became one of Ebtehaj's most loyal supporters, and, eventually, Governor himself of Iran's Central Bank and head of the Plan Organisation.[37]

Despite the affair of the union, Ebtehaj had no time for mere 'yes men' among his staff. He made it clear that staff members should feel free to submit suggestions and ideas, argue their views, and make recommendations – an unusual requirement in a country where it was normal for anyone submitting a report to his senior to end with some such polite turn of phrase as 'awaiting your orders, which will be immediately carried out'. Moreover, he was always willing not only to listen but to change his mind if and when he found the argument convincing.[38] In the event, of course, the final decision was his.

Inevitably, Ebtehaj's individual and 'new broom' approach evoked a mixed reaction both inside and outside the Bank. In February 1943, a Bill was presented to the *Majles*, signed by 64 of the deputies, asking for an alteration in the Bank Melli's statutes so as to require the Cabinet to prepare a short-list of suitable people for the Bank's Governor and Deputy Governor positions for the *Majles* to make the final choice of candidate. Ebtehaj's unpopularity, it seemed, was growing with the deputies, merchants, and many members of the Bank Melli staff. However, he managed to weather that particular storm, and worked hard to gain the confidence and support of the deputies and merchants as well as his staff. The deputy who presented the Bill to the *Majles* soon became one of his firmest supporters, and Millspaugh, who had been consulted by the *Majles*, gave it as his opinion that there were probably fewer than half a dozen people in Iran who would be equally suitable as Governor.[39]

Within the Bank Melli, therefore, Ebtehaj introduced new standards of professionalism, competence and honesty. At the same time, he endeavoured to expand its level of expertise in line with his ambition to extend its central banking functions: it was during his administration, for instance, that the economic research and intelligence unit of the Bank began to work effectively when its incompetent head was removed and replaced by Abol Qassem Kheradjou, the man who was in later years to head the Industrial and Mining Development Bank of Iran.[40] He then sought to use this newly-tuned instrument to bring all financial, currency and foreign exchange affairs in Iran under his control. The following two chapters will describe his resulting battles with the Allies and with the Imperial Bank. Meanwhile, Ebtehaj was also soon in conflict with the American Financial Mission in his country, for Dr Millspaugh considered himself in overall control of economic and financial affairs. It was not a claim which Ebtehaj could for long leave uncontested.

In November 1942 Millspaugh had been appointed Administrator General of Finances by the Iranian government on a five-year contract – a contract which was ratified by the *Majles*. The work of his Mission was to cover all fields of Iranian government finance and taxation; accounting, budgetary control and auditing; customs, tariffs and trade; and general economic and financial matters. The government agreed not to enter into any financial engagement without his written approval, and he was to be consulted by the government before any decision on any financial question was taken. He also had the power to sack officials of the Ministry of Finance.

The first seven members of the American Mission, headed by Millspaugh, arrived in Iran on 29 January 1943. At first Ebtehaj supported the Americans. His initial attitude when he heard about the Mission in 1942 was that Iran did not need foreign advisers, and he told Millspaugh this when he met him first. But the relationship between them could not initially have been better according to Ebtehaj: 'I knew about his background and whatever I had heard was that he tried to serve Iran. So I had a sympathetic view.' Millspaugh, for his part, believed that Ebtehaj belonged to 'a reputable group' of Iranian administrators, even if he was known to express 'a vehement nationalism'.[41] During 1943 and the first part of 1944, Ebtehaj and Millspaugh maintained a respectable working relationship. Millspaugh backed Ebtehaj in early 1943 when he was under attack in the *Majles*. Millspaugh, in turn, enjoyed Ebtehaj's support for the Full Powers Act of May 1943, a measure designed to clarify the Mission's extensive powers. And in each of his monthly reports, Millspaugh went out of his way to stress the excellent cooperation given to the American Mission by Ebtehaj and the Bank Melli.[42]

Millspaugh, however, attracted growing opposition from many quarters, opposition which focused on the sweeping economic powers vested in him. While profiteers objected to his attempts to restrain the wartime black market, reformers complained he had done too little. Nationalists objected to Americans being in charge of all key economic departments – with the notable exception of the Bank Melli. Pro-Soviet elements had their own reasons for opposing the Mission. In May 1944, Ebtehaj warned the United States Embassy that a full attack was about to be launched on Millspaugh in the *Majles*, which would be widely supported. Only Ebtehaj's intervention, or so he informed the American Chargé, had prevented thus far the introduction of a bill to repeal all of Millspaugh's economic powers. Ebtehaj advised, as a compromise, that Millspaugh should voluntarily transfer these powers to one of his American colleagues and concentrate on his financial responsibilities. Millspaugh rejected both this proposal and the Prime Minister's subsequent suggestion that a new Ministry of National Economy should be created to absorb the economic powers held both by the American Mission and the Ministry of Commerce and Industry.[43]

By June 1944 there was serious tension between Ebtehaj and Millspaugh. Ebtehaj had heard enough adverse comment on Iran's economic efficiency at the Middle East Financial Conference held in Cairo in April (see Chapter 3), to cause him, on his return, to look critically at the way in which Millspaugh was exercising his economic powers. Millspaugh's rejection of his well-meant advice, which would have allowed these powers to remain with the American Mission, confirmed his suspicion that Millspaugh was no longer worthy of support. In mid-June 1944, he joined the opposition forces in the Cabinet and *Majles* who were determined to deprive Millspaugh of his economic powers. On the other hand, Millspaugh objected forcefully when he was not consulted about Ebtehaj's appointment to head Iran's delegation to the Bretton Woods Conference in July. Although he still respected Ebtehaj's competence, he increasingly regarded him as a very large thorn in his flesh. 'What I desire to do', he told the American Embassy, 'is to put Mr Ebtehaj in his place here and avoid the necessity of removing an official who is able and honest and can be useful.'[44]

It was not long before the tension between the two men had escalated into a bitter feud. The independence of the Bank Melli was called into question by Millspaugh, and clashes occurred on a range of technical issues, including Ebtehaj's decision to divide the revenue obtained from the sale of gold coins between Bank Melli's profits and reserves and the right of the American Mission to inspect the Bank's books. Both before and after his visit to the United States for the Bretton Woods Conference, Ebtehaj wrote letters to Millspaugh accusing him of being senile, incompetent, and having evil intentions towards Iran. Millspaugh's reaction was that either he would have to go, or Ebtehaj.[45] On 7 October, he finally wrote to Ebtehaj, dismissing him for rudeness, refusal to cooperate, and interference in matters outside his proper sphere of activity, basing his action on Article 8 of his contract which gave him powers to dismiss Ministry of Finance personnel.[46] He also wrote to all the Bank's correspondents saying that he had dismissed Ebtehaj and warning them not to recognise him.

By this time, relations between the two were so bad that Millspaugh and Ebtehaj were each convinced that the other was quite unstable. In a letter to the Iranian Prime Minister in November 1944, Millspaugh listed Ebtehaj's mental condition as the first of the seven reasons why he had dismissed him:

> On occasions, my Iranian friends have referred to Mr Ebtehaj's mentality. My experience with him after his return from the Cairo Conference convinced me that what had been told me was correct. His arrogant, dictatorial, insulting, and otherwise unreasonable behaviour on several occasions toward the Minister of Finance and toward the Treasurer General and myself revealed lack of mental balance, uncontrollable temper, an exaggerated ego, and dictatorial drive, all of which clearly disqualifies him for a position that requires dignity, conservatism, reserve, calm deliberation, and willingness to listen to the views of others.[47]

Ebtehaj was, and has remained, convinced that Millspaugh was completely unbalanced, especially having heard some years after the American's departure from Iran that he had been in a mental hospital for nearly six months.[48]

Millspaugh was sufficiently unpopular in Iran to stand little hope of defeating Ebtehaj. The Iranian government ruled that Millspaugh did not have the authority to dismiss him, and Ebtehaj remained at his desk. After losing this battle, Millspaugh's power waned. In January 1945 the *Majles* deprived him of all economic powers. He resigned and left Iran in the following month. His defeat meant that Ebtehaj's campaign to bring Iran's financial system under the aegis of the Bank Melli, and develop the latter's central banking functions, continued from strength to strength.

Considerable strides in this direction had already been made by the end of the War, including the separation of Bank Melli's functions into two distinct departments, an Issue Department and a

Banking Department, a move which served to clarify its central banking role. While he was still at the Bank Rahni, Ebtehaj had been drawn by the Ministry of Finance and the Prime Minister into the negotiations on Iran's currency problems (see Chapter 3). Once he became Governor of the Bank Melli it did not take him long to ensure the Bank Melli's pre-eminent position in all future discussions and policy decisions on currency questions. Moreover, the necessity to protect the *rial* and maintain public confidence in it at a time of mounting inflation became one of his chief concerns. One tactic he employed was to bring into the country some of Iran's gold reserves, held in Canada and South Africa, mint the gold bars into *pahlavis* (crown coins), and sell them to the public. Each shipment of gold was given maximum publicity. Ebtehaj even invited groups to visit the Bank Melli vaults to see the gold, starting with the *mollas*, 'who had contact with the public in their mosques, in their preachings, in their Friday prayers'. The tactic worked. When the coins were minted and offered for sale 'there was a gold rush'.[49] While the sales of gold *pahlavis* did not succeed in reducing the very high commodity prices prevailing, they were successful in bringing down the inflated prices for property and land because they provided an alternative field of investment.[50] In November 1943, Ebtehaj had another bright idea to strengthen and support Iran's currency. Since the silver price was so volatile, he decided that gold should replace silver in Iran's currency reserve. Some 1,600 tons of silver were accordingly offered for sale in the open market, both locally, and, more importantly for Iran's foreign exchange reserves, overseas.[51]

The operation of Iran's foreign exchange was another area which Ebtehaj was determined to bring under the Bank Melli's control. He had not agreed with the introduction of exchange controls in the 1930s, but given their existence, he was determined that their administration was the proper function of the Bank. He fought a long and hard battle to abolish the Exchange Control Commission, which had been set up under the aegis of the Ministry of Finance to administer exchange controls, and have its functions taken over by the Bank Melli. When this proved unsuccessful, he worked to ensure that direction of the Exchange Control Commission was vested in the Bank rather than in the Ministry of Finance. This battle was eventually won.[52]

The overall thrust of Ebtehaj's policies after the end of the war was to conserve Iran's resources for economic development, a matter which increasingly dominated his thinking. Policies on a range of issues stemmed from this basic strategy. One of his major campaigns, for example, was to reduce the reserve ratio required for Iran's note issue. In 1932, when the Bank Melli effectively took over the issue of banknotes, a decree was enacted that the note issue should have a 100 per cent metallic cover. This was done to convince people that the new national notes were just as good as hard currency. In fact, the actual cover was far in excess of the notes issued since it included gold, silver and foreign exchange in circulation as well as the specie held by the Bank Melli. Two years later, the permitted level of the note issue was more than doubled and the metallic reserve, now limited to the specie actually held by the Bank Melli rather than in circulation, was reduced to 60 per cent. Thereafter, with the authorisation of successive increases in the note issue, which increased from 170 million *rials* in 1932 to 2 billion *rials* by June 1941, this ratio had started to slip. War and occupation, and the need for still further currency issues, caused further slippage, and by the end of 1942 the ratio of the metallic cover had fallen to a mere 19 per cent. In order to restore the situation, and permit the further expansion necessary, a Note Reserve Control Board was set up in November 1942. It was empowered to expand the note issue, so long as the new notes were fully backed. At the same time, a law was enacted which stipulated a return to a note reserve ratio of 100 per cent.[53]

Paradoxically, this insistence on 100 per cent effective gold cover for Iran's note issue was Ebtehaj's idea. It was aimed at preserving the gold and gold-backed sterling bought from the British authorities against their local currency needs during the Allied occupation. Ebtehaj was absolutely determined that the fruits of the 1942 Financial Agreement (see Chapter 3) should not be wasted, but saved in order to finance economic development after the war. In his view, the best way of ensuring this was to have a strongly backed currency until such time as a development plan was ready for implementation, and then to release the necessary funds by reducing the backing ratio of the currency to a more reasonable level. Unfortunately, however, this tactic was ruined by the fears of his opponents in the *Majles* after the war that any such reduction would fuel inflation. They recollected with horror the German inflation of the 1920s and were determined to prevent the same thing happening in Iran. Thus in March 1949 when a bill drafted by the Bank Melli, reducing the backing ratio for Iran's note issue to the 50 per cent Ebtehaj thought more rational at a time when the country's resources were needed for development, was approved by the Council of Ministers, the *Majles* refused to ratify it. Nor would the opposing deputies change their minds, despite the pressure Ebtehaj brought to bear over the next year or so and despite all the arguments he could muster – that Iran's currency was, for instance, over-backed by international standards (the United States currency was required by law to have a gold cover of only 25 per cent).[54] The issue was not finally resolved until the Mossadeq era in the early 1950s, as will be seen in Chapter 5.

The Bank Melli's credit policies were also part of the basic strategy. During the War and immediate post-war period, a policy of quantitative and qualitative credit control was pursued in an attempt to counteract the inflationary pressures caused by deficit spending and Allied military expenditure. The Bank refused to finance the holding of excessive stocks, and also raised the bank rate and other interest rates. By the late 1940s, the reasons for the strategy had changed somewhat. Credit policies were increasingly based on the principle that all credit granted by the Bank to traders and industrialists should be spent for productive purposes. Credit for speculative purposes was severely discouraged. Bank Melli cooperated with the newly-established Plan Organisation to provide loans for assisting industry and for importing machinery. In addition, government was urged to regard balancing the budget as a priority; Ebtehaj made it clear that he thought that the Bank's practice of lending the government money to meet current expenses should be discontinued, and arrangements made for the gradual repayment of loans already given so as to release the money for use in 'productive' enterprises.[55]

By 1950 Ebtehaj had made the Bank Melli a powerful force in Iranian life. The old corrupt image from the days of German management had been vanquished. Iran's first technocrat had built an efficient financial institution. By the time he left Bank Melli, it was much stronger than in the 1930s, despite the invasion and occupation of Iran by the Allies, and it had made considerable headway towards developing on central banking lines. Moreover, he had given the Bank a cadre of efficient officers and a set of coherent policies.

In a historical perspective, Ebtehaj's significance in reforming and creating institutions which were capable of undertaking the tasks of modern economic management stands out. Many contemporaries, however, saw matters in a different light. As will be seen in Chapter 4, the Imperial Bank of Iran was infuriated by Ebtehaj's policies, especially his efforts to gain for the Bank Melli some authority over the commercial banks, and convinced that they were motivated by personal animosity. Many opponents within Iran, and foreign observers, complained of Ebtehaj's egotism, and became convinced that his overall ambition was political power at the highest level. In 1945, a confidential report to Washington, by the Office of Strategic Services (the predecessor of the CIA) noted fears that Ebtehaj was 'attempting to build himself up to the point where he can eventually pull a Coup d'Etat and possibly set himself up as dictator'.[56]

Ebtehaj was not, in fact, aiming at supreme power, as was testified by his refusal to take up offers of the Prime Ministership. But his ambitions for the Bank Melli and his abrasive style caused a steady accumulation of opponents and enemies. It was only a matter of time before they challenged him, and the 'fools' he so obviously would not suffer had their revenge. However, before turning to the events which led to Ebtehaj's dismissal from the Bank Melli, we need to examine his attempts to make Iran a respected power on the international economic scene in the 1940s.

3

PUTTING IRAN ON THE MAP

Just as Third World nations frequently lack the appropriate modern institutions necessary for development, so they have suffered from domination by the great powers of the First and Second Worlds. Although Iran avoided the fate of colonialisation, it was nevertheless a victim of its geopolitical position as a buffer state between Russia and the British Empire, and as the locus of Britain's major oil interests in the Middle East. The reality of Iran's position in the world community was sharply highlighted in 1941 when the illusory autarchy of Reza Shah collapsed: as soon as his regime was perceived to present a threat to Allied interests, his country was occupied and he was forced to abdicate. Iran's geographical situation and the crucial importance of its oil continued to ensure its strategic value, both as an all-weather supply route to the Soviet Union during the war, and, with the onset of the Cold War, as a cardinal factor in East–West relations.

Ebtehaj's role in the shaping of appropriate domestic institutions in Iran was paralleled by his efforts to improve Iran's international standing, and thus increase his country's bargaining power in world affairs. This was a constant theme of his policy, and he was prepared to delve into the smallest of details in order to achieve his wider goals. Soon after he became Governor of the Bank Melli, for instance, he asked if the British Legation's Financial Counsellor could see to it that the *rial* was quoted alongside other currencies in *The Times, Economist,* and similar journals. The request was passed on to the Bank of England which undertook to arrange matters.[1] Ebtehaj wanted Iran on the map. In this sense he counts as a great Iranian nationalist – although it was an altogether less xenophobic form of nationalism than that of many of his contemporaries.

The existence of someone of Ebtehaj's calibre at the head of

Iran's national bank was in itself important for Iran's international image during the 1940s – the more so since there was both a lack of continuity in government and evidence of considerable corruption and inefficiency in most areas of the country's administration. The wholly different image presented by the Bank Melli was recognised internationally, and appreciated accordingly.[2] Ebtehaj was held in considerable respect in government and financial circles in the United States and Britain, and his opinion was sought regularly on a broad spectrum of issues – from finance and development to changes in the constitution. His influence with the Shah was also recognised.[3] Stewart Alsop, the American columnist, who visited Iran in 1947, singled out the quality in Ebtehaj which probably explained more than anything else the respect in which he was held in the West. Finding 'Iran's financial genius, Abol Hassan Ebtehaj' one of the three most interesting characters on the Iranian political scene – the other two being the Shah and Prime Minister Qavam – he described him as 'a man of great intelligence who speaks his mind with quite un-Oriental directness'.[4] This opinion was echoed by the American Chargé, James Somerville, in 1949, in a remarkable analysis of Ebtehaj's worth:

> From the view point of the Economic Section of the Embassy, Ebtehaj has during the past four years been by far the most important and active contact. He has great natural ability and an extremely quick mind and considering all that he has to do keeps remarkably informed on the questions of the day. He is one of the closer friends of the Shah. . . . He has been frequently used by the Shah to convey messages or to secure information on matters of importance both economic and otherwise. He has been the principal dynamic force in pushing the idea of economic development in Iran, and in this connection has dealt directly with the World Bank and with various American Engineering companies. . . . On various occasions Ebtehaj has gone out of his way to give the embassy assistance in matters which were not directly his concern, but where for one reason or another an impasse has been reached. . . . In dealing with Ebtehaj, it is necessary to bear in mind that he has a very low "boiling point" and not infrequently gets excited and angry. On the other hand, dealings with him are unusually satisfactory in the sense that one can always be sure that he says exactly what is on his mind. Furthermore, reliance can be placed on those things that Ebtehaj states as

facts. He is not a gossip-monger or woolly minded. . . . He has an unusual ability for stating a case, and, in this connection, during his several visits to the United States he has made a very favorable impression on most officials with whom he has come in contact. Certain World Bank officials stated that they regard him as outstanding among Middle-Eastern officials having to do with economic matters.[5]

Ebtehaj's involvement with Iran's external relations began with the serious currency and foreign exchange problems which afflicted the country following the introduction by Britain of strict exchange controls throughout the Sterling Area in August 1939, and later its occupation by the Allies. By 1939 Iran was already suffering from foreign exchange shortages as a result of Reza Shah's rapid industrialisation programme. The revenue from oil royalties, payable in Sterling and Iran's main source of foreign exchange, was usually spent as soon as it was received – for the most part outside the Sterling Area. Britain's exchange controls, which restricted the use to which foreign countries' Sterling could be put, was therefore a major inconvenience. Over the following two years there were extended and unproductive negotiations between Iran and Britain on the issue. Iran sought to persuade Britain to allow it a proportion of the oil royalties in 'hard' currencies – dollars or gold – that could be used to buy essential goods in world markets. Meanwhile, Britain strove to ensure that the Anglo-Iranian Oil Company received the local currency it required to operate within Iran. The British government eventually and grudgingly conceded that Iran could convert up to £6 million of its royalty payments into gold – and thus into dollars – provided 'that the friendly political relations between the Iranian Government and His Majesty's Government remain . . . unimpaired'.[6] However, there were a number of other complex subsidiary issues, and a formal 'payments' agreement on these lines still had not been signed by the time of the Allied invasion in August 1941.

The Allied occupation further dislocated Iran's fragile economy. Inflationary pressure had been evident since the mid-1930s, but it was greatly aggravated by the Allied insistence in September 1941 on the devaluation of the Iranian currency from the official rate of 68.80 to 142 *rials* to the £ Sterling, by Allied military spending in the country, and by wartime shortages compounded by widespread speculation and hoarding. By the autumn of 1942, Allied expenditure in Iran was in the region of some 400 million *rials* a month, price levels had more than doubled within the space of a year, and public confidence in the *rial* had been badly damaged.[7]

One result of the occupation was a prolonged currency crisis. Instead of a shortage of Sterling, a problem arising out of the massive expenditure necessitated by Reza Shah's industrialisation programme and exacerbated by the introduction of British exchange controls, the Iranian government faced a severe shortage of *rials*. The obvious answer was the issue of more paper currency, but the Iranian government, already faced with a steep decline in the ratio of the metallic cover and apprehensive about adding to inflationary pressures, was reluctant to permit this.

The shortage of local currency posed serious problems for the British authorities in Iran, and they pushed hard for an expanded note issue. They were able to manage in the short run by using the Imperial Bank to grant the British military an overdraft, and supply them with all the available local currency. By threatening that the Imperial Bank would be ordered to close its doors, the Iranian government was forced to increase the note issue by 700 million *rials* by the end of March 1942.[8] However, a more permanent solution was clearly necessary, and, in the end, this meant resurrecting the moribund 'payments' agreement negotiated prior to the Allied invasion. For its part, the Iranian government was determined to use the need to expand the note issue to force a revaluation of the *rial* against Sterling from the rate fixed after the Allied occupation, and to restore confidence in the currency by increasing its gold backing. The *rial*, it was argued, was seriously undervalued, and Iran was in effect paying for Britain's war expenditure in the country. In addition, Iran badly needed goods from Britain against its Sterling holdings, together with an option to convert unused Sterling into gold to restore the level of the note issue cover and confidence in the currency.[9] Not surprisingly the British authorities were reluctant to accede to any revaluation of the *rial*, and they also proved no more happy with the idea of granting Iran gold conversion rights than they had been in 1940 since it was feared that this would open the door to similar requests from other Middle Eastern countries and even Latin America.[10]

It was at this stage, in April 1942, eight months before he became Governor of the Bank Melli, that Ebtehaj was included in the discussions. Over the following years Ebtehaj was involved in the negotiation of a series of international financial agreements which had considerable importance for his country's economic fortunes, although the complexities and apparent dullness of such matters have meant that historians have generally preferred to neglect them and focus instead on Mossadeq's more colourful clashes with the Anglo-Iranian Oil Company.

Ebtehaj brought a new strength to the Iranian side of the negotiations, and it soon became evident that he had a thorough appreciation of the issues involved. He made it perfectly clear privately that gold conversion of Iran's Sterling balances should be the basis of any agreement reached, and that it should be easy to persuade the British authorities of the justice of this. The Prime Minister asked him to talk to the British Minister, Sir Reader Bullard, although with no real hope of any success as Bullard had so far proved impervious to every suggestion.[11] However, Ebtehaj skirted this problem by taking the matter up directly with William Iliff, the newly arrived Treasury representative and Financial Counsellor at the British Legation. Despite the fact that Iliff had been sent out specifically to ensure that Britain's advantage in any payments agreement was maintained,[12] in the course of a series of meetings during April 1942 Ebtehaj managed to persuade him of the justice of Iran's claim to gold conversion for its Sterling, arguing that since Britain had occupied Iran by force, and had brought the Soviets in, the least that the British government could do was to pay for its military expenses in gold. Iliff agreed to 40 per cent gold conversion. This was less than Ebtehaj wanted, but at least the principle was established, and Ebtehaj was convinced that he would be able to push the percentage up by holding firm. Before he could carry the argument further, however, the Minister of Finance pre-empted the situation and agreed with the British authorities on 40 per cent.[13] A Financial Agreement was finally signed on 26 May 1942, under the terms of which the Iranian government undertook to ensure an adequate supply of currency to finance all commercial and financial transactions between Britain and Iran, the Sterling/*rial* rate was set at 128 (a compromise between the 140 wanted by the British and the 80 wanted by Iran), and Britain agreed to convert 40 per cent of Iran's unused Sterling balances into gold.[14]

The crisis was not yet over though. By August 1942, the currency situation was again tense because of unanticipated objections to the Agreement and a consequent delay in its ratification by the *Majles*. There was no mechanism for the issue of notes without recourse to the *Majles*, and inevitably such recourse would bring up the subject of the gold conversion percentage which was considered to be too low. Once more Ebtehaj was brought into the negotiations. He was one of the four members of a commission set up to study the currency question and advise government on a policy for the note issue.[15] Before long, he emerged as the chief liaison between government and the British Legation in an attempt to amend the Financial Agreement, and the leading exponent of the government's argument for a higher gold conversion ratio. On 14 October 1942, at a meeting in the Legation attended by Bullard and Iliff, Ebtehaj presented Iran's case to Richard Casey, Britain's Minister of State Resident in the Middle East and a member of the British War Cabinet.[16]

By the autumn of 1942, the whole currency issue was just one bone of contention among many between the Allies and the Iranian government. The occupation had badly disrupted food supplies, not only because of heavy Allied purchases of food but also owing to constant Soviet obstruction of the shipment of wheat and rice from Iran's grain-rich but Soviet-occupied northern provinces. The southern and central provinces, and especially Tehran, were short of grain and famine seemed perilously close. The queues of starving people pleading for bread outside one of Tehran's many bakeries, which Ebtehaj passed on his way to the Legation for his meeting with Casey, lent considerable force to the conviction he expressed that Britain had a duty to recompense Iran in some measure for the rigours of the occupation. He warned that if Britain envisaged the establishment of friendly post-war relations with Iran, a more sympathetic attitude would have to be adopted. His arguments appeared to strike home, helped, no doubt, by the fact that they echoed the growing concern of the American authorities in Tehran – and he made a lasting impression on Casey. The Allies eventually took steps not only to import a reserve of grain, but to release supplies from Azerbaijan. However, a *quid pro quo* was required – the immediate settlement of the currency crisis.[17]

Alleviation of the food crisis bolstered the authority of the Iranian government and enabled it to deal with the currency crisis before frustration over the shortage of notes for Allied purposes drove Britain into adopting such contingent measures as forcibly taking over Bank Melli and the Imperial Bank.[18] In mid-November 1942, as explained in the previous Chapter, a new Currency Law was passed setting up a Note Reserve Control Board to regulate the issue of notes. At the same time, a supplement to the Financial Agreement was agreed, which increased the gold conversion ratio to 60 per cent, retrospectively to May. Although Ebtehaj was unable to secure the 100 per cent ratio he thought justified, he did contrive to obtain the next best thing – an assurance that the remaining 40 per cent of excess Sterling balances would be guaranteed against possible Sterling devaluation by being linked to the price of gold – and to persuade the *Majles* that this was, in effect, as good as 100 per cent gold conversion. The Supplementary Agreement was signed in January 1943, and the amended Financial Agreement was finally ratified by the *Majles* in June.[19] The British government felt it had made a major concession in signing it. 'The whole Agreement', a Bank of England official observed, 'was forced on HMG by the pressure of the military and political situation',[20] a circumstance which Ebtehaj had not only foreseen but contrived to turn to Iran's advantage.

As a result of the Financial Agreement, Iran's holdings of gold kept pace with the expansion of the note issue during the war, and the country also acquired substantial Sterling balances which were guaranteed by the price of gold. Moreover, even though it did not give Iran the 100 per cent gold conversion provided for by the United States Agreement negotiated in 1943, it did provide a windfall profit of nearly half a million pounds in 1945. When the buying price of gold in London changed on 8 June of that year, Ebtehaj invoked the gold price guarantee despite heavy hints from the Foreign Office that other countries with similar payments agreements had accepted that the change in price was only a technical one and had agreed not to ask for an adjustment in their Sterling balances, and the Treasury had to authorise the adjustment of Iran's balances.[21] In addition, the Agreement provided a precedent for the negotiation of similar agreements with the Soviet Union and the United States in 1943. The Soviet–Iranian Agreement was less generous than the Anglo-Iranian one, but the United States was, as might be expected, able to provide more generous terms: the provision to Iran of dollars against all *rials* required by the American authorities in Iran, the exchange of the dollars into gold, and acceptance of the principle of a variable exchange rate.[22]

The Anglo-Iranian Agreement of 1942 was a triumph for Iran, especially as it was so much more favourable than anything the British government had intended. It is particularly striking that it was signed at a time when Iran was under Allied occupation and the British were in a position to impose military sanctions as a last resort. However, it was the precedent the Agreement set for Anglo-Iranian financial relations after the war which was to prove to be its greatest value.[23] By 1946 the Iranian *rial* had become for Britain, in the words of Iliff, 'a very hard currency which ultimately the

Persians may be able to force us to acquire only against goods or gold'.[24]

By the time Ebtehaj became embroiled in Iran's post-war financial relations with Britain, his reputation as a tough negotiator was based on more than the wartime financial agreements alone. He had successfully represented Iran outside its own borders during 1944, ensuring for his country a serious voice in financial and economic deliberations on both a regional and international level.

Ebtehaj led Iran's delegation to a Middle East Financial Conference which was held in Cairo from 24 to 29 April 1944. The Conference was sponsored by the Anglo-American Middle East Supply Centre and attended by Ministers and technical experts representing the Allies and 11 Middle Eastern governments. Lord Moyne, then British Minister for the Middle East, was President of the Conference and his United States counterpart was one of eight Vice Presidents. The other seven were drawn from among the Middle Eastern delegations present, and included Ebtehaj.[25] The purpose of the Conference was to review how Middle Eastern currency and banking systems were standing up to the strain of wartime conditions, and the conclusions were, as might have been expected, complacent.[26] The real importance of the Conference for Iran was in the status imparted through being an active participant – the fact that Ebtehaj, as leader of Iran's delegation, was one of the Vice Presidents did much for his own if not the country's self-confidence – and the forum it provided for discussions and the exchange of information on a regional basis. Ebtehaj certainly returned to Iran strengthened in his desire to assume control over the country's exchange policy as a result of discovering that other Middle Eastern countries were in urgent need of dollars but were finding it almost impossible to get them from the British Treasury. It seemed to him necessary, in these circumstances, to conserve Iran's dollar holdings for useful and productive purposes – a course of action only possible if foreign exchange came under the direction of the Bank Melli.[27] He was also determined to do something about his discovery in Cairo that Iran was not using its import quotas efficiently and was considered the worst country in the Middle East in this respect.[28] It was a discovery that was taken just as seriously by the Iranian government as by Ebtehaj, and one which reflected badly on the Millspaugh Mission which was in charge of organising such matters.[29]

Within a few weeks of his return from Cairo, the Prime Minister appointed Ebtehaj to lead Iran's delegation to the International Monetary and Financial Conference to be held in July 1944 at Bretton Woods in the United States. The other members of the delegation were drawn from Iran's Embassy in Washington and therefore had no problem in attending. Ebtehaj, however, had somehow to make his way from Iran to the United States – a civilian trying to cross half the world in wartime. It was no easy task, but he tackled it with his customary drive and determination. He cabled Iran's Minister in Washington that he was leaving Tehran on a Monday and would arrive in Washington on the following Wednesday, and asked him to make appropriate hotel reservations. Arriving in New York on Wednesday as planned he at once telephoned Iran's Legation in Washington and was outraged to discover that no arrangements had been made for him. Indeed it transpired that the Minister was not even in Washington – he was in New York at the Waldorf Hotel. Ebtehaj promptly telephoned him there and complained bitterly. The Minister, for his part, expressed complete amazement that Ebtehaj was actually in New York. Neither he nor anyone else at the Embassy had taken Ebtehaj's cable seriously – it was unthinkable in wartime for the journey from Tehran to New York to take such a short time. Unthinkable or not, Ebtehaj had managed it. He had set off without the least idea of how his journey would proceed, but, armed only with an official *laisser passer*, prepared to argue his way on to whatever air transport – military inevitably – was going in the right direction. He went from Tehran to Abadan, from Abadan to Cairo where he was joined by members of the Egyptian and Greek delegations, from Cairo to Tripoli and finally, after various other stopovers, arrived at La Guardia airport:

> I had to go and fight. Nobody took any notice of a civilian, everyone was so busy you know . . . it was after the landings in Italy and I think before the landings in Normandy . . . they didn't care a damn about the Bretton Woods Conference, they didn't know what Bretton Woods was. I had a VIP document, but what did they care. They were afraid even to have a civilian on military 'planes but I forced my way and got there on time on Wednesday.[30]

The Bretton Woods Conference was organised under the auspices of the United Nations to consider the problem of cooperation in international trade and payments. It had its origins in a determination that the alleged mistakes of the 1920s and 1930s –

especially the ill-fated attempts to restore the gold standard – should not be repeated in the aftermath of the Second World War. The two principal pundits at Bretton Woods were John Maynard Keynes, Chairman of the British delegation, and Harry Dexter White, Under-Secretary of the United States Treasury, each of whom had a different idea of what should be done, although their objectives were very similar. The outcome of the Conference, which followed White's plan more closely than Keynes's, was the foundation of two related institutions, the International Monetary Fund (IMF) and the International Bank for Reconstruction and Development (which became generally known as the World Bank). Both the IMF and the World Bank were established in Washington in March 1946, and, by the end of 1950, had a membership of 49 countries.

Iran was a founding member of both institutions, and, in 1950, one of still only eight members from its immediate region (the others being India, Turkey, Egypt, Lebanon, Syria, Iraq and Ethiopia). Its attendance at the Bretton Woods Conference had evoked a mixed response. From the Iranian point of view it was a very high profile event. Millspaugh, for instance, objected strongly to Ebtehaj's appointment as Chairman of Iran's delegation, observing that even if he never accomplished anything in the United States he would return with greatly enhanced prestige in Iranian eyes and 'judging by the effect of the Cairo Conference on him, he would be utterly impossible to handle'.[31] Certainly Ebtehaj's trip to the United States attracted much advance publicity in Iran, and it seemed clear that great things were expected of it in terms of the country's status, contacts made, and in discussions with the State Department. The Shah asked Ebtehaj to see President Roosevelt on his behalf and deliver a personal letter to indicate the mutual friendship and goodwill between Iran and the United States.[32]

From the perspective of Bretton Woods, Iran's participation in the Conference was of little moment. At the end of May, Keynes wrote, in pejorative tones, that

> Twenty-one countries have been invited which clearly have nothing to contribute and will merely encumber the ground, namely, Colombia, Costa Rica, Dominica, Ecuador, Salvador, Guatemala, Haiti, Honduras, Liberia, Nicaragua, Panama, Paraguay, Philippines, Venezuela, Peru, Uruguay, Ethiopia, Iceland, Iran, Iraq, Luxemburg. The most monstrous monkey-house assembled for years.[33]

It was the only reference to Iran or its delegation he made. How-

4. Heads of delegations at Bretton Woods, 1944

PUTTING IRAN ON THE MAP

ever, there is no doubt but that Iran's presence at Bretton Woods, and its role as a founder member of the IMF, enhanced the country's status internationally. Ebtehaj was one of the 11 members of the Conference Steering Committee alongside Keynes, Mendès France and others. He also became one of the eight 'permanent' governors of the IMF, although Keynes dismissed these governors as 'ornamental personages, who receive no salary and only function on occasions, which may be no more than once a year'.[34]

In terms of relations between the United States and Iranian governments, Ebtehaj's visit to the United States was nearly a disaster. At a meeting with State Department officials on 26 July 1944, he told them that he was in Washington for two reasons – to meet with President Roosevelt and hand over to him in person the Shah's letter, and to discuss the problem of Millspaugh. He was unable to see the President, and, on the subject of Millspaugh, he was informed that any attempt to engage Soviet experts in Millspaugh's place would mean forfeiting America's friendship. Although he knew nothing about any such prospect, Ebtehaj's reaction was characteristic; such matters, he intimated, were nothing to do with the United States. Great offence was caused as a result of these interchanges. Ebtehaj

> expressed deep dissatisfaction at the trend of relations between the United States and Iran and stated bluntly that it appears the United States has refused the hand of friendship extended by the Iranians.[35]

His dissatisfaction was based on a series of incidents, starting with President Roosevelt's attitude at the famous 'big three' Tehran Conference in 1943, when, unlike Stalin who observed the correct formalities and called with due courtesy on the Shah, he merely waited for the Shah to call on him. The State Department's attitude on the Millspaugh issue and Ebtehaj's failure to obtain an interview with Roosevelt to deliver the Shah's letter compounded the problem, and he threatened to urge the Iranian government not to humiliate itself further but to look elsewhere for friendship and help.[36]

The lengths to which the United States government went to repair the damage to Iran's – and Ebtehaj's – esteem are an interesting reflection of its wish not to offend Iran. The State Department, and particularly the Secretary of State, Cordell Hull, put themselves out to soothe Ebtehaj's ruffled feathers. Cordell Hull at once asked Ebtehaj to come and see him, and as Ebtehaj later recollected,

> I was deeply impressed by him. He told me he had been greatly upset that President Roosevelt had not called on the Shah in Tehran & had expressed this feeling to FDR upon his return. He assured me of USA's friendship for Iran & asked me to convey this assurance to the Shah and to the Iranian people. ... He asked me to come and see him whenever I came to Washington.

Ebtehaj spent only 20 minutes with Cordell Hull, but it was a meeting both men remembered many years later.[37] President Roosevelt also did his best to repair the damage. Ebtehaj had left the letter with the Iranian Minister, pending instructions from Tehran, and, in due course, the Minister passed it on to Secretary Hull who handed it to Roosevelt on 21 August. Immediately, the enormity of the diplomatic blunder became evident. The contents of the letter were a reassurance to Roosevelt of Iran's willingness to cooperate with the United States both during and after the War and an expression of hope for 'more comprehensive understanding and mutual aid'. Ebtehaj was to discuss details. At the beginning of September, Roosevelt wrote to the Shah apologising for not having been able to see Ebtehaj, giving as his reason the fact that he had had to go to the west coast and Hawaii. The Shah's reply made it clear that any temporary irritation had now been allayed.[38] Honour had been served.

Ebtehaj was unable to attend the inaugural meeting of the IMF and the World Bank in March 1946, but thereafter he attended as often as possible. When he was no longer Governor of the Bank Melli, and thus no longer eligible to attend in an official capacity, he continued to be invited to the annual meetings. Many useful friendships were formed at these meetings and contacts made, and the informal socialising was invaluable in the enhancing of reputations. At a meeting in Washington in 1952, for instance, Ebtehaj met the Deputy Governor of the Bank of England, George Bolton, who introduced him as 'the fellow who saved . . . Iran's currency [in the War]'.[39] Ebtehaj came to know well such influential men as John McCloy, President of the World Bank from 1947 to 1949; his successor, Eugene Black, President from 1949 to 1963; and C.F. Cobbold, Deputy Governor (1945–49) and later Governor (1949–61) of the Bank of England; and to earn their respect. Indeed their respect for and trust in Ebtehaj was often to be of considerable service to Iran.

Neither the IMF nor the World Bank started operating properly until 1947, and the first country outside Europe and Latin America to obtain a loan was India, in August 1949. However, as early as October 1946 Iran had put forward an informal application for a large long-term loan ($250 million) for economic development purposes. While no immediate response was forthcoming on the loan, although it was clear that the size of it was unacceptably large, the Bank's staff investigated Iran's development programme and provided the country with technical advice. It was through the Bank that Iran obtained the services of consultants to study its Seven Year Development Plan and recommend measures for its implementation. Iran was one of the first Middle Eastern countries to be visited by the Bank's top executives – in March of 1949 its Vice President, Robert Garner, included Iran in his itinerary, reported favourably on the country's development possibilities and indicated that the Bank would in principle be prepared to participate, albeit on a less grandiose scale than Iran might wish, in the financing of some of the planned development projects.[40] Needless to say, Ebtehaj was in the forefront of these initial efforts to enlist the World Bank's active help and advice for Iran's development programme.

Meanwhile, before submitting formal applications to the World Bank, or elsewhere, for assistance with a capital development programme, it was essential for Iran to know the amount of finance that would be available from its own resources for such development. By 1946, Iran had accumulated Sterling balances amounting to over £20 million, as well as the gold acquired under the terms of the 1942 financial agreement. While British military expenditure in Iran would cease as soon as British troops evacuated the country, and Iran would lose the Sterling which paid for it, the country's Sterling income from oil revenues and from the local expenditure of the Oil Company seemed set to grow.

Already in 1945 it was evident that two schools of thought were forming in Iranian government circles over what should happen to the Sterling/*rial* rate of exchange when the 1942 Agreement expired, in relation to providing finance for a development programme. The Minister of Finance led a school of thought which advocated devaluation of the *rial* to 150 to the pound Sterling and a reduction in the metallic cover of the note issue to, say, 50 per cent in order to provide funds – both in local currency and foreign exchange – which government could use for various development projects. Ebtehaj led an alternative school of thought which still placed great merit on a heavily backed currency and the conservation of the country's gold reserves, until such time, at least, as the country was ready for these resources to be used in a systematic way for planned development. In the meantime, if anything, he favoured a revaluation of the *rial* in order to express what he considered to be the relative strengths of the two currencies.

The end of the Anglo-Iranian Financial Agreement in March 1946 focused attention on how financial relations between Iran and Britain were to be conducted thereafter. It signalled, to the relief of the British authorities, the end of the gold conversion and guarantee clauses. Sterling was by now in a fragile state, and any seepage of Britain's gold reserves was looked upon with alarm. Britain's freedom of manoeuvre was constrained by its financial dependence on the United States. At the end of 1945, Anglo-American agreement was reached for a substantial post-war loan to Britain, in return for which Britain promised to take steps to avoid discrimination in international trade and to seek a settlement of its Sterling debts either by wholesale cancellation or by freezing those which could not be cancelled. When the American loan became available in mid-1946, however, Britain could not prevent most of it leaking away through the drawing down of Sterling balances.[41] The terms of the Financial Agreement with the United States, when it became operative in July 1946, meant that Britain had to agree not only to make currently acquired Sterling convertible into dollars within one year, but also to negotiate the release of Sterling balances already held, and their convertibility. In order to protect its own position, Britain was thus forced into making agreements with individual countries to ensure that the release of such balances was gradual.[42]

It was against this background that post-war Anglo-Iranian financial arrangements were worked out. During early 1946, there were fears in the Foreign Office that Iran would insist on a change in the Sterling/*rial* exchange rate, to Britain's disadvantage, and also continue to demand gold conversion to the extent of 60 per cent or more.[43] Ebtehaj soon made it clear that for the time being Iran would observe the terms of the Bretton Woods Agreement and maintain the existing rate.[44] Nevertheless, he had stiff demands in other areas. He wanted the immediate settlement of accumulated Sterling balances, or at least specific indications as to the extent of release Britain would concede; the retrospective convertibility into gold of oil royalties from May 1942 to March 1946 and 100 per cent convertibility thereafter until such time as the Anglo-American Agreement arrangements for current Sterling earnings came into force; and the conclusion of some satisfactory arrangement for the convertibility of Sterling earnings from other than oil sources. In short, Ebtehaj insisted that Iran required access to its Sterling and gold reserves for capital development purposes, greater recompense for the fact that Iranian oil was one of Britain's best dollar earners, and access to convertible foreign exchange. And he was prepared, if necessary, to use the Oil Company's local currency requirement to force the issue.[45]

The Anglo-Iranian Oil Company's need to buy *rials* left Britain in no real position to bargain.[46] While Ebtehaj did not achieve all his desiderata, the financial arrangements entered into by Iran and Britain at the end of November 1946 ensured the continuation of Iran's gold conversion facilities until full convertibility of Iran's current sterling earnings, under the terms of the Anglo-American Agreement, came into force. Between 2 March (when the 1942 Agreement ended) and 31 October 1946, 60 per cent of the net increase in Iran's official holdings of Sterling area currencies was to be convertible into gold. Thereafter, if the amount of Iran's Sterling balances at the date when full convertibility was introduced exceeded the total at 31 October 1946, there was to be 100 per cent gold conversion of the excess. Moreover, the British government undertook to implement the provisions of the Washington Agreement, so far as Iran's current Sterling earnings were concerned, no later than 15 July 1947. In return, Iran agreed to abandon any claim against the Oil Company for the payment of royalties otherwise than in Sterling, to provide an adequate supply of local currency to finance all current transactions between Iran and the Sterling area, and not to restrict unreasonably the sale of Sterling for current transactions. The arrangements were, however, to be kept secret as they were potentially very embarrassing for Britain. Other nations might demand what Ebtehaj had secured for Iran.[47]

In July 1947, Britain introduced Sterling convertibility in line with its obligations under the Anglo-American Agreement, and, on 15 July, Iran was given transferable account facilities. By that time, Britain had reason to appreciate the fact that Ebtehaj was prepared to stick to his side of the bargain, and was also prepared to contemplate entering into a further agreement to meet the new situation regarding the status of Sterling. Not only had the November 1946 arrangements not been made public, and Britain saved from the embarrassment of explaining to other Sterling holders why Iran was getting such favourable treatment, but an understanding had been arrived at with Ebtehaj that until a new agreement had been made Iran's accumulated balances would not, after the introduction of convertibility on 15 July, be drawn upon to any significant extent except after consultation.[48] It was a 'gentlemen's agreement' which soon proved its worth.

Within weeks of the introduction of convertibility, Britain was in the throes of a 'convertibility crisis', and had to retreat from the terms of the Anglo-American Agreement. Sterling stopped being freely convertible, and Britain had to resort to a series of bilateral arrangements instead.[49] On 30 September the British Treasury reached an agreement with Ebtehaj, initialled *ad referendum* by both sides, on Iran's position. It was finally ratified at the end of October, and backdated to take effect as soon as convertibility was suspended on 20 August 1947. Because of the favourable nature of the deal to Iran, the negotiations were again cloaked in great secrecy, and when agreement was reached it took the form of a Memorandum of Understanding between the Bank of England and the Bank Melli, communicated in an exchange of letters, rather than an official agreement between the two governments. The main features of the arrangement were that Iran's Sterling accounts would have transferable account status; that the Sterling balances on these accounts would carry a guarantee against depreciation in terms of gold; that transferability to the American account area was permissible for essential goods not obtainable in Sterling; and that such transfer facilities were to be used only to the extent that Iran's own dollar resources were unobtainable.[50]

A Bank of England official pinpointed the significance of the arrangement, in its reliance on goodwill, when he observed –

> In view of the importance of the oil concession, it seemed better to rely on Ebtehaj's assurances, confirmed by the Persian Government, as to the use of their Sterling in the American Account area than to give the Persians 60% outright in gold (on which they would sit) and have to meet possible demands for dollars, etc, over and above that.[51]

The British need to protect the Anglo-Iranian Oil Company's business was, indeed, a major factor in explaining why Iran was able to twist the British government's arm. However, Ebtehaj undoubtedly used his advantages to good effect, earning admiration from British Treasury officials:

> Ebtehaj is entirely a modern European in his financial outlook and probably some distance ahead of his Government. He held all the cards and knew it, so we did not waste any time in disputing that . . . Ebtehaj is regarded as one of the most

intelligent people in Iran. Certainly I should hope there are not many more intelligent.[52]

It is noteworthy, too, that the Memorandum of Understanding was not an official agreement, but merely an understanding, and that it was based on Ebtehaj's personal promises that hard currency expenditure would be minimised and kept to absolutely necessary objects. Sir Wilfred Eady, who initialled the Memorandum on the Treasury's behalf, noted in a letter to Ebtehaj that the arrangement rested 'largely on a basis of mutual trust and recognition of one another's points of view'.[53] Ebtehaj had clearly proved that his word was good.

Iran's adherence to the spirit of the Memorandum of Understanding did more to ensure its claim to be considered seriously by the British government than almost anything else, and Ebtehaj's role in this was clearly recognised. The Understanding was renewed each year until the oil nationalisation crisis in the early 1950s, and the only real hiccup was in 1948 when the Committee with whom Ebtehaj had negotiated the arrangement refused at first to renew it. Ebtehaj went directly to Sir Stafford Cripps, then the British Chancellor of the Exchequer, who told him that greater assurances were required that the Memorandum would be observed strictly. In reply, Ebtehaj later recollected,

> I told him about a Council of Ministers' Decree that had been passed, authorising a Deputy to buy dollars. The Exchange Commission had refused because the beneficiary was travelling to France. The beneficiary protested. I refused to overrule the Exchange Commission. He saw the Prime Minister who called me to ask me to explain how the Bank Melli refused to observe a Council of Ministers' Decree. I explained that if we were to do that, we would be violating another decree ratifying the Memorandum of Understanding. The Prime Minister agreed. I told Cripps I could not show a better example of how we operated.[54]

Cripps took the point. He instructed that the Memorandum of Understanding should be renewed. Ebtehaj's reputation proved the best guarantee available.

Moreover, the value of the gold guarantee against depreciation of Iran's Sterling balances, which Ebtehaj had insisted upon, was soon to be forcibly underlined. When Sterling devalued in dollar terms by 30.5 per cent in September 1949, Iran was recompensed for losses incurred. Its Sterling balances and royalty earnings were worth 44 per cent more than they had been.[55] However, despite considerable pressure from his own colleagues in the Bank Melli, and from the management of the British bank, he resisted suggestions that the Sterling deposits of the Anglo-Iranian Oil Company held by the Bank Melli and the British bank should also be revalued. He was insistent that the devaluation guarantee did not apply to such British-owned Sterling balances, and in persuading both his colleagues and the Council of Ministers to endorse his view proved once again his adherence to the strict terms of the Memorandum of Understanding. Four years later, in 1953, Prime Minister Mossadeq attempted to have Ebtehaj prosecuted, along with the Prime Minister and Finance Minister of the government which had supported him, for his failure to collect the additional £2.2 million odd deemed to have been due from Britain on account of the Oil Company's deposits.[56]

By 1950, Ebtehaj had achieved a great deal in the way of improving Iran's international reputation and standing. Iran had emerged well out of the prolonged foreign exchange negotiations with the United Kingdom. The country had secured a voice in international financial affairs through its early membership of the IMF and the World Bank. And while western governments were alarmed at the political instability in Iran in the late 1940s, Ebtehaj at least provided a continuity of policy in financial and economic affairs. Everywhere Ebtehaj went he – and through him Iran – earned respect. The American Chargé in Tehran in 1949 observed that there was 'a remarkable measure of agreement' about Ebtehaj even amongst his critics – 'and that is as to his personal and financial integrity'.[57]

Yet more than the efforts of one technocrat was required to transform an administration run according to age-old traditions on the one hand, and to influence western perceptions of an alien culture on the other. Ebtehaj and others – including the young Shah – did their best, but as so often Iran found itself trapped by paradox. To achieve the economic and political regeneration needed at the end of the War, and to stand firm as a bastion against Communism, Iran required financial and military aid from the West, which meant effectively the United States. However, it became increasingly clear in the late 1940s that such help would not be forthcoming to the degree necessary until Iran showed significant signs of economic and political improvement. Ebtehaj's 'integrity' was not enough. In the wake of the collapse of Republican China, Washington became convinced that financial aid to 'corrupt' governments was simply 'money poured down a rat-hole'.[58] Iran was told that unless it reformed its administration and purged government of undesirable elements it could expect little help. When the Shah visited the United States in autumn 1949 in the expectation of receiving the sort of financial aid being given to Turkey and Greece – other 'frontline' states in the struggle against Communism – he got little more than lectures from the Truman Administration on the necessity of carrying out reforms and ending corruption.[59]

Ebtehaj's accomplishments were, in the end, insufficient to counter Iran's growing internal difficulties and compensate for the lack of the American loans which would have given much needed – and expected – aid, and thus have taken the pressure off the financing of Iran's burgeoning development plans. Instead, Iranian politicians turned to the Anglo-Iranian Oil Company to provide the extra finance required. Meanwhile, Ebtehaj was himself one of the casualties of a deteriorating political situation, and the escalating international difficulties confronting his country.

4

CHALLENGING THE BRITISH BANK

Ebtehaj's fight to create modern economic institutions in Iran, and to raise the international status of his country, was matched by a campaign to challenge the power of his old employer, the Imperial Bank of Iran. His desire to restrict the influence of western businesses such as the Bank was one shared by many of his fellow countrymen and, indeed, by generations of people in the Third World as a whole, faced with the domination of their economies by foreign corporations.

In twentieth-century Iran the reaction against western business interests has been particularly strong, a phenomenon related in part to the powerful grip exercised on the economy by foreigners and the links between foreign businesses and the imperial powers who had interfered in Iran's affairs. Until the late 1920s the 'modern' sector of Iran's economy consisted almost entirely of foreign, overwhelmingly British-owned institutions. Iran's struggle against the largest and most politically significant of these, the Anglo-Iranian Oil Company, has predictably attracted the greatest attention. The Oil Company was a symbol of the humiliating foreign domination of Iran. The terms of its concession were attacked for their patent unfairness, with varying degrees of intensity, from soon after the First World War right through to nationalisation by Mossadeq in 1951.[1] However, it is now forgotten that at the same time as the nationalist crusade against Anglo-Iranian was gathering pace in the 1940s, Ebtehaj was engaged in an equally dramatic dispute with the Imperial Bank, the second most important British institution in Iran.

The Bank, with its imposing branches spread all over the country, and its historically strong links with the British Foreign Office, was as much a symbol of the power of British business as the Anglo-Iranian Oil Company. And to Ebtehaj the Bank was the principal stumbling block to his plans to build up the Bank Melli to take its rightful position as Iran's central bank, with full powers over the country's monetary and credit policy. He believed that such control was necessary, not only because it reinforced the status and position of the Bank Melli, but also because in the end the central bank was the only source on which the Iranian government could rely for large borrowings, and so that a coherent financial strategy could be developed to underpin what, in Ebtehaj's view, was Iran's most essential and basic requirement – planned economic development.

This was not a policy which was calculated to endear Ebtehaj to many sectors of the Iranian commercial and financial community since it was bound to curtail their freedom of action in all sorts of ways. Indeed, within weeks of taking over the Bank Melli, Ebtehaj's unpopularity was already evident.[2] And by the late 1940s, when his campaign was well under way, criticism against him in the local press for such policies as credit restriction, the expansion of the note issue, exchange control, and the control of imports – all directed towards a reduction in the cost of living and the conservation of both local and foreign resources for development – was rife. At one stage, in May 1948, when the Imperial Bank was finding 'Ebtehaj's whole attitude . . . thoroughly uncompromising' and 'extremely anti-foreign' with 'not the slightest evidence of any goodwill towards us or the Oil Company', he had no fewer than 38 libel cases in the Courts against various local newspapers who were accusing him of ignoring the interests of the merchant community.[3] Just as Ebtehaj's overall strategy was aimed at the state of the economy in general rather than against the interests of certain sections of it, so his policies were not so much directed exclusively against the Imperial Bank as towards expanding the role of the Bank Melli.

Nevertheless, Ebtehaj had definite ideas about the place of foreign banks in the economy of a country like Iran. He believed that they should be obliged to operate in such a way as to bring maximum benefit to the Iranian economy, and that they should not be allowed to act as if they were locally owned. Foreign banks, he argued, should be confined to certain carefully defined roles – such as the finance of Iran's foreign trade. In practical terms, Ebtehaj fought to impose a series of obligations and restrictions on foreign banks. The most important of these were that they should transfer capital into the country rather than operate solely on local deposits; that their profits should only be remitted abroad in relation to the amount of capital brought into Iran; that their dealings in foreign exchange should be subject to control by Bank Melli; and that they should have no branches outside Tehran.[4] It was an agenda for conflict.

Ebtehaj's views applied to all foreign banks. However, there were only three such banks in Iran when he took over the Bank Melli – the Imperial Bank; the Irano-Soviet Bank, founded in 1924 and involved solely in the finance of Irano-Soviet trade; and the Ottoman Bank, which had opened three branches in Iran in the early 1920s, and a fourth in 1930. Furthermore, the only one of the three which presented any challenge so far as the Bank Melli was concerned was the Imperial Bank, since the Russian Bank's role was very specific, and the Ottoman Bank, which had been refused authorisation to deal in foreign exchange in the 1930s, closed its Tehran office – its last remaining Iranian branch – in 1948.[5] It was the Imperial Bank, therefore, which bore the full force of Ebtehaj's strictures against foreign banks.

It was unfortunate that it was also the Imperial Bank from which Ebtehaj had resigned because of its refusal to promote him to equal management status with its British employees. The fact of the former relationship between them, and in particular the rancorous dispute about compensation which followed his resignation, coloured in the Bank's eyes every action Ebtehaj took to define the role of foreign banks, and in Ebtehaj's eyes every fulminating reaction of the Imperial Bank. The Bank saw everything Ebtehaj did in terms of a personal vendetta, and the more this influenced its attitude towards him, the more it became a reality as Ebtehaj increasingly lost patience with the Bank's apparent inability to appreciate the changed circumstances in Iran after the Second World War.

The Imperial Bank also had fundamental objections to Ebtehaj's vision of the role of Bank Melli. It was regarded as outrageous that Bank Melli was not only a central bank but a commercial competitor. In fact, the combination of central and commercial bank in one institution was not unusual in the 1940s. British bankers in Australia were at this time equally up in arms about the Commonwealth Bank there which also combined the two roles, though it is unlikely that the insular directors and senior management of the Imperial Bank knew much of the angry conflict in Australia.[6] They saw only an embittered ex-employee in a country many of them still regarded as culturally and racially inferior to their own.

It is significant that the Imperial Bank's policies received surprisingly little sympathy from a quarter from which it might have

CHALLENGING THE BRITISH BANK

expected support – the Bank of England. When Ebtehaj was in London in October 1947, he poured out his woes about the Imperial Bank to two Bank of England officials, accusing the Bank of allowing 'their past position to cloud their attitude to present developments'.[7] It was an accusation which Bank of England officials seemed to feel was to some extent justified. Claude Loombe, an Adviser to the Governors (and in the 1960s to become Chairman of the British bank) remarked that in his opinion there was 'a substantial measure of truth in what Mr Ebtehaj says about the general attitude of the Imperial Bank'.[8] Henry Siepmann, one of the Bank's Executive Directors, found Ebtehaj's fulminations understandable 'if account is taken not only of the present but also of the past' and thought that any 'ideas about whether the Imperial Bank of Iran is entitled to perpetual exemption from the march of time' should be revised.[9]

The Bank of England viewed the clash between Ebtehaj and the Imperial Bank with realism, arguing that in view of the strong position Ebtehaj held in Iran it was the more incumbent on the Imperial Bank to 'effect a sincere rapprochement with him if they are to safeguard their position'.[10] However, Bank of England officials were also realistic enough to realise how difficult any such 'sincere rapprochement' would be. As Siepmann commented, rather wryly, 'I doubt whether matters can be prevented from going from bad to worse without changes in the personal representation of the Imperial Bank at the very top.'[11] 'At the very top', Lord Kennet, the Imperial Bank's Chairman, who visited Iran in 1946 and 1948 (the first visits ever made by a chairman to the countries where the Bank was represented), was convinced that Ebtehaj's whole attitude arose from 'an animus' against the Imperial Bank, and that the British Embassy in Tehran would do well to bring pressure to bear on the Prime Minister and Minister of Finance for his removal. This was an extraordinary suggestion, and the British Ambassador was quick to point out that it would put the Embassy in an 'impossible position with the Persian Government'.[12] The Imperial Bank's management in Tehran were equally blunt and more personal in their attitude, successive Chief Managers referring to Ebtehaj's attitude as 'jealous and inimical'; that of 'a megalomaniac with an extremely anti-foreign complex'.[13]

Such views – expressed in 1947 and 1948 – glossed over the fact that until he became Governor of the Bank Melli in 1942, relations between Ebtehaj and the Imperial Bank had been cordial despite the compensation troubles which followed his resignation from the

PLANNING AND POWER IN IRAN

Bank. In 1939–40 Ebtehaj was apt frequently to telephone the Bank's Tehran management to talk over issues of mutual interest in a friendly way.[14] As late as January 1942, the Imperial Bank's Chief Manager observed that 'Mr Ebtehaj shows himself very fair in his direct intercourse with us'.[15]

The relationship between Ebtehaj and the Imperial Bank began to turn sour when Ebtehaj took over the leadership of the Bank Melli. Over the following eight years, Ebtehaj sought to impose restrictions on the Imperial Bank in pursuit of his objective of centralising on the Bank Melli all of Iran's exchange, currency and financial affairs. Slowly, inch by inch, Ebtehaj implemented his policies. He was frequently forced to compromise by the determined opposition of the embattled Imperial Bank, which resorted increasingly to asking for help from the British Embassy. Moreover, many elements within the Iranian government were sceptical of or even hostile towards his views, and it was noticeable that whenever Ebtehaj was out of the country pressure against the Imperial Bank waned. Yet, over time, the will of the Imperial Bank to stay in Iran was worn down by the sheer energy and persistence of Ebtehaj.

The first clashes came over the matter of foreign exchange. Ebtehaj's determination to bring Iran's exchange control laws under the full control of Bank Melli meant not only eliminating competing Iranian institutions such as the Exchange Control Commission, but also curbing the Imperial Bank's exchange business since it and Bank Melli were the only two banks in the country authorised to deal in foreign exchange. The Allied occupation of Iran meant that Ebtehaj's freedom of manoeuvre was necessarily circumscribed during the War. Nevertheless, he secured in 1943 an agreement which reduced the large profits the Imperial Bank was making from foreign exchange operations,[16] and in the following year he audaciously captured for Bank Melli the accounts of the United States Army in Iran, which had hitherto been held by the Imperial Bank.[17]

After the end of the War in 1945, tension increased between Ebtehaj and the Imperial Bank. Foreign exchange continued to be a major cause of conflict, while two other issues served to exacerbate the growing bad feeling – Ebtehaj's requirement that compulsory deposits should be made with the Bank Melli, and the date on which the Imperial Bank's concession was due to end.

Once the War was over, Ebtehaj renewed his attempts to bring the Exchange Control Commission and all foreign exchange operations wholly under the Bank Melli's authority. As part of his campaign, in

September 1945 he informed the Imperial Bank that he intended to cancel its right to deal in foreign exchange. The Bank of course objected strongly, but Ebtehaj was ready for this and argued his case for the cancellation of its exchange authorisation before an informal meeting of the Cabinet. The Imperial Bank was not prepared to give up without a fight, however, the key privilege which made its continued existence in Iran profitable, and its Chief Manager called upon the British Embassy for help. In October 1945 the Ambassador took up the Bank's case with both the Shah and the Minister of Finance. The diplomatic pressure worked, although the fact that Ebtehaj was ill and had to be taken to hospital was an unlooked for bonus for the Imperial Bank. While he was indisposed and unable to exert his formidable influence, the Iranian Cabinet agreed to a new exchange agreement with the Imperial Bank.[18]

Ebtehaj soon resumed the offensive on another front: the question of placing a percentage of deposits with the Bank Melli. It was a question which applied in theory to all the banks in Iran, local and foreign, but again, in practice, it was the Imperial Bank which was mainly concerned since, after the Bank Melli itself, it was by far the largest deposit-taker in Iran. The issue was thrown into sharp relief by the fact that by the end of 1945 the Bank Melli was suffering from a severe liquidity problem, made worse by the Soviet-inspired breakaway of the province of Azerbaijan into a separate state and the consequent flight of deposits away from local banks to the greater safety of foreign banks. In contrast, the Imperial Bank was highly liquid in the immediate post-war period. By January 1946, it held total deposits of 1600 million *rials* (£12.5 million), of which 1137 million *rials* (£8.9 million) was held in cash. These cash reserves were largely held in notes, and out of a total note circulation in Iran of some 7500 million *rials*, 1000 million were in the Imperial Bank's treasuries. Even its Chief Manager felt obliged to admit the justice of Ebtehaj's contention that the Imperial Bank should keep as large a proportion of its funds as possible with the Bank Melli.[19]

Ebtehaj felt that the Imperial Bank was not making anything like an adequate contribution to help the finances of the Iranian government at a time when the latter was experiencing grave financial difficulties, and he was determined that it should be compelled to do more. Moreover Bank Melli was at the limit of its own ability to lend to government with safety. Indeed it had such a chronic shortage of cash, that Ebtehaj was desperately worried about its ability to survive a run if there should be one.[20]

At first Ebtehaj tried to arrive at an understanding with the

Imperial Bank. If it would cooperate with his scheme to deposit with the Bank Melli a certain percentage of its total deposits, he offered to forgo recourse to governmental decree and merely conclude an agreement with the Imperial Bank in writing. While the Chief Manager of the Imperial Bank was sympathetic towards the idea of keeping substantial balances with the Bank Melli, however, he rejected the idea of any definite percentage, maintaining that the amount should be at the Imperial Bank's own discretion.[21] Ebtehaj promptly resorted to legislation, and in mid-July 1946 a decree was issued by the Council of Ministers requiring all banks to keep with the Bank Melli, free of interest, 30 per cent of their demand and 15 per cent of their term deposits. The Imperial Bank again appealed to the Foreign Office for help, and again support was forthcoming, although William Iliff, the former Treasury representative in Iran, felt bound to point out that Ebtehaj's case had 'some logic on its side':

> It is nowadays a well-established practice for commercial banks to be required to deposit a specified part of their reserves with the Central Bank, and I do not think that the Imperial Bank would be on firm ground in fighting the Persian Government, if the latter decided to make such a requirement a feature of Persian Law.[22]

In the event, pressure from the Foreign Office, as well as a change in the Iranian government in August 1946, did contrive to delay the implementation of the compulsory deposits decree, which gave the Bank a chance to argue for a reduction in the percentages required. Finally, in October, a compromise was worked out, and a new decree was issued by the Council of Ministers in November. Under its terms, all banks were obliged to deposit 15 per cent of their demand and 6 per cent of their term deposits with the Bank Melli, and to hold, in addition, Treasury Bonds equivalent to a further 15 per cent and 6 per cent.[23] But this was not to be the end of the affair. The Bank Melli's liquidity difficulties were exacerbated by a law passed by the *Majles* in January 1948 which decreed that because of the dangers of inflation there should be no further issue of bank notes even against 100 per cent cover. At the time, the notes held by the Bank Melli throughout the country amounted to some 500 million *rials* while its deposits were in excess of 300 million *rials*. Any sudden withdrawal of deposits – as had happened in early 1946 as a result of the Azerbaijan crisis – would present the Bank with huge problems in meeting its obligations. And failure to meet its obligations could cause it to be declared bankrupt. It was a threat of which Ebtehaj was only too well aware, and which he had great difficulty in remedying. In the end, it led to his insistence that the percentage of their deposits which banks were obliged to place with the Bank Melli be sharply raised — a demand which meant renewed confrontation with the Imperial Bank.

Ebtehaj's difficulties with the Imperial Bank over foreign exchange and the compulsory deposits issue caused him to view its presence in Iran with an increasingly jaundiced eye, and the end of its 60-year concession in Iran began to present an attractive prospect. As far as the Imperial Bank was concerned, the concession was due to end on 30 January 1949, 60 years from January 1889 when Naser al-Din Shah had signed the original document. The concession's end was viewed with no particular misgiving, moreover. The Imperial Bank simply assumed that as a registered company it would continue to operate as before, the only difference being that it would start paying Iranian income tax, exemption from which having been for some time its only remaining privilege under the concession. Ebtehaj had other ideas. He had taken the advice of Iranian lawyers, and had concluded that using the lunar calendar, which had been in use in Iran in the nineteenth century, rather than the solar calendar, the Imperial Bank's concession was due to expire in April 1947. This was an unwelcome bombshell, especially as the Imperial Bank found itself the target of a vituperative press campaign. Once again the British Embassy and Foreign Office were appealed to, and once again they brought pressure to bear on the Iranian government on the Imperial Bank's behalf. Eventually, the Iranian government ruled in October 1947, when Ebtehaj was conveniently out of the country, in the Imperial Bank's favour. Its concession was deemed to end in January 1949.[24] Ebtehaj had lost another round.

The contest, however, continued, and between 1946 and 1948 he did achieve some progress on the control of foreign exchange. The introduction of a system of exchange purchase certificates in March 1946 for certain specified commodities provided the occasion for yet another assault on the Imperial Bank's foreign exchange authorisation. Although Ebtehaj again failed to persuade government of his case, the Bank Melli was granted overall control of the purchase of foreign exchange, and the Imperial Bank was ordered to follow its instructions. Then, in July 1948, a new foreign exchange decree was introduced which further curbed the Imperial Bank's business — the system of exchange purchase certificates was extended to all permitted imports and the Bank Melli was given an official allocation of £2 million Sterling to provide the necessary funds. Ebtehaj flatly refused to share this with the Imperial Bank, an attitude which inevitably provoked a furious response. Once more Ebtehaj was forced to compromise.[25]

Each confrontation made relations between Ebtehaj and the Imperial Bank more acrimonious. On a personal level, the difficulties were exacerbated by an unfortunate incident involving one of the Imperial Bank's two senior local staff members. Early in 1946, at a time when Ebtehaj was subject to a particularly damaging campaign of vilification by a section of the Tehran Press, the Bank Melli's Chief Inspector drew his attention to a letter and article passed on to him by the editor of one particular newspaper who happened to be a friend. The letter was signed by Ismail Dehlavi, Assistant to the Imperial Bank's Chief Manager, and it asked that the enclosed article – highly disparaging of Ebtehaj – be published. The article was in Dehlavi's handwriting, instantly recognisable to Ebtehaj since Dehlavi had been in his department in the days when he was still with the Imperial Bank. Ebtehaj was outraged, and immediately contacted the Bank's Chief Manager, Vivian Walter, who promised to look into the matter. In due course Walter informed Ebtehaj that he had investigated the affair and that although the article was in Dehlavi's handwriting, he had not actually written it. A friend had been the author and had shown it to Dehlavi who had made a copy of it – complete, as was evident, with erasures and insertions. Ebtehaj asked Walter whether he was really expected to believe this story, and indeed whether he himself thought it was true. Walter replied that he believed Dehlavi. He probably felt bound to support a member of his staff, but in the circumstances it was an unfortunate line to take. The proud and highly sensitive Ebtehaj was quick to take offence, believing Walter's statement to mean that the Imperial Bank associated itself with the views expressed in the article. To make matters worse, the Ambassador, Sir Reader Bullard, made it clear that he accepted Walter's assurance that Dehlavi had not written the article. It seemed to Ebtehaj that the word and opinion of an Englishman were all-important, even when contradicted by the laws of evidence and commonsense, and the incident increased his animus against the Bank.[26]

Walter's retirement in early 1948 ironically made matters even worse. Despite the Dehlavi incident, Ebtehaj at least had considerable respect for Walter. He had neither respect nor liking for

Walter's replacement as Chief Manager, Leslie Payne. The sentiments were reciprocated. In fact the new Chief Manager felt that any attempt to appease 'this megalomaniac, Ebtehaj, any further' was completely useless, 'and we should fight him at every step.'[27] As Claude Loombe of the Bank of England lamented sadly, he was 'unfortunately not the type to promote that degree of collaboration and friendship with Ebtehaj that is so necessary'.[28] With the end of its 60-year concession on 30 January 1949 in sight, this boded ill for the Imperial Bank.

Yet during 1949, albeit with difficulty, it looked as if the Imperial Bank had managed to secure a respite from Ebtehaj's attacks. Agreements in March and November of that year confirmed the Bank's right to continue to operate in Iran and deal in foreign exchange, although it was obliged to transfer £1 million capital to Iran, hand over 55 per cent of its total deposits to Bank Melli and close a number of its provincial branches as a 'goodwill gesture'.[29] However, the respite proved illusory. A bitter argument developed over the Imperial Bank's decision to treat deposits by importers against letters of credit in the same way as ordinary customer deposits, handing over to Bank Melli 55 per cent of total deposits rather than 55 per cent of customer deposits and the 100 per cent of deposits against letters of credit previously required by Bank Melli in order to discourage inessential imports and reduce the money supply. As usual, the Imperial Bank turned to the British Embassy and Foreign Office for help, complaining that Ebtehaj had reneged on the terms of the March Agreement, and it was decided that the best way of dealing with the situation was to take advantage of Ebtehaj's presence at the IMF's Annual Meeting in Washington and ask the Chancellor of the Exchequer, Sir Stafford Cripps, to discuss the issue informally with him there. Ebtehaj agreed to Cripps' suggestion that he should submit to arbitration on the matter by the Governor of the Bank of England.[30]

The Governor refused to arbitrate, but did agree to talk to both Lord Kennet of the Imperial Bank and Ebtehaj and give his 'personal and informal opinion on certain questions outstanding between Bank Melli Iran and the British Bank of Iran and the Middle East' (as the Imperial Bank became known from March 1949) – particularly questions relating to deposits against credits established abroad in foreign currency, and to availability of foreign exchange. His opinion, informal or not, was unequivocal on the point which had so enraged Ebtehaj. Deposits by importers against letters of credit had not been covered by the March 1949 Agreement.

On the other hand, he felt that it was unreasonable for the British bank, as an authorised foreign exchange dealer, to be denied access to the foreign exchange it required.[31]

Ebtehaj's attitude towards allowing BBIME access to foreign exchange had inevitably been affected by the argument over importers' deposits against letters of credit, and it seems clear that the opinion of the Governor of the Bank of England and the good offices of Sir Stafford Cripps might well have resulted in a softening in this direction. Characteristically, however, the November foreign exchange agreement was negotiated while Ebtehaj was out of the country, and when he returned to Tehran at the end of 1949 he refused to abide by it. Instead, while Ebtehaj bent his efforts towards getting the agreement replaced by one signed with him, and towards settling the question of the percentage of deposits against credits to be handed over, Bank Melli continued to deny BBIME access to foreign exchange. Meanwhile, BBIME's business was showing ominous losses as a result of the restrictions imposed upon it. Its available resources were greatly diminished by the obligation to place such a high proportion of its deposits, interest free, with the Bank Melli, while the continued lack of access to official exchange meant that its foreign credit business was grinding to a halt. By March 1950, deposits had also dropped by some 29 per cent as a result of the Bank's inability to provide foreign exchange facilities for its clients.

It seemed that BBIME's business was finally on the way out, and Ebtehaj's long campaign to establish the supremacy of the Bank Melli over the monetary and credit policies of the country had succeeded. As indeed it had: by mid-1950, BBIME's Board had decided, for various reasons, drastically to reduce its operations in Iran and concentrate instead on its expansion elsewhere in the Middle East. But when this decision was made, Ebtehaj was no longer at the helm of the Bank Melli. The catalyst for BBIME's decision was not its conflict with Ebtehaj, although this had clearly raised considerable doubts about the viability of a foreign bank doing business in Iran, but the escalating oil crisis and Iran's increasingly vulnerable position in the front line of the Cold War.[32]

Ebtehaj was himself a victim of the difficulties in which Iran found itself by 1950. Criticism of him in government circles which had often been fierce in the past finally grew too great for even the Shah's championship to save him, and in July 1950 he was dismissed from the Bank Melli. In many ways, it was a miracle he had survived so long since his uncompromising policies and his insistence on an independent role for the Bank Melli had antagonised successive Ministers of Finance, not to mention other members of post-war governments. He had very definite ideas on what needed to be done to effect the economic regeneration of Iran – such as, for instance, the reduction of the backing of the country's note issue in order to release funds for financing the new development plan, the strict control of consumer imports in order to conserve foreign exchange for capital goods, and the reduction of interest rates to bring down the cost of living – and was prepared to forge ahead with the necessary measures in the teeth of sometimes considerable opposition, whether such opposition came from the government, the bazaar or British bankers. The British Ambassador remarked in 1949 that Ebtehaj had 'constituted himself the sole champion of his countrymen against "exploiters" from within and without. Uncharitable people say his aim is to establish a controlled economy with himself as financial dictator.'[33]

As early as September 1945, the then Minister of Finance, Mahmoud Bader, had told the British Embassy's Commercial Counsellor in confidence that Ebtehaj's pretensions not only to control foreign exchange but to dictate to government what its financial and fiscal policies should be were intolerable, 'and neither he nor the Government, and he was sure no Government in the future, would accept this dictation from the Manager of its own Bank'.[34] However, over the next few years neither Bader nor his successors were able effectively to bring Ebtehaj under control. As the Imperial Bank's Chief Manager pointed out, it was 'difficult for any Minister to make a public stand against nationalistic arguments such as those invoked by Mr Ebtehaj'.[35] In fact, post-war governments were rarely in office for long enough for any one minister to carry on a sustained attack against Ebtehaj, and the Shah's continued support for him was proof against intermittent sniping.

Nevertheless, there was a groundswell of discontent over his policies from all sides, which gathered momentum as Iran slid ever closer to economic and political crisis. By 1950, with political stagnation and economic paralysis internally, the absence of any substantial economic and military aid from the United States and the growing difficulties with the Oil Company, Iran was in a dangerously unstable situation. The American State Department observed with anxiety what they regarded as the growing power of the Tudeh Party, Iran's faltering economy, and 'the incredible disorganization, confusion and uncertainty among the Government leaders'.[36]

As Iran descended into one of its periodic quagmires, Ebtehaj was at odds with almost everyone in government circles as well as the British bank and the bazaar. As one local newspaper observed, 'The Bank Melli Iran is an independent Government in itself which has apparently severed its relations with the Imperial Iranian Government.'[37] The criticisms of Ebtehaj crossed the board. The *Majles* did not like his intransigent stand on the note reserve cover with its implied threat that until he got his way Bank Melli would not give the development plan the financial backing it required. The merchants did not like the control of imports and the restrictive credit policies he introduced, accusing Ebtehaj of exacerbating the effects of the economic depression which stemmed from the particularly bad harvest of 1949–50 and which was forcing them into bankruptcy. BBIME, usually backed by the British Embassy, accused him of conducting a vindictive personal campaign against its continued presence in the country.

Ebtehaj never wavered from his conviction that he was absolutely right and everyone else was absolutely wrong, but with so many opponents in so many quarters it was only a matter of time before he fell from power. The blow fell in the middle of 1950. On 26 June, the Shah appointed a new Prime Minister – a strong man whom he hoped would succeed in effecting the administrative reforms required before the Americans would consent to grant Iran the long hoped-for loans – General Haji Ali Razmara, the Shah's Aide and Chief of Staff of the Army. Within 22 days of his appointment, Ebtehaj received a letter from Razmara dismissing him as Governor of the Bank Melli.

The reasons for Ebtehaj's dismissal are shrouded in mystery. According to his own recollections, Razmara visited him at his home before he became Prime Minister in an apparent attempt to test Ebtehaj's reactions to his possible elevation. He went so far as to say he himself would be honoured to serve under Ebtehaj if the latter were to accept the Prime Ministership, but when Ebtehaj made it clear that he had no intention of doing any such thing, the two men moved on to what Ebtehaj took to be the real purpose of his visit – Razmara's own appointment, his Cabinet team, and his programme. When Razmara was eventually appointed, Ebtehaj was contacted by Ala, then Minister of Court, and told that Razmara wanted Ebtehaj to join his Cabinet as Minister without

Portfolio, while still remaining Governor of the Bank Melli. Ebtehaj felt that he could not accept joint cabinet responsibility with people whose ideas and principles he did not share; he asked Ala to convey his thanks, but to decline as his health did not permit the taking on of any additional burden of work.[38]

5. Ebtehaj and Hussein Ala, 1955

A somewhat different emphasis comes from a United States Embassy report of a conversation with Razmara in July 1950. According to this account, Razmara stated that he had found it impossible to continue working with Ebtehaj and had decided to remove him as Governor of the Bank Melli. But he had tried to obtain Ebtehaj's cooperation, offering him various alternatives to dismissal — to remain as head of the Bank Melli under the direction of the new Ministers of Finance, Dr Taghi Nasr, and National Economy, Dr Morteza Azmoudeh; to enter the Cabinet as Minister without Portfolio while remaining Governor of the Bank; or to resign. Ebtehaj had been unwilling to carry out the instructions of the two responsible ministers, and had also refused to enter the Cabinet. 'Ebtehaj appeared to want full authority in the bank but no responsibility before the public. On these conditions, the Prime Minister said, he had no alternative but to ask for Ebtehaj's resignation.'[39] In appointing Taghi Nasr as Minister of Finance, however, Razmara was in fact obviating any possibility of cooperation from Ebtehaj, since the two men had clashed in the past and Ebtehaj was known to be highly critical of Nasr's competence. Ebtehaj would not serve under Nasr.[40]

There is evidence of a concerted campaign to get rid of him as Governor of the Bank Melli – involving British and American officials as well as Iranians.[41] In 1956 Ebtehaj learned of one aspect of American manoeuvres against him. During the visit of the head of the World Bank, Eugene Black, to Tehran, Ebtehaj had arranged for him to have lunch with the Shah. Before the lunch, Black and some of his colleagues had a formal meeting with the Shah, at which Ebtehaj was present, regarding the negotiations for the World Bank's loan to Iran. At this meeting, Black remarked to the Shah that he was 'lucky to have Mr Ebtehaj'. After a moment's hesitation, the Shah commented: 'You know why we removed Mr. Ebtehaj from the Bank? It was because *your* Government promised to pay us $100 million if we dismissed him. We did this and we did not receive one Dollar.'[42]

Whatever the reasons behind it, Ebtehaj's actual dismissal came as a bolt from the blue: he had after all survived a number of previous attempts to unseat him. As Ebtehaj later recollected,

> On a Summer afternoon, the 18th July 1950, when most of the members of the staff of the Bank Melli Iran had left, Ebrahim Zand was announced. Zand was at that time Governor General of Azerbaijan. . . . Upon entering my office he handed me the letter of dismissal, addressed to me by General Razmara, . . . which read as follows . . . "While recognising the services rendered by your Excellency during this period and thanking you, seeing that the Government's decision is to carry out changes in its economic policy, His Excellency Zand has been appointed Governor of Bank Melli Iran and is hereby introduced".[43]

There was nothing left for Ebtehaj to do, but to hand over to Zand and close the door on his remarkable eight years as Governor of the Bank Melli.

PART THREE
PLANNING IRAN'S FUTURE

5

'EXPECTATIONS UNLIMITED: RESOURCES LIMITED'

Ebtehaj's role as the initiator of Iranian planning in the 1940s is seldom acknowledged. This Chapter looks at the evolution of his vision of planning, and his first attempts to apply these ideas to Iran.

Governments had, of course, intervened in the process of resource allocation from time immemorial. Even in late Victorian Britain – the closest approximation to a neo-classical market economy ever seen – governments did not leave the provision of the police or postal services, for instance, to the price mechanism. In other countries of that era, such as Tsarist Russia or Japan after the Meiji Restoration, governments intervened more directly to build railways and establish new industries. Nineteenth-century Iranian governments lacked the resources for such intervention, although Naser al-Din Shah's efforts to develop Iran's resources with external help through the granting of concessions could be regarded as a form of state intervention. And while Reza Shah's industrialisation programme in the 1930s raised government activity to new levels as he attempted a rapid modernisation of the economy, projects were undertaken on a piecemeal and purely personal basis.

Economic planning, however, is wider than uncoordinated state intervention in the economy. It is a twentieth-century concept, pioneered by the world's first planned economy; the Soviet Union in the 1930s. Stalin's Russia opted for an extreme form of planning, where the ownership of the means of production was in state hands, and decisions on the total outputs of most goods were taken by the planners. The creation of a substantial industrial base by the Five Year Plans – a base which enabled the Soviet Union to withstand the assault by Nazi Germany after 1941 – attracted widespread interest, far beyond the confines of socialists or communists. After the Second World War, the idea of planning spread to many Third World countries, to some western European countries such as

France, and even, with the formation of the Commonwealth Development Corporation, to the British Empire. These states were attracted to the idea that their governments should have a view of the direction in which their economies should be moving – 'a plan'. They were usually less attracted by the Soviets' central planning system, and many opted for the use of 'indicative planning', which did not necessarily involve coercive official direction of resources and often retained a substantial role for the private sector. The word 'planning' came to cover a wide variety of economic systems, or – as the market-economists of the 1980s would regard them – sins.

Iran was one of the first wave of Third World countries to adopt economic planning. Its first Seven-Year Plan, finally adopted in 1949, pre-dated India's first plan by three years. Even China, one of the few developing countries to follow the Soviet model, did not embark upon its first plan until 1953. Turkey launched a Plan in 1947, but in the Middle East, economic planning in Egypt only began in 1952, and in fact until the late 1960s this 'did not involve much more than public investment programmes'.[1]

The idea of more systematic planning in Iran was first mooted in the late 1930s. Its leading exponent was Ebtehaj. Although he may have been aware of the dramatic changes Stalin's plans were bringing to the Soviet Union, his own planning philosophy evolved more from his observation of the problems of Reza Shah's economic programme in the 1930s. As soon as he became Controller of state-owned companies in 1936, Ebtehaj was confronted by the myriad inconsistencies and inefficiencies which resulted from the lack of communication between the ministries implementing the industrialisation projects, and the generally haphazard way in which large sums of money were wasted on useless projects. He was convinced that the industrialisation programme was going badly wrong because there was no attempt at any rational approach, and that what was needed was an economic coordinating body which could sit down and work out a 'plan'.

When Hossein Ala became Minister of Commerce in early 1937, Ebtehaj found someone who was prepared to lobby Reza Shah on his behalf. The result, as mentioned in Chapter 2, was the formation of an Economic Council to study, and attempt to find solutions for, Iran's economic problems. Ebtehaj was appointed its Secretary General. Ebtehaj later recollected that when, at the first meeting of the Council, he was asked to explain what its function was supposed to be, he used a very simple and homely analogy. If a grocer in a

Tehran side street wished to expand his premises, he would go and find a mason, tell him what sort of expansion he had in mind and ask for a costing –

> I said ... the purpose of this Supreme Council is to sit down and do what that grocer would do before he commits himself. If the mason tells him 'you can't have two rooms of the size you want with the money that you have', you have either to go and borrow enough money to do this or reduce the size of your rooms ... I said it is as simple as this and this is what planning means in my sense.

The grocer, Ebtehaj went on, was behaving rationally 'in the way that the Imperial Government of Iran is not doing'.[2]

At its tenth meeting, in the presence of Reza Shah himself, the Council announced that its 'prime duty [was] to prepare a general economic plan for the country', and in October 1937 the formation of a permanent committee charged with the 'preparation of a plan for increasing the productive capacity of the Country' was approved.[3] However, this first effort to plan economic development in a more rational way was short-lived. Ebtehaj had been very surprised that Reza Shah had permitted the establishment of the Council in the first place. When Ala had told him the good news, his reaction, as he later recollected, had been: 'You've misunderstood, he can't agree to planning, everything he does is against planning.'[4] And so it turned out. Late in 1938, after some 20 meetings, Reza Shah suddenly adjourned the Council *sine die*.[5] Coordinated planning meant an unacceptable limitation on the dictator's whims.

The effective abolition of the Economic Council did not spell the end of the idea of planning, however. Rather, Ebtehaj's ideas expanded and developed during the next few years. He constantly preached the necessity for planning, freely expressing his doubts about the way in which government was proceeding with the industrialisation programme and advocating his own recipe for success. The Allies' removal of Reza Shah, and Iran's acute economic difficulties following the Allied occupation, led to a resurgence of interest in the idea of planning Iran's post-war future. In 1945 the government established a High Economic Council patterned on the Economic Council of 1937, whose primary task would be 'to prepare a general economic plan for the country'.[6]

As with the earlier Economic Council, the High Economic Council of 1945 came to nothing. But this time Ebtehaj, as Governor of the Bank Melli, was not prepared to let the opportunity pass. He wrote to the Minister of Finance informing him that in view of the country's urgent need for an economic plan he intended to establish a committee within the Bank Melli to start thinking about the preparation of such a plan, and he suggested that the same thing be done within the Finance Ministry. However, it was not until early 1946 and the appointment of Ahmad Qavam as Prime Minister that any serious work began.[7] In February 1946, Ebtehaj published a memorandum he had presented to the Prime Minister in 1939, which had postulated the necessity of an economic plan and the establishment of a planning organisation. The paper was up-dated to take into account the more critical economic and social situation the country was in as a result of the war.[8] And when Qavam became Prime Minister in March, he knew that at last he would get some support from government.

Qavam asked Ebtehaj to address the first meeting of his Cabinet on the subject of Iran's economic difficulties and how to set about solving them. The timing could not, on the face of it, have been worse. There had been a series of political shuffles during 1945, and there was no reason to believe that Qavam's government would remain in power any longer than others. Soviet troops were still occupying the north of the country – they were in fact only 40 kilometres from Tehran – and were refusing to honour their obligation under the Tripartite Treaty to leave. Iran's future seemed as fragile as it had ever been. Yet Ebtehaj, with Qavam's encouragement, was talking about planning long-term economic development. Recognising the irony of the situation, he told the Cabinet that if Iran survived the immediate danger, planning was 'the only salvation no matter what happens'.[9]

In April 1946, the Qavam government approved a decree which established an Economic Council under the Prime Minister's presidency. Qavam's statement defining for the members of the Economic Council the nature and scope of their task served also as a statement of intent to the nation, and was published as such by the press.[10] It is worth looking at closely, since it was pure Ebtehaj in its inspiration, from its analysis of the country's economic difficulties and prescription as to how to set about solving them, to its methodology of action and aspirations for the future.

Qavam started by reviewing the grave economic situation and the reduced standard of living of the Iranian people. He went on to say that the Economic Council had been formed to undertake the difficult task of 'ensuring the economic life of the country' on the basis of two general principles – the raising of the standard of living by both the increase of production and of consumption, and the ensuring of an equitable distribution of the goods produced. With this end in mind, the Economic Council was to study the more important problems and prepare a five-year plan, for

> it is only by improving and increasing economic activity, and in raising the general standard of living by a more equitable distribution of produce that one can build a new and lasting basis for the nation and guide our country in the ways of progress and prosperity.

Qavam then gave an indication of the framework within which the Economic Council should prepare its plan. His programme covered every aspect of the economic life of the country from foreign trade to municipal development, from industrialisation and labour relations to transportation and agricultural development, from the sale of Crown lands to the exploitation of mineral resources. The methodology envisaged was also laid out. The necessary instructions had been given to all competent ministries to enable them to put at the disposal of the Economic Council all the information it required to draw up a plan. The Council was to form sub-committees to which technical experts from ministries, and other competent persons, could be co-opted. It was to feel free also to take advantage of the existence of the Economic and Social Committee of the United Nations Organisation if required, and to request the assistance of its experts for consultation and to help draw up plans. In all its endeavours, Qavam pledged, the Economic Council would have the full support of government and of the Shah.[11]

The draft plan drawn up by the Economic Council within the next few months, on the basis of Qavam's programme, was, essentially, a first draft of the Seven-Year Plan adopted in 1949. The next step was to prepare a definite plan, and the Council recommended that the Cabinet appoint a Supreme Planning Council for this purpose, to study the size of plan that could be financed from the country's internal and external resources and to consider its legislative framework. This was promptly agreed, and the Supreme Planning Council came into being in August 1946.[12] Ebtehaj continued to be the dynamo at the centre of its activities. While he steered clear of involvement with the content of the plan, he was the man who had the ear of the Prime Minister, who decided how the organisation should work and issued the necessary instructions to individuals and ministries on the Prime Minister's stationery for his signature, and who constantly preached the message of planning to government, civil service, *Majles*, press, and the public. As Stewart Alsop reported in the *New York Herald Tribune* in 1947, it was Ebtehaj, who

> while the struggle with the Soviets was still on . . . came to the conclusion that it went deeper than boundaries and provinces, that it was a struggle which must sooner or later be won by the Soviets unless the squalid misery in which most of the people live could be alleviated. He preached this doctrine with endless energy, and both Qavam and the Shah have become enthusiastic converts.[13]

While the wholehearted 'conversion' of the Shah seems somewhat doubtful, Alsop did highlight a central feature of Ebtehaj's planning philosophy which was to underpin all his policies in the 1950s. Economic growth, he believed, was the solution to Iran's many-faceted problems. It offered, in his opinion, far better protection against external enemies than a huge army with expensive military hardware: it was an opinion which was to lead him into growing conflict with the Shah in later years. Ebtehaj also saw economic growth as a solution to Iran's domestic problems and faults as he perceived them. This aspect of his thinking was later commented upon by Khodadad Farmanfarmaian, who as a young economics lecturer at Princeton University had been persuaded by Ebtehaj in 1957 to return to Iran to work for the Plan Organisation –

> a basic tenet of his thought . . . was that once you raised the standard of living of people through deliberate economic development, all these political problems – corruption, inefficiency, jealousies etc . . . – will be wiped out from their awareness, from their conscience, from their character if you will. And as the standard of living went up, people would become more straightforward, more cooperative, and that you would get true social, political change from the development of the country.[14]

From the perspective of the late 1980s, Ebtehaj's faith in economic growth might be seen as a (very) rational man's misunderstanding of the irrational political and social behaviour of most of his fellows. It is easier to empathise with such views in the circumstances of the immediate post-war years. Yet it must be acknowledged that Ebtehaj's belief that economic growth would solve all problems led to an over-willingness to ignore or leave to others matters not strictly concerned with that growth, which was to have serious consequences.

The Ebtehaj view of planning was, and remained, a non-socialist one. He had no wish to see extensive public ownership of resources. Rather, he argued − in striking conformity with the model of development later developed by Alexander Gerschenkron − that the state had a duty in a backward economy to cut a path for private enterprise.[15] Years later, in 1961, he expounded his views to a San Francisco audience:

> some degree of national planning is essential to the high rate of investment that is required if underdeveloped countries are to break the vicious circle of poverty and stagnation. The government must be the planner. But the government will only be an originator of new activities, the chief engine of growth, a major source of innovation, and a large scale enterpriser to the extent that private investors and businesses fail to recognise or to exploit their myriad opportunities for expansion.[16]

The draft plan was presented to the Iranian cabinet as a seven-year plan for Iran's 'Reconstruction and Development': two years had been added to the original five envisaged to cater for the essential time required for study, research and appraisal of projects. The title of the document reflected very closely the purposes for which the newly established World Bank − officially the International Bank for Reconstruction and Development − had been created. Iran's development strategy was envisaged as being part of the ethos of the Bank and the IMF, and Ebtehaj hoped that the Bank would provide some $250 million of the funds needed to finance the plan.[17] Iran's plans were also in line with Britain's ideas as to the economic policies which should be pursued by Middle Eastern countries to raise the general standard of living of an area which was in the front line of the Communist advance. The British aim was that each of the Middle Eastern governments should be encouraged to draw up its own economic development plan, and that such British technical and specialist assistance as might be required should be provided. The British Ambassador in Tehran was instructed to express Britain's willingness to help.[18] The United States' Acting Secretary of State, Dean Acheson, also believed that economic development was Iran's best hope of preserving its political independence, and that 'our declared policy of economic assistance' should be implemented in full.[19]

As the scale of Iran's planning aspirations became clear, British,

American and even World Bank opinion became more reserved, especially when it came to any promise of financial help. The World Bank's response to Iran's informal application for $250 million (informal since the World Bank was still in its very early days) was that it would only consider applications for individual projects whose soundness had been tested by technical studies.[20] And the British and American governments agreed that they were unable to pledge their automatic support for Iran's application for a World Bank loan, unless it were to pass the test of the Bank's own objective appraisal procedures.[21] Privately, neither World Bank officials nor the British and American governments thought that Iran would get anything like $250 million even if its application was accepted, since the World Bank's operations would be limited by the unwillingness of the New York market to lend abroad.[22]

Prime Minister Qavam announced Iran's Seven-Year Plan to the nation on the eve of the Persian New Year in March 1947. It was, as the British Ambassador observed, a remarkable statement in which 'nothing has been forgotten from irrigation to lunatic asylums' – 'in effect a blue print for the total regeneration of Persia'. The only problem was that the expenditure envisaged was nearly 600,000 million *rials* (some £450 million) – the equivalent of about 14 years' annual government revenue at the time.[23] This was way beyond Iran's means, and even before 1946 ended steps had been taken to establish an independent and objective screening process to select the most appropriate projects. As the World Bank had not yet opened its doors officially, Ebtehaj asked Iran's Ambassador in Washington, his old friend, Ala, to find and recommend a firm of consultants to provide some expert and impartial help.[24] Ala came up with the name of Morrison Knudsen and Company Limited, of Boise, Idaho, a leading firm of consulting engineers and contractors, and in December 1946 the Iranian government invited Morrison Knudsen to send a mission to Iran to survey the whole country and advise on the practicability of the projects envisaged under the capital development programme.[25]

The Morrison Knudsen team, under the leadership of G.F. Dunn, Vice-President in charge of foreign operations, arrived in Tehran at the end of December 1946. The ten members were in the country for some four months, during which time the Bank Melli was their headquarters. Ebtehaj went out of his way to ensure that the team members were able to get on with their work with as few delays as possible, and the support services of the Bank were placed at their disposal. In July 1947, Morrison Knudsen presented their report. It was addressed to Ebtehaj. Referring to him as 'Our principal contact in Iran', the acknowledgements went on to state: 'We cannot rate too highly his unfailing courtesy, quick cooperation and instant grasp of our problems.'[26] It had been suggested that the consultants prepare a list of worthwhile projects which would total $500 million or more, from which alternative programmes of $500 million or $250 million would be selected. In the event, the Morrison Knudsen team presented the Iranian government with a report outlining three possible plans. The largest contained a list of projects estimated to cost some $1250 million while the cost of the projects in the smallest plan was some $250 million.[27] It was left to the Iranians themselves to decide on how large a programme the country could afford, and how it was to be financed.

With the Morrison Knudsen report in hand, in November 1947 the Iranian government appointed a new Supreme Planning Board, under the Chairmanship of Dr Hassan Mosharef Naficy and with Dr Ali Amini as its Secretary General, to make the necessary choices.[28] In January 1948, Naficy, a long-time and close friend of Ebtehaj, who had been the Anglo-Iranian Oil Company's legal representative in the 1930s and Minister of Finance in 1941, submitted the Board's recommendations to the Council of Ministers. His 'unusually able report', much influenced by Ebtehaj's ideas, provided the basis for the Seven-Year Plan Bill as it was finally enacted.[29] The recommendations of the Morrison Knudsen report were not entirely followed since 'many of the studies of the Planning Board on which Morrison-Knudsen based their report were incomplete'.[30] In fact, the plan presented was one which, in the British Ambassador's view, took into account 'Iran's limitations, particularly as regards finance and technical capacity',[31] and was, in the opinion of Foreign Office officials, 'more comprehensive and suitable for the needs of Persian development' than the Morrison Knudsen recommendations as it took 'into consideration aspects of the Persian economy not covered by the Morrison-Knudsen plan'.[32]

The Naficy Report presented a plan which was to cover seven years, the first two years of which were to be devoted to preparation and study. The cost was estimated at 21,000 million *rials* (£161.5 million), distributed in the following proportions: 23.8 per cent on agriculture; 14.3 per cent on mines and industries; 23.8 per cent on roads, railways, ports and airports; 14.3 per cent on aid to health, education, the police and other civil institutions; 7.1 per cent on the construction of cheap housing; while the remainder covered a wide variety of other projects. The large allocations to agriculture and infrastructure provided a contrast to Soviet plans of the 1930s, in which heavy industry had been given priority, but were very similar in emphasis to the 1947 Plan devised in neighbouring Turkey, which also hoped to attract World Bank or western financial aid of some kind. It was not until the 1960s that the plans of either country began to focus on heavy industrialisation. The Iranian Plan (also like its Turkish equivalent and the early Indian plans) was unsophisticated by later standards, consisting of a range of unrelated investment projects with no overall view of the total allocation of resources in the economy as a whole.

So far as financing was concerned, it was proposed that one third of the cost of Iran's plan should be met by a loan from the World Bank (of about $200 million, or £50 million), while the remaining two thirds were raised internally. Four ways of raising the latter were mentioned: the royalties and share in profits received by government from the Anglo-Iranian Oil Company should be made available in their entirety for the plan (£60 million); the cover of the note issue should be reduced from 100 to 50 per cent, which would release funds for the Bank Melli to lend to the plan (£35 million); the state-owned factories currently operated by the Industrial and Mining Bank should be reorganised by government and then sold to private investors (£8 million); and private investment and savings should be encouraged (£8 million).[33]

The most important aspect of the Naficy Report was its reflection of the Planning Board's concern to safeguard the plan from 'Iran's endemic corruption'.[34] It recommended that an independent authority, not subject to political changes, be set up to supervise the execution and expenditure of the plan. Within this authority, a hierarchy of control provided the necessary checks and balances: the organisation was divided into a permanent High Council of seven members, a Director General and subordinate officers, a Board of Supervision of six members, and a Technical Bureau. The appointment of foreign technical employees for a maximum of eight years was also envisaged.[35] Over the next few months various attempts were made to limit the independence of the proposed Plan Organisation,[36] but the Shah gave his support to those who wanted an independent authority. The creation of such a body in Iran was in direct contrast with practice in Turkey, where planning was executed by government ministries until the 1960s. And although, in 1950, India established a Planning Commission, this was an advisory body, chaired by the prime minister, and with policies 'always subject to wider political considerations'.[37]

'EXPECTATIONS UNLIMITED, RESOURCES LIMITED'

The nascent Plan Organisation had enormous autonomy. As Farmanfarmaian later observed:

> it had its own substantial financial resources earmarked. It had the authority to disperse directly. It could hire consultants to study projects or it could study the projects itself. It could tender out or directly choose the contractors for construction. ... It had the responsibility for the implementation or execution of the projects it had decided upon. It could borrow from abroad. It had its own separate auditors appointed by the parliament.[38]

This independence was very much a reflection of Ebtehaj's thoughts on the matter. He believed, in Farmanfarmaian's words,

> that Iranian traditional bureaucracy was inefficient and corrupt, and the task of development could not be left to them. He believed that a new organization with full authority and free of traditional fetters was needed. ... I termed this approach 'the wedge approach'. That is, a wedge-like organization to break into this soggy mess which was the inefficient, the effete, the tradition-bound Iranian government bureaucracy. Ebtehaj believed that without this type of approach to development, plans, programs and projects cannot be developed and implemented.[39]

Ebtehaj's views on the need for the Plan Organisation's 'independence' were thoroughly understandable: he had first-hand experience of the 'soggy mess' of the government machine. Yet, as with his faith in the virtues of economic growth, this approach had flaws, for the insulation of the planning process from politics was a hopeless ideal in any society, let alone Iran's. Farmanfarmaian's retrospective views are again of value:

> The very nature of planning and investment allocation is political ... The very nature of the Plan Organization, in spite of all the attempts to be insulated from politics, to be independent of the goings-on within the government, was highly political. Where there is money there must be politics ... I don't think you can proceed to develop economic models in vacuums, or organizational models in vacuums. These models have to somehow relate to traditions, to characteristics, to the politics and the political nature of things.[40]

The Planning Bill, including most of the Naficy recommendations, was put forward to the *Majles* for enactment in September 1948, and finally became law in February 1949.[41] Anticipating delays in the passage of the necessary legislation, at the end of August 1948 a credit of 25 million *rials* was voted, which was to be spent on preliminary surveys of projects. And to help in the screening process, foreign consultants were again appointed.[42] By this time, the World Bank had started operating and, with the need for a loan in mind, advice on consultants was sought from it rather than, as in the case of Morrison Knudsen, the American State Department. Once more Ebtehaj was closely involved, in conjunction with Ala in Washington.[43] There was also, at this time, another individual in Tehran observing the progress being made towards economic and social planning, and lobbying for the appointment of foreign consultants – Max W. Thornburg, an American independent industrial consultant who appeared to have appointed himself as unofficial adviser to the Planning Board. As early as March 1948, in commenting with unreserved praise on the Naficy Report and the Plan Bill based on it, Thornburg was stressing the role of consultants in the direction of the Plan.[44] Between them, according to the British Ambassdor, Ebtehaj and Thornburg were instrumental in getting the American group Overseas Consultants Incorporated (OCI) appointed to help the Iranian planners.[45]

It was the World Bank which first suggested OCI. Bank officials apparently did not hold a high opinion of Morrison Knudsen. On the other hand, OCI – a consortium of 11 American engineering firms which had been formed to work in Japan – had very relevant experience, and it was felt that if they could be persuaded to reconstitute themselves and interest themselves in Iran, this would be the ideal solution. Because Ebtehaj was lobbying hard for a substantial loan from the World Bank, he was happy to act on its suggestion, and he asked Ala to negotiate with OCI.[46] Thornburg was also apparently in favour of requesting OCI to reconstitute themselves to carry out in Iran a similar task to the one they had successfully carried out in Japan, and did much to persuade them to do so. Certainly he became the leader of the twelve-man advisory group OCI sent to Iran during the first year of the Plan.[47]

In any event, OCI were appointed in October 1948 to make a preliminary survey and report, and, as he was in Washington for the annual IMF meeting, Ebtehaj was present when the contract was signed.[48] In November, five OCI experts – all senior officials of their respective firms – arrived in Tehran, under the leadership of John Lotz, chairman of the firm of Stone and Webster, one of America's largest and oldest engineering corporations, to see for themselves what the general conditions in Iran were, look at the feasibility of the Plan, advise on which parts of it should be tackled first, and determine how many specialists would be needed to prepare detailed working plans for the actual execution of the Plan.[49] The preliminary report prepared by OCI on the basis of this visit approved the Seven-Year Plan Bill under consideration by the *Majles*, encouraged the Planning Board to go ahead with engaging some 35 to 40 American engineers and other experts to arrive in early 1949, and paved the way for their own appointment in February 1949 to proceed with the main task of detailed planning which lay ahead.[50] When the *Majles* eventually passed the Plan Bill, therefore, the new Planning Authority was ready to forge ahead without delay.

It had taken virtually four years for the concept of planned economic development to be accepted in Iran, and Ebtehaj had been the prime mover from the time the 1945 High Economic Council had started to consider planning as a solution for the country's post-war economic ills to the time the Bill was passed in February 1949 by the *Majles*. Not without some difficulty, Ebtehaj's dream of an independent central planning authority had been achieved, and the Plan Organisation established. At the centre of this Organisation was the Managing Director, appointed by the Shah on the government's recommendation for a three-year period and responsible to a full-time seven-man High Council, equivalent to the board of directors of a western corporation. The Organisation also incorporated a six-man Board of Control whose principal task was to oversee the finances.[51]

Yet paradoxically Ebtehaj was not directly involved with any of this. His position in the planning process remained an unofficial one of providing constant pressure to get the process of planning underway, organisational advice, and as much persuasive publicity both at home and overseas as was necessary. Most importantly of all, he continued to concern himself, as he had done since he became Governor of the Bank Melli, with the task of financing the plan. He had not, from the start, shown any interest in an official position within the Planning Authority, although the membership of the Supreme Planning Board owed much to his advice and nomination – Naficy, for example, was very much his representative and 'frontman' in this sense. Even when Naficy resigned from the chairmanship of the Supreme Planning Board in January 1949, unable to cope any longer with the delays and politicking which he and the Planning

Board had suffered all along, Ebtehaj could not be persuaded to take on the role of chief executive. Prime Minister Mohammad Saed actually wrote him an official letter at the beginning of 1949, appointing him head of the Plan Organisation in conjunction with his Governorship of the Bank. Ebtehaj declined the honour, however, saying that neither the statutes of the Bank nor those of the new Plan Organisation permitted this dual function, but that, as in the past, he would continue unofficially to serve the interest of the Plan Organisation.[52] While he clearly looked on the Plan Organisation as his 'child' (as he was later to describe it) and was proud of it, he preferred to remain Governor of the Bank.

From the point of view of the Plan's finances, it was important that he should do so since the task of finding the resources required was crucial to the Plan's implementation and success, but by no means easy. The sub-title of a talk on the Plan Organisation's role in the economy of Iran given by Ebtehaj in the late 1950s summed up the fundamental problem faced by Iran's planners: 'Expectations Unlimited: Resources Limited'.[53]

The Plan Bill envisaged, in much the same way as had the Naficy Report, that the Plan would be financed principally through revenues obtained from the Oil Company (600 million *rials* were to be earmarked for the year ending March 1949, but all revenues thereafter), helped by loans from the Bank Melli (4,500 million *rials* over the seven-year period, but no more than 750 million *rials* in any one year), a loan from the World Bank (up to $250 million), and credits from private institutions within Iran and commercial institutions abroad. Initially, in the year up to March 1949, 1,000 million *rials* would be required of the 21,000 million *rials* total, rising to a peak of 3,600 million *rials* in the last years of the Plan.[54]

By 1949, however, the prospect of a large World Bank loan was receding. From the beginning, in 1946, Bank officials had made it clear to Ebtehaj that Iran was unlikely to get anything like $250 million. Indeed, in September 1947 the Chairman of the Bank's Loan Department indicated that there was little likelihood of Iran receiving a loan at all for the time being.[55] Priority was to be given to financing European reconstruction. Moreover, all loans had to be raised by public subscription in the United States and subscribers would not come forward unless they were certain of the standing and financial position of the applicant. In the particular case of Iran, Bank opinion was that a loan of $250 million far exceeded immediate needs: most of it would lie idle for some years, and the IMF was not prepared to back the future political status of any country for more than two years ahead. Ebtehaj, however, was furious, and complained bitterly to British officials that Iran was getting nothing out of its Bank and Fund membership – on the contrary, 'it was now quite clear that the International Bank was simply a device for helping the European powers and not the impoverished peoples of the Middle East who really needed it'.[56]

British officials lobbied the World Bank on Iran's behalf, arguing that the political interests of the West required that a more lenient policy should be adopted. Iran was one of the few countries bordering the Soviet Union which still looked towards the West, they pointed out, and it was imperative that this should continue to be the case. Both British oil interests and those of the United States in the Persian Gulf were at stake. Iran was trying to do something to regenerate itself economically and raise living standards, and it was incumbent on the West to give all support to these efforts.[57] Meanwhile, Ebtehaj continued to lobby the Bank at every opportunity, despite constant reiteration that the large loan he was after was out of the question.[58]

Nevertheless, he was realistic enough to know that the large loan initially hoped for was unlikely to materialise, and in 1949 there was a distinct change of emphasis in his line of attack. World Bank officials had indicated, unofficially, that the Bank might be able to help in a more limited way by providing finance for individual projects.[59] Thus when the Bank's Vice President paid a brief visit to Iran in the spring of 1949, Ebtehaj stated that there was no immediate need for the loan – in fact, it would probably not be required for some 18 months to two years. On the other hand, an assurance from the Bank that some sort of loan would be forthcoming eventually would be enormously helpful to the Iranian government, and it would make the Plan more palatable to the Iranian people if, by way of a token gesture, the Bank were to make a loan for one or more specific projects.

Ebtehaj took the argument further, stressing that while help from the World Bank was Iran's right by virtue of its membership of and annual subscription to both IMF and Bank, Iran was in the business of self-development. The country, he argued, did not need any direct economic grant or loan for development purposes; it was quite capable of self-sufficiency and was not in the market for handouts. However, this was not to say that such practical help as could be afforded by the United States' aid programmes or the military assistance missions would be unwelcome. Indeed, in view of regional strategy imperatives and the Shah's determination to strengthen Iran's military establishment, adequate military aid rather than any economic aid was what Iran needed. This was a controversial stance to adopt – particularly in 1949 when Iran's requests for economic, as well as military, aid from the United States were gathering momentum – and Ebtehaj's attitude, spelled out to State Department officials in September 1949 on the eve of the Shah's first visit to the United States, in search of aid, caused confusion in Washington and consternation in Tehran. His discussions at the State Department had taken place at the behest of the Shah and the Iranian Ambassador, Hossein Ala, and State Department officials took his views to imply that Iran had made no request to the United States government for economic aid and did not want it.[60] What Ebtehaj had in fact meant, as Ala was later at pains to point out, was that Iran could use its resources either for financing economic development or for re-equipping the armed forces, but not both.[61]

The change of emphasis, with regard to the financing of development, away from dependence on a sizeable World Bank loan, was important. It meant that, in addition to the budgeted revenues from oil, the first stages of the Plan would have to be financed out of Iran's accumulated reserves of foreign exchange so far as external expenditure was concerned; and through the release of resources obtained by reducing the note cover, the transfer of deposits from the Imperial Bank of Iran to the Bank Melli, and drawing on the Bank Melli's cash reserves, so far as internal expenditure was concerned.[62]

Ebtehaj's whole strategy since 1942 had been directed towards the garnering of resources to provide the necessary finance for postwar development. He had done his best to tie up excess Sterling earnings during the War in the note issue reserve and to ensure that these earnings were either convertible into gold or guaranteed by the price of gold. Furthermore, the agreements negotiated with the British government on the status of its Sterling balances in 1946 and 1947 further strengthened Iran's finances. However, while the currency position was good in theory, Iran suffered from a recurring shortage of funds for even its current budgetary expenditure, and the problem of raising sufficient additional revenue for its development plans was acute, particularly as it was necessary to persuade government ministers to relinquish the use of royalties and other earnings from the Oil Company, and to reduce their borrowing from the Bank Melli. It was not that Iran did not have the necessary funds, and the expectation of increasing revenues in the future; it was a problem of cash flow. Ebtehaj's task was not only somehow to contrive to raise sufficient revenue for the Plan, but also to tighten up government expenditure and ensure that such additional revenue was not frittered away by government in its usual hand-to-mouth fashion.[63]

In 1947, when the Plan was still in its initial draft stage, Ebtehaj was already looking at ways and means of raising the necessary local currency, having committed himself under the Memorandum of Understanding with Britain to conserve Iran's foreign exchange as far as possible for essential imports only. The task was a particularly difficult one in a country where there was little internal investment and no money market to speak of. Ebtehaj favoured the reduction of the gold cover of the note issue as a means of increasing government revenues, but this idea met with much criticism because of the spectre of inflation. The difficulties he encountered in trying to get his March 1949 Bill to reduce the note issue cover passed by the *Majles* have already been mentioned. Ebtehaj's other financial policies were similarly geared to ensuring that the Bank Melli was in a position to provide funds for the Plan – this was, for example, one of the main reasons behind his concern for the Bank Melli's liquidity and his insistence that commercial banks, such as the Imperial Bank, should place a percentage of their deposits with Bank Melli.

Meanwhile, the Plan Organisation itself was going through enormous difficulties. Although it had been established on a more satisfactory legal and structural base than might have been expected given its difficult rites of passage, its progress was slow and less than successful. And this despite the fact of a large staff of able engineers and administrators in Tehran, led by the OCI team, which had been appointed in February to produce a detailed report on how the Plan should proceed, and then, in the autumn of 1949, to oversee the execution of it. Part of the reason was inherent in the situation: it was not easy to build up a totally new structure like the Plan Organisation, with its 500–700 employees, while at the same time expecting it to handle projects worth millions of *rials*. There were bound to be pressures and inefficiencies at all levels, especially given Iran's unstable political situation and generally venal administration. But some disastrous decisions, like that to take over the corrupt and moribund Industrial and Mining Bank and the bankrupt state-owned companies it ran (a decision Ebtehaj warned would sabotage the Plan's chances of success), together with bad publicity and bad timing, also played a part; as did the Razmara government's attempt to decentralise the planning process by diverting funds to the provinces which would have their own individual development plans. The Plan Organisation was established at a time when Iran was sliding into a calamitous period of economic and political chaos, and it did not prove immune from the malaise affecting the country as a whole.

Less than a year after its inception, Max Thornburg, leader of the OCI team, observed that the Plan Organisation was 'so nearly completely dominated or victimised by political or private interests ... that ... there probably is little to choose between the Plan Organization and any government organization'.[64] British officials at the time took a more optimistic view of the Plan Organisation's capacity, although this probably said more about their lack of understanding of both Iran and the planning process than about the Plan Organisation.[65] However, there were a few achievements in this period, notably the introduction of tractors in the extreme north of Azerbaijan to relieve the considerable agricultural distress in that area, although this was too far from Tehran to have any impact on the Plan Organisation's deteriorating public image.

Ebtehaj's dismissal from the Bank Melli on 18 July 1950 meant that for the next few years he left the problems of planning behind him. By this time the Plan Organisation was in major difficulties. A serious internal dispute about the form of its organisation had arisen, with decentralisation to the various provincial ministries being advocated by the Razmara government and by Max Thornburg and his OCI team, but bitterly opposed by Plan officials. In addition, the Plan Organisation was stripped of the independence so prized by Ebtehaj: from July 1950 the approval of a *Majles* Plan Commission had to be obtained before any new project was undertaken. And the shortage of money, already acute as a result of having had to spend most of its allocated funds on such existing commitments as subsidies for the state-owned factories it had inherited, became more of a problem as the oil dispute gathered momentum and the vital revenues upon which the Plan depended were frozen, and as the foreign exchange reserves which had been hoarded for the Plan's use had to be used for the imports of wheat to alleviate the effects of bad harvests.[66]

The nationalisation of the oil industry by Mossadeq in 1951 finally spelled the end of any hopes that Iran's First Plan might succeed. Oil revenues came to a virtual standstill towards the end of that year, and remained unavailable until the dispute was finally settled in September 1954. Funds for development no longer existed. Ironically, in the midst of the political and financial disturbances of the Mossadeq years, the dispute over the reduction of the note issue cover was finally resolved. After Ebtehaj's long crusade, the solution to the problem seemed ludicrously low key. Because Mossadeq ruled by decree, he was able merely to expand the currency as and when required without bothering about the ratio of its backing, and in this way the historic linkage between the note issue and the necessity for 100 per cent cover was finally broken. The metallic backing of the currency had fallen to 40 per cent by the end of 1954, a ratio which was formally recognised by the Currency Stabilisation Act of that year.[67]

Meanwhile, Ebtehaj had missed most of the mounting political and economic confusion which culminated in the nationalisation of the oil industry. After his dismissal from the Bank Melli in July 1950, the Shah had named him as Iran's Ambassador to Paris, and he did not return to Iran until 1954. The Ambassadorship was not something Ebtehaj wanted. When the post was offered to him, he at first declared his intention of turning it down. He was persuaded to change his mind by Ala, who convinced him of the necessity of leaving Iran for a time to prevent any possibility of being accused of exerting his influence unduly or intriguing against Razmara's government.[68] Soon after taking up his post as Ambassador to France, Ebtehaj was also accredited, in the spring of 1951, as Iran's Minister to both Portugal and Spain.

Ebtehaj hated being an ambassador. He found, he said, nothing constructive about the role – 'I don't like this manner of "Excellence, Monsieur l'Ambassadeur", and "mes hommages" and kissing ladies' hands. ... [but] I did my utmost to serve my country.'[69] And indeed, whatever he thought of the role, he contrived to ensure that Iran's Paris Embassy, during the difficult period of oil nationalisation and Mossadeq's rise to power, became one of the most active and efficient of Iran's embassies (it in fact headed the efficiency list published in a Foreign Ministry circular). As with the Bank Rahni and the Bank Melli, he lost no time in introducing order and discipline into his new area of operation – even going so far as to request Tehran to allow him to cut down on the large number of superfluous counsellors he had in comparison with other embassies.

His main interest, however, lay in trying to do something constructive for the many Iranian students in Paris – he was very keen that a permanent residence for them should be established at the University and hoped that Sarkis Gulbenkian, whom he knew well, might be persuaded to finance this. However, before he could achieve anything, he was dismissed in 1952, and it was his involvement with the students which was the cause. On the advice of the Chief of Police in Paris, and with the agreement of his colleagues, he had banned a reception being held by the students to celebrate the Persian New Year, because of the strong possibility of trouble between the Tudeh faction among the students and the others. In the event, the Embassy's own formal reception was marred by a demonstration by the Tudeh students. The Foreign Minister in Tehran advised Ebtehaj to take a diplomatic 'holiday' to allow tempers to cool, but Ebtehaj was determined that he should either be supported or dismissed. He was dismissed.[70]

It was not long before Ebtehaj was offered another job — this time as Adviser to the Managing Director of the IMF in Washington. It was a move that had been under discussion for some time. In July 1950, after he left the Bank Melli, Ebtehaj had informally discussed with a United States Embassy official in Tehran the possibility of obtaining a position either with a private international banking corporation or with the IMF or World Bank. The request was transmitted to the State Department which was asked to pass it on to the Chase Bank in New York for its advice, in the following terms —

> Ebtehaj has resigned [sic] as Governor Bank Melli. I regard him as possibly ablest banker and administrative executive in ME. Although Iran Government will probably offer him new position, possibly as Ambassador, he would prefer independently find satisfactory position international banking field.[71]

United States' officials in Washington were also asked to investigate the possibility of persuading the Iranian government to retain Ebtehaj and appoint him as Iran's alternate executive director to the Fund, under Pakistan, a move which might moderate somewhat the World Bank's obvious concern at his removal from the Bank Melli.[72] This was not, however, the kind of thing which could be arranged in a hurry, and meanwhile Ebtehaj had accepted the Paris appointment.

Nevertheless, the wheels had been set in motion, and in 1952 when it was learnt that Ebtehaj was relinquishing his Ambassadorial post, he received a telegram from the IMF asking him to go to Washington as Adviser to the Managing Director. Anxious by this time to return to Iran, Ebtehaj telegraphed Hossein Ala, now Minister of Court in Tehran, telling him of the Washington offer and asking him how Mossadeq would react to his return instead to

Tehran. Ala's reply was diplomatic but quite definite. Mossadeq was not very enthusiastic that Ebtehaj should return, but would be very pleased if Ebtehaj accepted 'this important assignment with the Fund'.[73]

Ebtehaj spent the next two years in Washington with the IMF, first of all as Adviser to the Managing Director, and then as Director of the Fund's Middle East Department. It was the peak of the McCarthy era, a fact which influenced Ebtehaj's thinking since he found the scare tactics of the McCarthy Commission, in the context of a democracy like the United States, profoundly shocking. It was also the start of the Eisenhower Administration, and Ebtehaj held no brief at all for Eisenhower or his policies. However, he made good use of the time to make useful contacts in Washington and become acquainted with how the Fund and the World Bank worked. He also began thinking and talking about the relevance of his views on planned economic development across a broader spectrum than merely Iran, and this led him to consider the need most developing countries had for foreign aid. Ebtehaj became at this time a fervent exponent of the principle of multilateral as opposed to bilateral international aid and a promoter of the establishment of an autonomous internationally-administered aid agency.[74] Interestingly, the International Development Association was founded in 1960 as part of the World Bank group to fulfil just such a function.

In 1953, Mossadeq was overthrown in a coup which had the support of both the American CIA and British agents. Many would now regard the Eisenhower Administration's decision to support the British in the oil dispute, and the American role in the coup, as the turning point in post-war American–Iranian relations.[75] Although Ebtehaj knew the main CIA operatives involved, Allen Dulles and Kermit Roosevelt, both of whom had been in Tehran, the former as one of OCI's report writers, he had no foreknowledge of the coup. However, with the Shah's restoration to power, he was able to think seriously about returning to Iran.

Ebtehaj did not know Mossadeq well on a personal level and had met him only briefly, but it was natural that the two men should know each other by repute. Mossadeq, for his part, had a rather ambivalent attitude towards Ebtehaj. While the latter had been in Paris, for instance, Mossadeq had expressed appreciation of the way in which the Embassy was run, but he had not wanted Ebtehaj to return to Tehran. Then, when Ebtehaj was in the United States, Mossadeq conceived the idea of bringing him back to Tehran to manage the National Oil Company. One evening he had called in the Chairman of the Joint Oil Committee of the *Majles* and the Senate, and said that he had decided to recall Ebtehaj to take charge of the National Oil Company. The Chairman, who welcomed the proposal, at once convened the Committee and put the proposition to them. It was rejected out of hand, the reaction being that 'if an Englishman were appointed as head of the Oil Company he would serve Iran better than Ebtehaj'. When the Chairman went to report this outcome to Mossadeq, he found that members of the Committee had arrived before him, and Mossadeq acted as if he had not instructed the Chairman to put up Ebtehaj's name.[76]

These incidents are interesting in the way they reflect Mossadeq's character as Ebtehaj saw it. He had no sympathy for the characteristically naive and ill-informed view of Mossadeq, held by a wide spectrum of British opinion, as a 'lunatic' and chronic opium addict.[77] There was no doubt in Ebtehaj's mind but that Mossadeq was 'an honest patriot', although he regarded his associates as incompetents. However, Mossadeq was, in his view, 'a man who knew what he did not want but had no idea of what he wanted'; thus he had embarked on the nationalisation of the oil industry with no apparent regard as to what the outcome might be. While Mossadeq could stir people *against* targets such as the British Oil Company, Ebtehaj wanted to mobilise Iranians *for* the development of their country.[78]

When the Shah was restored to power in Tehran in 1953, Ebtehaj's contract with the IMF still had six or seven months to run, but he at once gave notice that he would not be renewing it. The Fund's Managing Director tried to dissuade him from taking any such hasty step, suggesting instead that he should return to Iran at the head of a Fund mission to test, so to speak, the warmth of the water. But Ebtehaj refused. He was determined to go home. His friends and colleagues all thought that he was only saying this because the Shah had asked him to return, but they were wrong. He had no idea what he was returning to. It seems clear, nevertheless, that the Shah did have his recall in mind. In October 1953, the American Ambassador reported that he had already suggested to the Shah and the Prime Minister, General Fazlollah Zahedi, on several occasions the importance of recalling Ebtehaj to help sort out the country's finances. The Shah was obviously in favour, but the Prime Minister, while acknowledging Ebtehaj's ability and declaring his hope that his talents would eventually prove useful, wished to postpone his recall, because 'in view of [Ebtehaj's] pro-British reputation he would encounter difficulties if he would assign important work to him at this moment'.[79] Ebtehaj returned on his own initiative in August 1954, when his contract with the IMF had expired, and the first contact he had with the Shah was when the Shah sent for him three days after his return. At this initial interview, moreover, he gave the Shah fair warning that although he was determined to do something to serve his country, in so doing he was quite likely to be the same 'nuisance' that he had been before he left.[80]

A few days later, the Shah recalled Ebtehaj and said he had two jobs suitable for him. One was to head the National Oil Company, but he added that this job was of little importance since the oil industry would in fact be run by foreigners. The other was to run the Plan Organisation, and he pressed Ebtehaj to consider this option. Ebtehaj reminded the Shah of the circumstances of his departure from the Bank Melli – how he had been dismissed without even the benefit of an interview, treated worse than a menial servant, because he had made enemies and had insisted on independence of action. It was the same Ebtehaj who would go to the Plan Organisation. He went on to make it absolutely clear that his acceptance of the post would be conditional on being allowed to do the job without interference, in his own way, taking orders from no one, not even the Shah himself, unless he agreed with them. This would undoubtedly create an awkward situation since he might well be accused of disobeying the Shah's orders and ignoring the government.

> I feared that he would find it very difficult to ignore these protestations. I said he might attach no importance to these remarks five times, ten times, twenty times, but in the end I was afraid that he would be influenced by these repeated objections coming from all sectors of the ruling classes. . . .[81]

As was his wont, the Shah's response was indirect. He gave no specific assurances, but he did observe that he wanted the oil revenues to be in the hands of someone who was immune to any outside influence. Ebtehaj took this to mean that he would have the Shah's support for running the Plan Organisation in his own way.

Ebtehaj had two further reservations: he wanted to know what the attitude of the Prime Minister, General Zahedi, was to his possible appointment and be assured of his support, and he wanted information on the current status of the Plan Organisation before finally making up his mind. The Shah told him that the Prime Minister had agreed to his appointment, but urged him to talk to

6. The Shah with members of the government and Ebtehaj in 1957

General Zahedi himself. Ebtehaj did so. The General not only confirmed that Ebtehaj would have his full support, but assured him that he had no intention of interfering in the Plan Organisation's affairs. He also arranged with the Plan Organisation that Ebtehaj be given access to its files. Some ten days later, having done all he could to ensure that he would have the freedom of action he felt was necessary, and with some notion of the magnitude of the problems ahead, he told the Shah that he was prepared to accept the assignment.[82] Finally, he was to have direct control of 'his child'.

6

EBTEHAJ'S ALTERNATIVE GOVERNMENT?

The First Seven-Year Development Plan had given formal recognition to the concept of economic development as a national goal in Iran, and represented a first attempt at allocating the country's resources according to a development strategy. It had created, also, a planning authority which could operate outside the 'soggy mess' of the government bureaucracy.

Yet the physical achievements of the First Plan were meagre. The effort of building the new organisation and creating the planning machinery proved much greater than had been envisaged. The new Organisation was hamstrung by the fact that not only did the expected foreign (including World Bank) loans not materialise, but also that, because of government expenditure needs, only a small proportion of the ear-marked oil revenues actually reached it, even before the oil crisis began to bite in 1950. Oil revenues were cut off altogether after the nationalisation of the Anglo-Iranian Oil Company in 1951.[1] What the Plan Organisation needed was a resumption of the oil income on which its finances depended, and a degree of continuous, strong executive management to re-establish its credibility as a feasible independent authority. In 1954, it got both: the oil dispute was finally settled and a new agreement provided for the resumption of the vital revenues, and Ebtehaj was appointed head of the Plan Organisation. Over the following four and a half years he unscrambled the mess into which the First Plan had degenerated; restructured the Plan Organisation; prepared a Second Seven-Year Plan, which was to lay the foundations on which Iran's fast growth in the 1960s was based; and enlisted the World Bank's aid for Iran. During Ebtehaj's period at the Plan Organisation, according to one western expert writing in 1967, 'Iran's development effort achieved a success never won before or since.'[2]

When Ebtehaj took over the Plan Organisation, the First Plan was in disarray. It was virtually bankrupt, with many foreign contractors owed money which the Organisation did not possess.[3] The Plan Organisation itself was riven by disharmony. After submitting their detailed report on the projects to be tackled in the First Plan, the consulting group, OCI, were re-engaged to assist with the actual execution of the Plan. Iranian–American cooperation did not long survive this venture into the field of practical implementation, however, and by the autumn of 1950 the consultants and the Iranian officials were at odds with each other. In December 1950 OCI decided to withdraw their services completely, and their contract was cancelled as from 1 January 1951. The basic problems lay in the different perceptions of the western consultants and the Iranians on how the Plan should be implemented, combined with the fact that, after mid-1950 in particular, the Plan Organisation did not have a strong leader who could withstand political interference. The Iranians were looking for quick and concrete results whereas 'the essence of the plan . . . was to create from the first the conditions necessary to industrial development by improving the educational, health, and agricultural standards of the country'.[4]

The First Plan was also beset both by the suspicions of the landed and mercantile élite who perceived it as a threat to their economic and social supremacy, and by conservative *mollas* who looked on any programme of industrialisation and modernisation as a threat to the traditional Islamic way of life.[5]

During the early 1950s, the Plan became almost moribund, and complete collapse was only averted by help from President Truman's 'Point Four' programme, a scheme launched in 1949 to assist Third World countries by the grant of technical assistance. Under a contract signed in October 1950, Iran became the first beneficiary of Point Four aid, and it was inevitable in the circumstances that the United States Overseas Mission (USOM), as the technical assistance team was referred to, should find itself largely abandoning its original brief to involve itself in a rural improvement programme. Instead, it became strategically necessary during the years between 1951 and 1954 to give aid and assistance on a largely *ad hoc* basis to various industrial projects which were part of the Plan's programme, rescuing those for which firm contracts had already been entered into and which were deemed to be crucial to Iran's industrial expansion. By mid-1954, some 38 of the projects approved by USOM were originally engineering and construction projects started under the First Plan.[6]

Ebtehaj's first reaction to the problems which confronted the

Plan Organisation was to decide that the First Plan should be ended prematurely, and replaced with a new development plan, and that the Organisation should be totally restructured. His immediate task had to be to discover what contractual commitments had been entered into before he took over. No consolidated list of commitments by the Plan Organisation existed and data had to be collected from whatever files were available. Nor had there been any attempt to coordinate them or relate them to the country's resources. When this basic information had been garnered, the commitments were sorted through to find out which were irrevocable and which were still open to critical scrutiny.

After conducting this audit, and in expectation of continued American aid until Iran's oil revenues started flowing again, Ebtehaj formulated an interim programme which would serve both to round off the First Plan and lead into the Second Plan.[7] This programme, which was approved by a *Majles* commission in February 1955, and for which some 8 billion *rials* was budgeted,[8] included contracts for the construction of 6000 kilometres of first-class roads, the improvement of six airports and a number of ports, a programme of municipal development, and the construction of two cement plants. The rationale for going ahead with these contracts was that they were projects 'for which the highest priority seems essential regardless of the nature of the overall [new] plan'.[9] Nevertheless, Ebtehaj was determined to re-assess the procedures by which even these contracts were awarded. He wanted to end the prevailing system of contract-hunting through local agents, and of contractor-led turnkey projects, both of which were open to all sorts of abuse, and he made it clear that in future all contracts would be properly appraised, supervised by international engineering consultants and executed after being properly put out to competitive tender.[10] The ports contract, for example, was given to a Danish group, Consortium Kampsax, rather than the British consortium which had been in the running for it under the pre-Ebtehaj regime.

The First Plan ended officially in September 1955. It was, as a recent study concludes, 'a plan that fell far short of expectations', with only 53.6 per cent of the planned expenditures actually spent.[11] Yet Ebtehaj had brought some order into the confusion, and he lost no time in turning his attention to the future. His goal was to restore credibility to the Plan Organisation and to the concept of planned development. Perhaps Ebtehaj's greatest achievement was that having insisted on being allowed the independence of action he felt the job required, he succeeded, against all the odds, in remaining at

7. Ebtehaj inspecting potential harbour sites in the Persian Gulf 1956/7

the head of the Plan Organisation, giving it purpose and strong direction, for just long enough to establish its viability. He was able in this time to build up and staff an Organisation capable of surviving without him and of carrying Iran's planning efforts on into the 1960s and 1970s, despite opposition by powerful groups within the political system. The fact that under him the Plan Organisation became a 'government within a government' was merely the logical extension of the 1949 legislation which had established it as 'an unorthodox planning-and-executing agency outside the regular machinery of government' being enacted under the direction of a strong personality driven by the imperatives for getting things done in Iran.[12]

Ebtehaj felt, and generated to others, a tremendous sense of urgency to get things done. He both saw the enormity of what had to be achieved, and realised that his own tenure at the Plan Organisation was unlikely to be of long-term duration. His energy and urgency had an electrifying effect on his staff, as Khodadad Farmanfarmaian later recalled:

> He used to drive us to the end of our wits, used to drive us to the point where we as young men (Ebtehaj was my senior easily by thirty years) just couldn't continue, we would fall asleep behind our desks. But it wasn't because he used his position or power. It was because he used arguments. It was because he made us feel the urgency of development in Iran. It was because he made us love – it is true – he made us love that organisation. It was because he made us love Iran, he made us understand the urgency of the problem of the Iranian people.[13]

Those who argued for caution, or warned of the dangers of Iran going 'too fast', were likely to produce a messianic explosion from Ebtehaj about Iran's needs for development. Thus, in 1957, a World Bank official who warned of possible inflationary and other problems found himself receiving a characteristic Ebtehaj lecture:

> Iran has resources, vast resources. The way to develop a country is not to listen to economists, who always say "No, don't do this, don't do anything". If America in her early days had listened to economists she would never have developed. America can say: Thank God, in our early years we had no economists. If a patient will surely die unless he has a serious operation, and he might not survive the operation, is there any sensible person who would say: don't operate? That is Iran's

position. Of course, there are dangers in doing things, in spending money for development. But unless that chance is taken, Iran will surely die.[14]

Urgent action required competent administrators if it was to be effective, and Ebtehaj was determined to improve the quality of the personnel at his disposal in an Organisation which had become, in his opinion, 'just another broken down Government administration' whose staff had no notion of its proper function and thus no faith in what they were doing.[15] He brought into the Organisation a number of officials of proven reliability, and sought to recruit some foreign experts. One of the first decisions he had made was that the focal point of any new structure should be two bureaux, one technical and one economic, staffed by the most highly-qualified experts who could be found, internationally or within Iran, and he lost no time in requesting the World Bank for help in establishing the most obviously necessary of these – the Technical Bureau.[16] He also arrived at conclusions about the priority areas of development – which were to be roads, ports, railways, airports and cement works – and resolved that in each of these fields the Plan Organisation should rely initially on the advice and supervision of foreign engineering consultants.

In the difficult area of the Plan Organisation's relationship with the ministries, Ebtehaj established the former's position by pursuing a policy of definition by challenge, and his successful arguing of the case for ear-marking the bulk of the oil revenues for development purposes finally ensured, to all intents and purposes, Plan Organisation control over the development activities of other departments.[17] It was the right strategy for a man in a hurry, but it fuelled resentment of Ebtehaj elsewhere in government, and in the long term did little to improve the quality of the bureaucracies he despised. There were, Farmanfarmaian remembered,

> tremendous jealousies by other ministries. . . . All the limelight was on the Plan Organization and those who labored in shadows obviously would be jealous of those who had the limelight . . . the ministries [could not] be expected to improve unless they were given specific development responsibilities under proper supervision. We raised this question with Ebtehaj. We argued for the transfer of responsibility for implementation of some projects to the ministries under proper supervision, reporting and auditing of the Plan Organization. We argued that ministers should have a chance

to go through a process of trial and error just as we were experiencing in the Plan Organization. ... Ebtehaj wasn't at all convinced. He said, "I'll do it when they improve". But then, how could they improve without the challenge of the responsibility for projects?[18]

Relations between Ebtehaj and the staff he had inherited were also not always easy, and he dismissed some men who might well have proved useful. He made it painfully clear when he felt people were incompetent, and this caused strong resentment, particularly in the light of his elaborate plans to employ foreign experts both as consultants and in key positions within the Plan Organisation itself. The ruthless battle he conducted against corruption made him many enemies amongst those who were used to regarding 'commission' as a deserved perquisite of public office or of business dealings. In consequence, Ebtehaj's relations with many of those with whom he needed to cooperate rapidly deteriorated: notably the Prime Minister, General Zahedi, a number of government ministers and many of the *Majles* deputies. He also failed to win the support of the business community who saw his plans and methods as cutting right across their interests. He remained, as a result, very dependent on the support of the Shah.[19]

Ebtehaj's relations with the Shah were the key to the Plan Organisation becoming a 'government within a government', and to an extent reflected the Shah's own move from 1954 on towards personal government. Without the consistent support of the Shah over the four and a half year period Ebtehaj was in office, he could not have won the various battles he had with government or withstood his increasing unpopularity with the majority of the *Majles* and the general public. As it was, the Shah backed Ebtehaj 'to the hilt, as he never backed any of his Ministers or security chiefs'[20] — indeed, in the view of one observer,

> The Shah's determination in standing by Ebtehaj as long as he did was the most impressive argument in favour of His Majesty's claim that he was determined to bring progress and stability to Iran.[21]

Ebtehaj's great weakness was the lack of his own political power base. He had neither the interest in developing such a base nor the political skills necessary. Moreover, his family connections generated little 'influence'. His two brothers both married foreign wives. Ebtehaj's own first wife was well-connected — but (as related in Chapter 8) he divorced her in the mid-1950s causing a considerable social scandal. In short, Ebtehaj could remain powerful only so long as the Shah let him.

The Shah's support was put to the test almost immediately Ebtehaj took over the Plan Organisation. Prime Minister Zahedi's impatience for quick results led him to ignore the assurance he had given Ebtehaj before the latter's acceptance of the job, that he would not interfere in the day-to-day working of the Plan Organisation, and it was not long before he and Ebtehaj were at loggerheads — particularly over Ebtehaj's schemes for the employment of foreign consultants and contractors.[22] Ebtehaj announced that while the Prime Minister was entitled to ask him questions, he was not going to brook any obstruction or interference.[23] By March 1955, the differences between Ebtehaj and Zahedi were such a serious obstacle to all public business — Zahedi had even gone to the length of setting up a committee to propose a three-year development plan in opposition to Ebtehaj's seven-year one — that it was clear that their differences were irreconcilable.[24] In one incident, later related to Farmanfarmaian, Zahedi attempted to overawe Ebtehaj by force after he had refused a request from the Prime Minister —

> Zahedi . . . was Prime Minister and a General, at that, he was tough too . . . he wasn't going to just back out. Zahedi sends a tank with soldiers to Plan Organization. . . . And Ebtehaj stood his ground and called the Shah and said, "I just want you to know the Prime Minister has sent a tank and soldiers to the Plan Organization". And apparently the Shah interceded and the tank was withdrawn and Ebtehaj [was] left alone. He would not be intimidated by anyone.[25]

The Shah ultimately assured Ebtehaj of his full support, and made it clear to Zahedi that he was not prepared to dispense with Ebtehaj. There was nothing left for Zahedi to do but resign.[26] He was replaced as Prime Minister by Ebtehaj's friend and ally, Hossein Ala.

This was not the end of the difficulties and confrontations Ebtehaj faced from various ministries and the *Majles*. Opposition to him remained fierce throughout 1955, manifesting itself most evidently in the differences between the ministries and the Plan Organisation over the extent of their responsibility for economic development. The financing and construction of the Karaj Dam came to symbolise, graphically, the points at issue.

Before Ebtehaj joined the Plan Organisation, a contract for the construction of this Dam on the Karaj River, some 40 kilometres north-west of Tehran, had been signed with the American engineering firm Morrison Knudsen, and a semi-autonomous agency called the Karaj Dam Authority (KDA) established under the direction of the Minister of Agriculture. For Ebtehaj, the contract encapsulated everything he disliked. The KDA operated independently of the Plan Organisation and yet was involved in a project which was clearly in the remit of the Plan Organisation and for which the Plan Organisation would ultimately have to find the funds. In the meantime, the KDA had arranged that the United States' Export–Import Bank (EXIM Bank) should provide credits for the financing of the project, credits which were tied to EXIM Bank's nomination of Morrison Knudsen to build the Dam. However, it appeared that Morrison Knudsen's costs would be about one billion *rials* higher than a French engineering consulting firm had estimated for the same job. Even worse, although two years had elapsed, no start had yet been made on the project, and EXIM Bank was demanding further studies before it would make the necessary loans. Ebtehaj made his views on the Karaj Dam quite plain. He saw no need for the involvement either of the American consulting engineers, or for American financing. Recourse to independent engineering advice on the design of the Dam had given him to understand that a cheaper French design would be perfectly appropriate, while the American design was unnecessarily costly. And he had concluded that it would be possible to finance the project without loans from EXIM Bank, particularly if such loans were to be tied to American firms and American goods regardless of their relative value.[27]

Given these fundamental disagreements, the argument inevitably came to rest on which was the final decision-making authority – the KDA under the direction of the Minister of Agriculture, or the Plan Organisation under Ebtehaj. There was no outright winner: Ebtehaj did not succeed in doing away with the KDA and bringing the whole project directly under the Plan Organisation. A compromise was reached whereby the KDA was to be run as an independent authority by a three-man board. The Minister of Agriculture was to chair this board, but Ebtehaj became a member and nominated the third member. Moreover, the project was to be financed not by way of the EXIM Bank credits, but directly from Plan Organisation funds, and the construction contract went to international tender.[28]

The battle for control, symbolised by the Karaj Dam and other such conflicts, was finally resolved – for the time being at least – at the end of 1955 when the Shah made quite clear his decision to back to the hilt the Plan Organisation and Ebtehaj's ideas of economic development and financial management. A bill was submitted to the *Majles* renewing the Organisation's overall authority for carrying out a new development programme and outlining the categories of projects in this programme.[29] Yet, the Shah's backing for Ebtehaj over the next few years did not mean the end of criticism and conflict. Clashes between the Plan Organisation and government were an inevitable result of the Plan Organisation's autonomy, and these clashes grew in intensity over time. Political pressures made Prime Ministers envious of the funds to which Ebtehaj had access, and relations between Ebtehaj and Dr Manouchehr Eqbal, who took office as Prime Minister in April 1957, were no better than they had been with General Zahedi. Ebtehaj's position, which appeared to be very secure after the end of 1955 remained, in reality, exceedingly vulnerable.

With characteristic vigour, Ebtehaj persuaded the World Bank to serve as a recruiting agent for the Plan Organisation. He was attracted to this international organisation not only because of his own personal experience of it and the IMF but because he had no wish to be dependent on any single nationality of foreigners. The Bank's response to Ebtehaj's request that it should recruit foreign experts for Iran was at first negative – such a function was not seen as part of its normal role, and the officials approached by Ebtehaj were reluctant to assume the responsibilities which would be created. However, Ebtehaj visited the World Bank in Washington early in 1955 to present his ideas and arguments in person. The President of the Bank, Eugene Black, whom he had first met in 1947, and who held him in very high regard, was soon persuaded of the necessity of helping him find the people he needed.[30]

A senior member of the Bank's staff, Hector Prud'homme, who in the early 1950s had been part of an abortive mission to Iran by the World Bank to find a solution to the oil dispute, was detailed by Black to identify suitable 'experts', as well as someone to lead the team who would be able to work closely with Ebtehaj and be absolutely free of any private or national vested interests in making recommendations for the award of contracts. Prud'homme started on this task before any formal agreement had been signed, and at once encountered the first hiccup – appropriate payment for the Technical Bureau personnel –

> We were talking not to people who were looking for a job, but to firms and their staffs who were active, and the word was

around that Iran had a way of delaying and complicating payments on contracts. The sense of some responses was: "It sounds like a challenging job, and I presume I would have an attractive employment contract in hand, but so-and-so tells me I could wait a long time before being paid".[31]

To solve this problem, Prud'homme promoted a scheme, which with Black's encouragement was adopted, whereby Iran would deposit with the Bank the funds needed to cover the salaries of the Technical Bureau personnel, and the Bank would have the function of employment agent and paymaster, shouldering the risk of having to find alternative jobs for the experts recruited if for any reason their contracts were cut short, but being guaranteed against loss by the Plan Organisation. The major difficulty of the scheme as it was adopted was that the annual payment by Iran to the Bank – initially $250,000 for the period to February 1957 but with provision for more if necessary – was to be a matter of public knowledge. While this ensured that the Bank could not be accused of making a profit out of the assistance it gave Iran, it did not disguise the fact that the foreign experts were being paid substantially higher salaries than their Iranian counterparts.[32]

Another difficulty was to find a suitable person to head the new Technical Bureau within the Plan Organisation in the limited time available, given that Ebtehaj wanted the Bureau personnel in Iran as soon as possible. However, this problem was overcome when, at Ebtehaj's suggestion, Prud'homme himself was nominated for the job and granted secondment from the World Bank.

In May 1955, Ebtehaj finally signed the formal agreement with the World Bank, the latter having safeguarded itself by ensuring that the scheme was fully supported by the Shah, the *Majles* and the government, and by reserving to itself the right to wind things up if at any time the scheme appeared not to be working effectively.[33] Under the terms of the singularly unusual agreement, the Bank agreed to engage for the Plan Organisation a group of eight highly ranked engineers of as many different nationalities as possible to form the Technical Bureau and supervise all technical and engineering affairs.

It took Prud'homme about six months to find suitable experts. In the interim, however, Black arranged for an American engineer, Walter Binger, to act as Ebtehaj's right-hand man and technical adviser until the Bureau was set up and staffed. Binger, a New York City engineer who had been Commissioner of Works and had supervised the engineering of, amongst other things, the East River Drive in New York City, spent four months in Tehran, leaving at the end of 1955 just as Prud'homme's team were beginning to arrive. Binger's services proved invaluable, not least in the encouragement and support he gave to the Plan Organisation's Iranian engineers, who often lacked self-confidence even when they had the required technical skills. His main task, however, was to go through the ever-increasing pile of project submissions and 'he just took them one by one in some order of priority, refusing to be dragooned or hurried just to pass things along'. Ebtehaj himself leaned heavily on Binger, and no contract or proposal was approved in the latter part of 1955 without his prior agreement.[34] Prud'homme's choices for the more 'permanent' members of the Technical Bureau proved equally felicitous and fulfilled Ebtehaj's requirement that there should be a spread of nationalities: besides Prud'homme himself (an American), there was a Frenchman, an Englishman, a German, an Italian, a Dutchman, a Belgian and a Norwegian. In Prud'homme's words, it turned out to be 'teamwork at its best', a judgement with which Ebtehaj concurred.[35]

Nor was the Technical Bureau the only area in which Ebtehaj requested the World Bank's advice and assistance. He turned to the Bank for help in identifying the best engineering consultancy companies, the provision of experts to appraise projects, specific project loans and even general bridging loans (another area in which the World Bank's response to Iran provided something of a precedent). Aside from the Bank, Ebtehaj looked to foreign foundations and universities for the sort of disinterested financial aid and technical advice he felt that official national aid and credit agencies could not supply. In 1958, for example, he persuaded the Ford Foundation to finance the second major bureau – the Economic Bureau – he wanted to establish within the Plan Organisation. When Ford agreed to provide the funding, the Foundation and Ebtehaj decided to ask Edward S. Mason, Dean of Harvard's Graduate School of Public Administration, to recruit the members of the Economic Bureau. Dr Khodadad Farmanfarmaian had already been appointed by Ebtehaj to head the Economic Bureau. After discussing the whole concept of the Economic Bureau and its functions with Ebtehaj, Dean Mason accepted the assignment, and the first Harvard Advisory Group team members began to arrive in Iran in May 1958.[36]

The Plan Organisation also continued to receive considerable American aid and technical assistance. As the oil revenues began to flow again, however, the USOM programme was re-directed from the capital investment projects it had had to deal with during the emergency of the Mossadeq period towards the provision of technical assistance for joint projects, usually financed by the Plan Organisation. During 1956–58 the Plan Organisation contributed $6.2 million towards USOM projects, and was directly or indirectly involved in 67 out of the 133 USOM projects.[37]

With the range of foreign help enlisted, Ebtehaj was able both to re-structure the Plan Organisation and to improve the way it operated. While the general structure of the Organisation remained much the same, internally it changed quite considerably. Ebtehaj had begun immediately to clean up the administrative mess he found when he took over the Organisation, waging a characteristically ferocious war on corruption, and insisting on punctuality and orderly administration. His plans for a Technical Bureau and an Economic Bureau within the Organisation were implemented. The Technical Bureau, operating directly to his orders, advised and assisted with the appraisal of projects and their implementation and guided the operating divisions on project preparation and execution. The Economic Bureau reviewed progress, collected and analysed economic information, studied the macro-economic and financial aspects of the Plan in the context of the whole economy, and prepared the framework of the Third Plan. Various other bureaux – to deal with public relations, projects and reports, finance – were also established. And the line organisation was improved and strengthened by the creation of an operations department, designed to coordinate the different operating divisions of the Organisation.[38]

On the operations side of the Plan Organisation, Ebtehaj had from the start strongly favoured the use of foreign consultants, selected after international tenders or on World Bank recommendation, to supervise the implementation of projects under the guidance and control of the Technical Bureau. By 1958 there were some 30 such firms, from Europe and the United States, in Iran, serving as consultants for a variety of industrial and infrastructure projects. The role of these foreign consultants was for the most part limited to the preparing of specifications, the adjudication of tenders, and the supervision of construction and installation. They could make recommendations, but actual decisions were made by the Plan Organisation. One notable exception to this general rule was the regional development programme in Khuzestan, for which an American consulting group was given executive authority.[39]

The employment of overseas consultants in a supervisory role did much to control the pervasive graft and corruption previously associated with construction contracts, as did the decision that contracts for major works were to be awarded on the basis of international tender. But Ebtehaj also introduced various new procedures specifically aimed at restricting the scope for corruption. Plan Organisation contracts, for example, could be declared null and void if there were any indications of bribery, even if such contracts were already in operation; and, in an attempt to eliminate one of the more common opportunities for bribery, if payments to contractors were not made within five days of receiving the relevant accounts, the person responsible for such payments was dismissed. It was less easy to control what happened further down the line and where the responsibility for implementation of contracts was shared with ministerial departments and the municipalities. Indeed, one great criticism of the Plan Organisation was that it was over-centralised, and lacked adequate representation in the provinces.[40] However, this was in part a reflection of the general weakness of the central government in the provinces, and more particularly the rural areas, in the 1950s. Large absentee landlords continued to hold sway in much of the Iranian countryside.[41]

As this was a very considerable constraint on the effectiveness of the Plan Organisation, Ebtehaj worked hard to improve its nation-wide administration which, in turn, necessitated the recruitment of competent management staff. When one of the newly-recruited Iranian managers, Dr Manouchehr Gudarzi, was made director of the social affairs operating division, he not only dismissed some 25 employees – a quarter of his staff – for inefficiency or dishonesty, but turned his attention towards the assignment of regional Plan Organisation directors to key areas throughout the country to monitor the progress of projects under way, make decisions on routine matters without reference to Tehran, and provide a channel for accommodating regional demands.[42] It was a step towards bringing the Plan to the people, though in practice the Plan Organisation never succeeded in generating much popular enthusiasm for the 'message' of planning: the general unavailability of newspapers and radio outside Tehran was a major obstacle to any popular dissemination of planning ideas.

Ebtehaj's four and a half years at the helm of the Plan Organisation vividly demonstrated his talent at institution building. He was adept at making things happen, and by 1959 he had transformed the almost moribund Organisation he had inherited. However, his determination to do things his way and his impatient style meant that he had made bitter enemies in the process – 'at a rate', according to one American observer, 'which showed some kind of negative genius'. Moreover, 'his very virtues as an economist became weak spots in the rough-and-tumble of Iranian politics', as his insistence on the importance of building a viable Plan Organisation and of laying the proper foundations for future development and long-term planning, and on putting in place a checks and balances system of project appraisal, came into conflict with the demands of politicians for rapid and visible results.[43] It was the combination of Ebtehaj's particular temperament and character with this conflict of expectation that was to cause his downfall.

Apart from rescuing what remained of the First Plan and rebuilding the Plan Organisation, Ebtehaj's major task was to see to the preparation and implementation of the Second Seven-Year Plan. Since the Plan Organisation's Economic Bureau was not yet in existence in 1954–55, preliminary work on drawing up the Second Plan was undertaken by 'a wide range of experts in different fields from the private as well as the Government sectors'.[44] Ebtehaj later recollected that he consulted with a number of his friends and colleagues and collected the names of 60 men (most of whom he did not know personally) who were considered to be the best qualified people in their own fields – from economists and engineers to lawyers and educationalists – and invited them to work together on drawing up a programme for the Second Plan. Although no remuneration for this task was offered, they accepted. A staff member of the Plan Organisation was named as secretary to the group, and Ebtehaj briefed it and attended its working sessions as often as his time permitted.

The Second Plan was completed in the space of about three months, but it was not until March 1956 that the Plan Bill was finally enacted. In the interim it had to be presented for approval to the Council of Ministers, the *Majles* and the Senate and it faced predictable criticism and discussion at each stage. Ebtehaj, who personally submitted the Plan to the Council of Ministers, told ministers that he was prepared to take into account any changes which they wished to make in the structure of the Plan on condition that the total disbursement over the seven-year period was not exceeded – unless the source of any excess funding required could be pinpointed. The Council's deliberations continued for some weeks, but in the end the Plan was approved almost unchanged: although every minister was unhappy with the share of the total allocated to his department, it soon became plain that any extra amount allocated in one direction would only reduce some other ministry's allocation.[45]

In June 1955, the Bill for the Second Plan was presented to the *Majles* where it again ran the gamut of comment and disapproval. In order to expedite matters, the *Majles* created a special Commission of 36 members, representing all interested bodies, to consider it, every session of which Ebtehaj attended in person. Like the Council of Ministers, each member of the Commission wanted an increase in the allocations he thought would be most beneficial to his own constituents, but although there were shifts in allocations, there was little basic change. There were, however, two major points of dispute – the extent of the authority granted to the Plan Organisation in controlling expenditure of the oil revenues, and the relative degree of authority of the Organisation and the various ministries. Both issues stemmed in large measure from the violent opposition Ebtehaj aroused amongst many of the deputies and ministers, and it was only pressure from the Shah which ensured that the Bill came out of the Committee only slightly amended, mostly in the direction of encouraging more short-term projects which would have immediate and visible results. The revised Plan Bill was presented to the *Majles* on 13 November 1955, and then went to the Senate. Opposition in the Senate proved to be more effective than in the *Majles*: the Senate President managed to persuade the Shah that the Director's authority ought to be somewhat circumscribed 'since the bill as written was too dependent on the personality of a Director who was liable to be changed'. A number of amendments were made which were intended to give Parliament closer control over the Plan Organisation's operations, but the influence of the Shah was sufficient to ensure that these amendments were less restrictive than they might have been. The amended Bill was then passed by the Senate on 21 February 1956, by the *Majles* on 28 February, and signed by the Shah on 13 March 1956, though the Second Plan period was deemed to have begun in September 1955.[46]

Despite the fact that the passage of the Bill had taken nine months, and had raised some serious issues, the new Bill was little different from the one presented in June 1955. There had been some quite large shifts in allocations, but this merely accentuated the fact that the Plan's programmes had been drawn up in general terms and that at the project level it was intended that there should be considerable room for manoeuvre. The Second Plan, like its predecessor, consisted of a series of sectoral investment projects, with no overall target other than a total expenditure of some 70 billion *rials* (about $921 million) and the general direction imposed on it by the Plan Act. It did not even cover the total activities of the public sector, was silent about the private sector, and gave no priorities to its wide-ranging but vague objectives, although there continued to be a strong preference for social infrastructure.[47] It was not, therefore, an attempt at 'comprehensive' planning – nor could it have been given the limited funds, and lack of data, trained planners, and inter-departmental coordination at the time of its writing – and individual ministries and *bongahs* (semi-independent organisations which administered some government enterprises) continued to sponsor their own projects.

The lack of a more comprehensive planning structure has been seen as a major contributor to the severe recession in Iran between 1960 and 1962, which came after accelerating inflation and general economic 'over-heating' forced the government in 1959 to seek the aid of the International Monetary Fund and impose an austerity programme.[48] Yet the positive achievements of the Second Plan need to be emphasised. It laid the infrastructural and organisational base on which a more comprehensive approach could be attempted. Moreover, after the stagnation of the early 1950s owing to the oil dispute, Iran achieved an estimated annual growth rate of GNP of about 7–8 per cent from 1955 to 1960, which was equivalent to a per capita rate of about 4.5 per cent. Over the same period there was an enormous rise in the level of capital formation. After the recession of the early 1960s, the average annual growth rate increased to 8–9 per cent and the per capita rate to some 5.5 per cent in the period of the Third Plan (1962–1967), and there was a further huge rise in the level of capital formation. By some measures, Iran in the 1960s achieved the highest growth rate of GDP per capita of any developing country, including such later economic 'stars' as South Korea and Taiwan.[49] During the first five years of the Second Plan – 1955–60 – the estimated 15 per cent of gross national product on average invested annually in various fields of development gave rise, together with accumulated reserves and foreign credits, to an estimated average annual increase in national income of about 5.7 per cent in real terms.[50]

To Ebtehaj and his planners, these growth rates spelled success. Ebtehaj was a 'growth man' who measured success by high growth rates.[51] In retrospect, some historians have criticised the obsession 'with the rate and pace of economic growth'.[52] Certainly, during the 1960s and 1970s this obsession became part of the Shah's grandiose and ultimately fatal design to make Iran one of the world's great powers. Ebtehaj, however, did not suffer from the Shah's later illusions. Nor was he alone in his interest in growth rates: as Farmanfarmaian later observed, 'growth' was the fashionable preoccupation of the 1950s and 1960s:

> The philosophy of the times, you know we were all deeply enamoured of economic growth. It wasn't that we were unaware of the necessity of improving as soon as possible the living standards of the masses, the problem of disguised unemployment and equitable income distribution. In fact, when you read the document of the third plan, it's very clear that we talk about these as the ultimate goal of development. But we do, however, state that unless there is growth, there cannot be much to distribute. ... we now, I myself am among these people, look back and say or think we should have perhaps have paid more attention from the beginning to this whole question of income distribution and unemployment.[53]

The funding for the Second Plan was to come largely from oil revenues, supported by some foreign borrowing, and only to a minor extent from local savings. According to the 1956 Plan Bill, the Plan Organisation was to receive around 60 per cent of total oil revenues up to March 1958, rising to 80 per cent thereafter. However, there was considerable competition for oil revenues from other government agencies, and by 1958 the Plan Organisation found that far from achieving the expected increase its share of Iran's oil revenues was being reduced.[54] This shifted the burden of financing the Plan towards foreign sources of capital.

Iran's past history had created a widespread and deep-rooted dislike of foreign loans and the sacrifice of sovereignty they were deemed to imply. The authorisation in the 1956 Plan Bill to raise up to $240 million in foreign loans had used a Persian word for 'loan' more accurately translated as 'credit', as credit did not have the unfortunate connotations of a loan.[55] Ebtehaj's willingness to borrow abroad – especially from the World Bank which was widely deemed to be 'American' – did nothing to enhance his popularity in the country. Ironically, no objection was made to lines of credit extended by such institutions as the American Export–Import Bank, although such credit was tied specifically to American goods and services, because no actual money changed hands.

Nevertheless, there was no shortage of offers to help Iran in its development effort. In November 1954, it had been announced in Washington that the United States would provide $127 million in aid during 1954–55. In 1956, Ebtehaj obtained 'without much difficulty' the promise of $40 million under new American legislation specifically aimed at giving assistance to developing countries (the Development Loan Fund or DLF), and he was also assiduously courted by the Soviet Ambassador who assured him that the Soviet Union would be only too happy to provide whatever loans and other assistance were necessary. What he really wanted, however, was a purely commercial loan to bridge the initial gap between revenue and expenditure, rather than any foreign government funding which might well have strings attached. He discussed the problem with John McCloy, Chairman of Chase Manhattan Bank and a former President of the World Bank, when McCloy was visiting Tehran in 1956, in the faint hope that Chase might be interested in making Iran a commercial loan, but was not surprised when McCloy said that his bank could not make a loan of the magnitude Iran needed. McCloy suggested that Ebtehaj approach the World Bank instead. When Ebtehaj pointed out that the World Bank had no provisions for making the sort of large non-specific loan he required, McCloy offered to discuss the matter with Eugene Black on his return to the United States. As a result Black agreed to visit Tehran and talk to Ebtehaj.[56]

There was no real precedent for what Ebtehaj was expecting. The World Bank's policy was to finance specific projects submitted by developing countries, but only after due appraisal and to the extent of the foreign currency component of the project's cost. Ebtehaj, however, in 1956, was not yet in a position to present specific projects. What he required was the equivalent of an overdraft facility which the Plan Organisation could use for its requirements of both foreign and local currency across the board. And, remarkably, this is what he got. In October 1956, after having heard that the Bank's management not only approved in general terms what the Plan Organisation was trying to do but also the firm management and 'outstanding personality' of Ebtehaj, the World Bank's Board decided to grant Iran a non-specific loan of $75 million.[57] The decision was formally confirmed on 18 January 1957, once the offer had been approved by the Iranian *Majles*. It was a decision brought about, in Ebtehaj's view, by the 'courage and magnanimity and farsightedness of Eugene Black'.[58] But it was also a decision which afforded several of the Bank's Board members particular pleasure, demonstrating as it did a more flexible and optimistic approach to the Bank's lending policy towards developing countries. As one of them remarked, 'I see that the old orchestra is going to play some new music, not the conventional waltz but maybe some rumba and perhaps a cha-cha-cha now and then'.[59] There was, of course, a recognition that the 'new music' being played for Iran would not be an appropriate precedent for every developing country – Iran had the advantage of an oil-based economy. And the terms and conditions of the $75 million loan reflected this: the loan was to bear interest at 5 per cent and be serviced directly by the oil revenues. Moreover, the Bank stipulated that for a two-year period Iran should not borrow from any other source, and that the Plan Organisation should cut back on its deficit by moving some of its first-half expenditures to the second half of the Plan period.[60]

Ebtehaj had considerable difficulty obtaining acceptance of the loan offer in Iran, but the Shah's strong support for it in the end ensured its approval by the *Majles*.[61] Ebtehaj also succeeded in convincing Eugene Black that it would be in the interests of both the World Bank and the Plan Organisation for the Bank to have a permanent representative in Tehran to monitor the use made of the loan. It was a suggestion which had at first been rejected by the Bank because of the assumption of responsibility implied, but Ebtehaj insisted. It suited him very well to have the World Bank counselling caution and requiring accountability as a counter-balance to the pressure within Iran – from the Shah down – to race ahead with implementation of Plan projects before all the necessary preparation had been undertaken.

Over the whole period of the Second Plan, Iran was to receive more foreign loans than the $240 million originally authorised in the 1956 Plan Bill. The Economic Bureau, which was given the task once it was set up of dealing with loans, was responsible for negotiating loans amounting to about $330 million, together with budget aid of about $30 million, between 1958 and 1962.[62]

Apart from the unique general loan of $75 million, the World Bank provided further project loans of $72 million in the late spring of 1959 for the extensive road building programme (nearly double the amount supplied by the DLF), and $42 million in February 1960 to finance the foreign exchange cost of the Dez Dam construction in Khuzestan, together with the concomitant electricity generating and distributing facilities. A formal application was made to the World Bank in September 1957 for help in financing the latter – a 'multipurpose project based on the Dez River, which was intended to be the initial step in a long-range program for the development of the Khuzistan area in southwestern Iran'.[63] Despite considerable doubts raised by the Bank's appraisal of the economic justification of the project for power generation (the Bank's consultants thought that a thermal project would make more sense than a hydro), it went ahead with a loan for roughly half of the cost of the first phase for the simple reason that by 1960 the Dez Dam was already under construction, and an investment of some $15 million had already been made.[64] In 1957, before World Bank officials had had time to read the Development and Resources Corporation's (D & R) Report, or make their own appraisal, Eugene Black taxed Ebtehaj with trying to force the Bank's hand by forging ahead with work on the Dez project. Ebtehaj assured him that this was not the case: the Bank should feel free to judge the project on its merits so far as financial support was concerned, but he felt it his duty to proceed without delay. Again Ebtehaj's sense of urgency was to the fore, and his foreboding that if he did not move he might not remain in a position to start the work. As he later recalled:

> As events turned out, the final report by D & R was submitted to the Plan Organisation in March 1959, one month after my resignation. I have not the slightest doubt that if I had acted according to the established traditions, Iran would not have had the Dez Dam or the cane sugar project in operation in early 1962.[65]

Compared with oil revenues and foreign loans, the mobilisation of local savings played a minor part in financing the Second Plan. However, a devaluation of the *rial* against the dollar in 1955 and a revaluation of the country's gold reserves two years later, both of which effectively expanded the money supply, made borrowing from the Bank Melli considerably easier and provided some resources for the Plan Organisation.[66]

By the end of 1958, the Second Plan's expenditure was 3.2 billion *rials* (or some $42 million) higher than the 31 billion *rials* ($407.9 million) originally estimated. Two of the Plan's sectors – agriculture and irrigation and communications and transport – had overspent their budgets, while the other two – public utilities and industries and mines – had underspent. This reflected the bias of the Plan Organisation under Ebtehaj towards long-term infrastructure development. His aim was to try to remove certain bottlenecks in the economy, notably in the transport sector. Above all, Ebtehaj believed that large-scale dams and irrigation projects were needed as a foundation for economic growth.[67] However, the bias towards large-scale projects was balanced in part by a programme of 'social improvement', undertaken in answer to the considerable pressure for more immediately visible benefits from Iran's growing oil revenues.

There were two sides to the social improvement programme; it incorporated both municipal projects in which the municipalities had a share, and capital projects undertaken in conjunction with the Ministries of Education and Health.[68] It was an imaginative attempt to spread the benefits of clean water, electricity, asphalted streets, schools, hospitals and so forth beyond the confines of Tehran to towns across Iran. As it was clearly impossible to carry out this sort of fundamental municipal development simultaneously in every town, because the necessary funds, implementing organisations and manpower were not available, a scheme had to be adopted that would be both fair and practical. Ebtehaj therefore decided to limit the application of the municipal development projects to towns where there were elected municipal councils. Priority was given to those towns whose elected councils undertook to provide 50 per cent of the cost of whatever project they wished the Plan Organisation to undertake – the Plan Organisation would provide the remaining 50 per cent as a grant and also the entire cost of preliminary engineering studies and their execution. The scheme had in theory two great advantages – decisions as to what projects should be undertaken, and where, would not be determined centrally but would depend solely on how much interest was evinced by the local councils, and there would be, in theory, no limit on the projects a town wished to have.[69]

Ebtehaj had considerable difficulty gaining acceptance for the municipal development programme. A majority of the *Majles*, and some of the Senate demanded that every town in Iran should benefit from the programme, whether or not it had an elected town council, and also that the Plan Organisation should pay the entire cost of each project. A bill was prepared to this effect. Ebtehaj, however, informed the *Majles* in his usual blunt fashion that if the bill were passed, there would be no municipal development programme at all since such an impossibly large programme would drain all available resources and sabotage the entire Second Plan. Although he had to agree to some speeding up of the programme, his arguments eventually won the day and the crisis passed.[70] In the meantime, three foreign firms of engineering consultants were selected to supervise the programme. Each covered a large area, and had to handle a range of projects which varied from the installation of piped water to the setting up of diesel-electric power stations, building of schools, or asphalting of roads. It was to prove a formidable task, and slow to get off the ground owing to the limited fiscal capacity of the municipalities and the physical difficulty of getting to projects located in remote areas.[71]

A unique feature of the Second Plan was the promotion of regional development – a systematic approach to the development of the land, water and mineral resources of an area to harness energy, provide irrigation, promote appropriate agriculture and industries, together with the provision of the social infrastructure and manpower training required. Khuzestan province, in south-western Iran, covering one eleventh of the country's area and containing nearly one eighth of its population, provided an ideal location for unified development of this sort: it had the huge advantage of embracing the drainage basins of five snow-fed rivers – the Karun, the Dez, the Karkheh, the Jarrahi and the Hendejan – suitable for harnessing for hydro-electric and irrigation purposes, and free from the complications of being touched by international borders; it had a vast plain suitable for intensive irrigated agriculture; it produced in the mid-1950s almost 4 per cent of the world's total production of crude oil; natural gas was abundant; and it had ready access to international trade routes at the Persian Gulf and to domestic markets via the Trans-Iranian railway and the expanding road network. Indeed, in times past, before the Mongol invasions, the irrigated Khuzestan plain had been the centre of prosperous agriculture (notably sugar-cane) and flourishing cities.[72]

In the mid-1950s, the possibility of harnessing the rivers in the Khuzestan region and of irrigating the plain was not new. The potential was there, especially once the establishment of strong central government, the discovery of oil and the construction of the railway had brought to an end the region's decline and isolation from the rest of Iran. The feasibility of irrigation projects in Khuzestan was investigated by the British during the Second World War, and the British and Indian governments even lent money in 1942 to a local cooperative called the Khuzestan Agricultural Society, managed by a Colonel Noel, in the hope of ensuring the rapid production of cereals during a period of acute shortage.[73] In the post-war decade, there was much discussion about the region's promise. However, although the United Nations' Food and Agriculture Organisation (FAO) selected it for special investigation, and their preliminary report (completed in early 1956) described the opportunity for comprehensive development of both the Karun and

8. Ebtehaj on the train to Khuzestan, late 1950s

EBTEHAJ'S ALTERNATIVE GOVERNMENT?

Karkheh river basins, FAO representatives were doubtful if anything could ever be accomplished in Khuzestan owing to the salinity of the soil and water, and the unbearable climate.[74]

By the late 1940s, consideration of the development of the Khuzestan river basins had become part of an overall policy of the West to combat the spread of Communism in the Middle East by encouraging and promoting economic development in the area. It was sometimes said that water and not oil was the true liquid gold of the Middle East, a region of deserts and, in most places, sparse rainfall; and major opportunities were seen to exist for irrigation, flood control and increased food production in countries such as Egypt, the Sudan, Syria, Jordan, the Lebanon, Iraq and Iran if the few major rivers were harnessed and their basins developed. Schemes centring on these rivers were given all possible technical assistance, and the prospect of financial help from the World Bank was raised.[75] But although there was much discussion of TVA (Tennessee Valley Authority)-style schemes in the Middle East, copious surveys undertaken, plans made, and some projects started, it was not until the mid-1950s that a TVA scheme in the Middle East – the comprehensive development of a region – was seriously addressed, and this was in Iran.

Ebtehaj had long been foremost amongst those Iranians who recognised the potential of Khuzestan, and when he became head of the Plan Organisation, a development scheme for the area was very much in his mind.[76] In September 1955, a meeting with David Lilienthal, former chairman of America's TVA, at the Annual Meeting of the IMF and World Bank in Istanbul, gave him the chance to take a first step towards the realisation of a dream. The meeting was particularly fortuitous since Lilienthal and Gordon Clapp (chairman of the directors of the TVA from 1946 to 1954, and head of the UN Economic Survey Mission to the Middle East in 1949) had formed in June 1955, in association with the American branch of the bankers Lazard Frères & Company, and with the encouragement of the World Bank, a new private company, Development and Resources Corporation, to provide planning and administrative services in resource development work to foreign countries. Having checked with Eugene Black that Lilienthal was the right man to approach, and been assured that there was no one better, Ebtehaj lost no time in inviting him on his own and the Shah's behalf to visit Iran to investigate development possibilities.[77] Lilienthal was interested. He recorded in his diary that

Ebtehaj is intense, cultivated, and utterly sincere. He is positively incandescent, impetuous and full of feeling. Without this kind of missionary zeal, I wonder if anything can be done to change the present conditions of what was once a great country.[78]

On Ebtehaj's return to Tehran he spoke to the Shah about his meeting with Lilienthal, and his idea (which he had not yet mentioned to Lilienthal) of sending him to Khuzestan to investigate the prospects for regional development. The Shah, who knew of Lilienthal, approved: this was to be the only authorisation Ebtehaj sought or obtained before going ahead.[79] Lilienthal, followed a few days later by Gordon Clapp, arrived in Iran on 20 February 1956, three days after the Shah had left for India on an official visit. The two men were already well-briefed on Khuzestan: when Ebtehaj had confirmed the invitation to visit Iran, he had told Lilienthal that Khuzestan was his particular interest and had sent him every scrap of relevant material available on the area. Once Lilienthal was in Tehran, moreover, Ebtehaj saw to it that he had an opportunity to talk to various people who might be able to pass on useful information about Khuzestan – members of the Point Four mission, for instance, and of the FAO team. To Ebtehaj's horror, the two FAO men voiced their conviction that nothing could be achieved in Khuzestan because of the problems of climate and salinity. Lilienthal appeared undismayed, however, remarking that the Imperial Valley in Southern California suffered from much the same problem. Later, to Ebtehaj's 'great relief' Lilienthal told him that

> what the so-called experts had stated was exactly what every single expert in the United States predicted and proclaimed with regard to the Tennessee Valley project before Lilienthal and others had started to work on it.[80]

As soon as Clapp arrived, Ebtehaj arranged for the two men to visit Khuzestan by special train to see the region for themselves. Upon their return, on 1 March, they reported verbally to Ebtehaj and a number of his senior colleagues. It was an enthusiastic report, and one which confirmed for Ebtehaj 'all the dreams I had concerning Khuzestan'. The heart of the programme, as tentatively conceived, was a system of dams in the headwaters of the region's rivers to permit the irrigation of the Khuzestan plain. The dams would also control floods, and make possible the generation of electricity. In addition it was envisaged that the region's mineral resources would be developed, including the large quantities of natural gas which were currently being burned off as waste. At a big party he gave for Lilienthal and Clapp the same evening, attended by the Prime Minister and other members of the government, Ebtehaj was, observed Lilienthal, 'so moved it was hard to believe' about the prospects which lay ahead.[81]

Ebtehaj lost no time in asking Lilienthal and Clapp to undertake the job of preparing an overall development plan for the Khuzestan area. Furthermore, he made it quite clear that he wished D & R to take full executive responsibility for implementing the plan when the operating stage was reached and for seeing to it that the people of the region benefited from the development taking place. Although Prud'homme had already warned Lilienthal that unless D & R were prepared to accept such responsibility nothing would ever happen, Lilienthal was amazed to find that Ebtehaj was of the same mind. It put D & R in a potentially awkward position given the political uncertainties of Iran, and the endless frustrations and delays inherent in tackling any sort of project. However, the problem of justifying such a high risk venture to D & R's New York associates was overcome when Lilienthal suggested that the programme of development be divided up into stages, starting with an initial six-month preparation stage. On 14 March, a mere and, according to Prud'homme, miraculous two weeks later, an agreement was signed with D & R, under the terms of which they 'were to plan and help carry out a long-range program of agricultural and industrial development of the Khuzestan region, along TVA lines'.[82] In a supplement to this agreement, signed in December 1956, D & R's responsibility was expanded still further when they assumed an executive role in the case of all projects in the Khuzestan region, not merely new projects. It was to be a totally integrated programme.[83]

D & R produced their preliminary report in the summer of 1958 and their final report a year later, just after Ebtehaj had left the Plan Organisation. Their proposals – the most important of which was that 14 dams should eventually be constructed – were accepted in principle by Iran's government. Implementation was to be undertaken initially by the corporation set up in Iran by D & R – Khuzestan Development Services. Later the Khuzestan Water and Power Authority (KWPA) was set up by the Iranian government as the organising authority. Recommended projects were so numerous and vast in their scale that their implementation would take decades, and depend on government's choice of priorities. However, a start on the programme of action was to begin at once so that there could be no question of the scheme becoming 'all surveys and no work'. This programme included the construction of a multipurpose dam on the Dez River, the erection of a high voltage electric transmission line between Abadan and Ahwaz, the development of a 10,000-hectare irrigated sugar cane plantation, together with mill and refinery, to produce 30,000 tons of refined sugar a year, and tests and demonstrations of chemical fertilisers on Khuzestan soils to help farmers increase food and fibre production.[84]

Although the unified regional development scheme for Khuzestan was unique in Iran in terms of its size and scope, there were other more modest regional schemes started during the Second Plan in the Seistan and Baluchistan regions.[85] Moreover, the Khuzestan scheme provided the model for further regional development schemes started under the Third and Fourth Plans.

The level of implementation and accomplishment during the Second Plan was surprisingly high despite complaints and criticisms of a slow start owing to Ebtehaj's insistence on reorganisation, proper feasibility studies, and competitive tendering, and despite constant shortage of cash after 1958. In 1957–58, for instance, two new branches of the Trans-Iranian railway were finally inaugurated, linking Tehran with Tabriz and Mashad and opening up thereby the fertile northern provinces of Azerbaijan and Khorasan. And by the end of the Second Plan period some 2500 kilometres of major highways had been constructed, and port facilities increased to cope with the growing volume of international trade. Huge strides had been made in some key industries: by 1961 the government owned four large integrated spinning and weaving plants and textile production had increased from 60 to 480 million metres annually; sugar production had risen from 85,000 to 227,000 tons and cement production from 100,000 to 1.2 million tons. Iran's first modern milk pasteurisation plant (a joint UNICEF–Plan Organisation venture) went into operation at the end of 1957. The construction of several large dams – on the Karaj, Sefid Rud and Dez Rivers – was well on the way by 1958 and although they absorbed most of the funds allocated to the agriculture and irrigation sectors, they were multipurpose in nature and when finished contributed a 9.3 billion cubic metre increase to Iran's water-storage capacity and 692 megawats to hydroelectric generating capacity. In addition, four smaller dams had been completed by the time Ebtehaj left the Plan Organisation, two of which were in Seistan; the large irrigation works on the Moghan plain in northern Iran had been finished; and various other

9. The Dez Dam

studies and investigations were in progress. Implementation of various projects in the first phase of development in Khuzestan had also started.[86]

Although the Plan Organisation under Ebtehaj did not attempt to play a major role in stimulating private industry, except in a small way through credits given to medium-sized firms by an Industrial Credit Bank owned by it, Ebtehaj was very much one of the moving spirits behind the establishment of the Industrial and Mining Development Bank of Iran (IMDBI) in 1959. In 1957, the World Bank had suggested to André Meyer, senior partner of Lazard Frères in New York, that Lazard should cooperate with Iran in setting up IMDBI, and that Meyer should consult with Ebtehaj who was currently visiting the United States. Ebtehaj was delighted with the idea and promised to put it to the Shah. Various difficulties delayed the project for the new Bank, but Ebtehaj continued to use his influence with the Shah, and when he succeeded in introducing André Meyer to the Shah during the latter's visit to Washington in June 1958, Meyer was informed that the project would go ahead. IMDBI opened in October 1959, under foreign management and with the World Bank acting as midwife. The largest contribution to its capital, $18.7 million, came from a portfolio of 'managed loans' which the Iranian government lent it. A third of the remaining $23.6 million capital came from an interest-free advance from the government, one third from the World Bank and the American Development Loan Fund in equal proportions, and the remaining third was equity capital. Despite the recession of the early 1960s, IMDBI proved to be a success from the start, and did much to help create a capital market in Iran. It attracted an excellent staff and within five years had made the transition from foreign to local management.[87]

Yet despite its accomplishments, the Plan Organisation under Ebtehaj experienced many difficulties and failures. Some of these were the result of inevitable conflict between high expectations and harsh realities: in Iran's case expectations were particularly high because of the resumption of, and growth in, oil revenues. Some were the result of the characteristic style and temperament of Ebtehaj himself, especially his inability to compromise or to accept that economic development could not be divorced from political realities. Perhaps the two greatest problems faced by the Plan Organisation in the 1950s were the lack of trained personnel and the dilemma of long-term versus short-term benefits.

By 1958 the shortage of sufficient qualified personnel was being acutely felt by the Organisation, and Ebtehaj was having to rely more and more on foreign advisers. This was not surprising for a country at Iran's level of development, but Iranian sensitivity to foreign 'control' was high and the image held in some quarters of Ebtehaj as 'anti-Iranian' and a foreign 'stooge' was reinforced. In fact, Ebtehaj regarded the use of foreigners as inevitable in the short term if anything was to be achieved, but also as an important means of transmitting scarce skills to Iran over the longer term. As he later wrote,

> I would *never* engage a foreign national if an Iranian was available who would do the job. But I would also never consent to engage Iranians as consultants and contractors, if they were not qualified for the job. For instance, at the time I took over Plan Organisation, there was not a *single* Iranian group with any experience of consultants or who possessed machinery for carrying out important building projects, such as dams or highways. However, I did everything possible to help Iranians to qualify themselves for such jobs. I carried out a project whereby Plan Organisation imported large quantities of modern, heavy machinery for important jobs for the construction of modern roads and irrigation projects and dams etc. The machinery and equipment were purchased by Plan Organisation at prices not available to any Iranian contractor. The machinery and equipment were sold at cost plus 6% per annum. In large consultants or construction contracts, such as the Khuzestan programme, Plan Organisation consultants like D & R were required under terms of their contracts to train Iranians, right from the start of their work, to engage and train *qualified* young Iranians to take over and run the projects as soon as they were completed. Thus we were able to fill most of the senior positions with Iranians with the highest university training and management experience.[88]

In 1956, Ebtehaj established a manpower development division in the Plan Organisation, with responsibility for training and education. But although the division did some basic statistical work, it was progressively weakened by politicking and was abolished in 1961. The first national manpower plan, on the basis of a survey undertaken in 1958, was prepared in 1960–61 – after Ebtehaj's departure – by the Economic Bureau, whose staff, like Ebtehaj himself, were only too aware of the importance of the question of human resources. However, the implementation of specific projects was very slow, and probably the most dramatic and effective manpower development programme in the Third Plan period – the establishment of an army-based literary corps – was not a product of that Plan at all.[89] Not that the idea of using the army as an instrument of training was new. On the contrary, Ebtehaj had on several occasions during the 1950s suggested to the Shah that this would be the most effective means of providing technical skills' training. But although, after some difficulty, he finally persuaded the Shah to his point of view, and went so far as to discuss the project with an American Point Four official in Washington, he had left the Plan Organisation before he could take the idea any further.[90] Ebtehaj's recognition of the urgent need for vocational training was also reflected in his insistence that it should be provided 'on the job' whenever possible. One of the D & R Corporation's primary tasks in Khuzestan, for instance, was the provision of such training, so that within a given time Iranians would be able to take over completely the institutions and plant created. In the end, however, one of Ebtehaj's more enduring successes was the recruitment of bright, often foreign-educated, young Iranians – men such as Farmanfarmaian and Gudarzi – into the Plan Organisation. These, like the young technocrats whom he had recruited to the Bank Melli (and there was some overlap), supplied Iran's Plan Organisation and other economic institutions with their senior management for the next two decades.

The difficulty over long-term versus short-term benefits was never satisfactorily resolved. It is a problem in any society or political system, but many observers came to the conclusion that there were special difficulties in Iran, with its 'residual bazaar mentality . . . [and] philosophy of quick profits, quick returns'.[91] Such factors did not rule out economic planning, but it did require 'the institutional design of planning' to 'take this cultural characteristic into account and design means for coping with any difficulties that may arise'.[92] Ebtehaj was perhaps not the man to adapt his methods to cultural characteristics he considered undesirable.

Ebtehaj's commitment to long-term planning led to continuing criticism that the Plan Organisation was undertaking projects too grandiose for Iran, which were costly to execute and which offered no prospect of early improvement in living conditions. In addition, certain projects – such as the development of port facilities and airfields – were looked on with deep suspicion as being of strategic rather than economic significance, and undertaken for the benefit of the West rather than Iran.[93] To some extent a compromise between the long- and short-term view was effected by the adoption of the social improvement programme, but this was not an easy programme to administer or to get off the ground quickly. By March 1958, only 66 per cent of the total budgeted expenditure had been spent – 103 projects out of a total of 1029 had been completed; another 185 projects were under actual construction; and about 700 more were at the stage of having specifications and tenders drawn up. The municipalities encountered great difficulty in meeting their share of expenditure on projects, and the Plan Organisation had to think up ways of coming to their aid – such as guaranteeing supplier's credit to them, and requesting a 25-year non-interest-bearing loan of around $80 million from the United States' Development Loan Fund, guaranteed by the Iranian government, for their exclusive use.[94] The planners could not work miracles.

Plan Organisation's financial difficulties increased towards the end of Ebtehaj's tenure as its director, moreover. This was partly because of the reduction in its share of oil revenues, and partly because of the expansion in its programme. Although short-term borrowing from the Bank Melli, and longer-term foreign loans, at first bridged the gap, borrowings never succeeded in catching up with the Organisation's need for cash in the second half of its programme. Because of the cut-back in the Plan's programme, necessitated by the cash shortage, some projects vanished entirely (such as the projected PVC plant in Khuzestan, part of the D & R programme), while the progress of others was adversely affected; and in certain sectors – rural development, health, education, and so on – funding was cut. The chronic cash shortage in the last years of the Second Plan led an IMF official to observe in 1961 that 'to all intents and purposes Plan Organisation is bankrupt'.[95]

In the end, as the following Chapter will discuss, Ebtehaj fell victim to his failure to compromise economic development and planning by bowing to the range of political pressures he faced, or to understand the political pressures faced by other government agencies. Yet his insistence on running the Plan Organisation in the way he did, brooking no interference and demanding the lion's share of the oil revenues, was an understandable reaction to the problems of planning in Iran. An American economist, a member of the first Harvard Advisory Group team, concluded that the specialised structure represented by the Plan Organisation in the 1950s was a 'necessary' condition for an Iranian development programme, although it was not a 'sufficient' condition. Three other conditions were also necessary – a managing director capable of minimising and managing the inevitable tensions between the Plan

Organisation and the ministries, the employment of a certain number of foreigners because the Plan Organisation itself exhibited to some degree many of the cultural 'anti-planning' characteristics that influenced Iranian politics and administration, and that the Plan Organisation and government should be under the discipline of periodic accountability to external financing institutions – preferably the World Bank and the IMF as bilateral aid was too political.[96] Whereas Ebtehaj, during his term of office, managed to achieve the latter two of these conditions, he did not achieve the first.

PART FOUR

THE CLASH OF VALUES

7

MORE EUROPEAN THAN IRANIAN?

In February 1959, Ebtehaj resigned from the Plan Organisation, his 'child'. He was never again to hold public office. Indeed, within three years Ebtehaj found himself incarcerated in one of the Shah's gaols after publicly criticising American support for the Shah's regime, which he accused of corruption and repression.

To some observers, Ebtehaj's fall from power sooner or later was inevitable, for his ideals and methods were alien to the society in which he lived. The First Secretary of the United States Embassy in Tehran at the time of Ebtehaj's resignation believed that he 'had forgotten how to think and feel as an Iranian; he was far more European – thus he was greatly trusted by Europeans and Americans and hated by most Iranians who came in contact with him'.[1] It was a point also made by a British observer, the historian Peter Avery, who commented that 'the fault of the zealous reformer lies in his forgetting to be, at the same time as he is a reformer, also an Iranian'. Part of Ebtehaj's trouble, according to Avery, 'was that he really *believed* in the necessity for changes to which his colleagues in many instances were only paying lip service'.[2] A similar, if rather more jaundiced view of Iran's planners was taken by R.K. Ramazani: they were, he observed from a post-Islamic Revolution perspective, 'really "alien Iranians" . . . insensitive to the non-economic roots of political alienation'.[3] Unfortunately for Ebtehaj, as the 1950s progressed comparable thoughts began to enter the Shah's mind, though for very different reasons. 'I don't understand this man', he once remarked, 'Iran has been good to him, yet he doesn't like Iranians. He calls us all thieves. He doesn't seem to believe in what we are doing. The worst thing is that he doesn't seem to like his country.'[4]

Any simplistic view that Ebtehaj was merely an alien implant into his society can be rejected. He did not conform to some of the usual forms of behaviour in Iran. He displayed, for one thing, an uncharacteristic directness in both his views and actions, as well as an uncomfortable honesty. However, this was symptomatic not so much of being 'more European than Iranian' as of his own particular character, and his position as a pioneer technocrat in a country which did not yet understand technocrats. Nor did this mean that he became any the less 'Iranian': indeed his temperament – proud, subtle, quick-tempered, thin-skinned, emotional – could be termed (at the risk of cultural stereotyping) peculiarly 'Iranian'. He certainly 'liked' his country. The problem was perhaps Ebtehaj's abrasive manifestation of all the characteristics of a technocrat – a strong belief in professionalism, and a corresponding dislike of corruption wherever it occurred.

These attitudes, pursued in Ebtehaj's distinctively energetic and self-confident manner, made enemies, and led to inevitable misconceptions as to his motives. He was frequently accused of being either an American or a British 'stooge', or both, and sometimes even – quite ludicrously in his case – of being pro-Russian.[5] In fact, as the British Ambassador observed to the Shah in 1955: 'anybody who knew him could not conceive [of] him being the stooge of anyone.'[6] Certainly Ebtehaj looked to the West, and in particular to the United States, when he required the technical help and managerial skills which were not readily available in Iran, or when he needed help in the financing of Iran's development effort. But this reflected the actions of a realist rather than a 'stooge'. The help, skills and funds had to come from somewhere. Ebtehaj made great efforts to steer away from purely bilateral aid, as his recourse to international institutions whenever possible demonstrated, but the World Bank and similar agencies could not provide all the help and finance required.

Ebtehaj bore the brunt of the prevailing mythologies in Iran about the western powers. Since the 1907 Agreement between Russia and Britain, which had carved Iran up into 'spheres of influence', it had been part of Iranian mythology that Britain was behind any and every political or economic shift in the country – from the fall of the Qajar shahs and the rise of the Pahlavi dynasty to Mossadeq's rise and fall; from the occupation in World War One to the occupation in World War Two. It was a mythology which long outlasted any real influence Britain had in Iran – there were even those, incredibly, who at the time of the Islamic Revolution, maintained that Ayatollah Khomeini was in the pay of the British. The mythology about the United States was of much later origin, and was still in its infancy in the 1950s. However, American involvement in the downfall of Mossadeq provided a dramatic yardstick, and, with the escalating military aid received by the Shah, ensured that the United States soon came to occupy the place Britain had once held as one of the two baleful influences dominating the Iranian scene. It was all too easy for the critics or enemies of Ebtehaj – or any public figure – to whip up public opinion by suggesting that he was a British or American 'stooge'.

Ironically, while some of his own countrymen vilified him for being an arch-servant of the West, many westerners looked on Ebtehaj as being 'anti-foreign, particularly anti-British', as expressing a 'vehement nationalism', and as taking 'no pains to conceal his belief that he was equal or superior in ability to Americans'.[7] These views were just as misleading. Ebtehaj was no more anti-foreign than he was a foreign 'stooge'. His circle of friends and acquaintances was highly cosmopolitan. He had no difficulty, and indeed derived much enjoyment, in the early 1950s, from living and working in Europe and then America. Equally, he made no attempt to remain in the West at a time when he could easily have done so, and left an important job with the IMF, of his own volition, to return to Iran. He was, as some perceptive British and American officials realised, 'no more pro-American than he is pro-British'; 'actually . . . a highly patriotic, but very thin skinned Iranian, with nationalistic or even chauvinist tendencies'; 'a sincere patriot' with a 'genuine desire to improve Persia's economic position'.[8] They were views which in the end came to be shared by many Iranians, even former critics.[9]

While Ebtehaj was attacked in public as a 'stooge' of various parties, his methods raised the ire of many in Iran's political élite in the 1950s. Over the years, the resentment of ministers at Ebtehaj's consistent refusal to allow them to participate in development projects, except under his direction, grew. Each year from 1954 to 1959 there were problems at budget time as successive Prime Ministers and Ebtehaj argued over the disposition of the oil revenues, and it became more and more intolerable for the former, exposed to constant public demands for expansion of government functions but cries of anguish at any attempt to increase taxation, that Ebtehaj should be in the position of being able to spend oil revenues lavishly at his sole discretion. Furthermore, Ebtehaj's reliance on foreign advisers and consultants to provide the expertise and disinterested competence required to oversee the implementation of plan projects both hurt the pride of many Iranians and excluded them from what they considered their right – a chance to benefit financially from the expenditure of government funds.

There is also evidence that some American officials, from both the Embassy and such aid agencies as Point Four, were willing to support anti-Ebtehaj elements in the Iranian government. This was certainly the opinion of David Lilienthal, who confided to his diary in December 1956, that

> it has been evident to us that the U.S. Embassy and the U.S. Point IV effort is out to discredit Ebtehaj if they can, a deliberate and at times it appears to be a malicious business. At our visit with the American Ambassador, Selden Chapin, the other day ... he repeated all the gossipy things that the members of the Embassy staff had said about Ebtehaj. This campaign has been intensified since the flat policy laid down in Washington by Harold Stassen, head of Point IV during this Administration, that Point IV must be "integrated" into the regular old-line Ministries. Those Ministries, of course, are against Ebtehaj, or anyone else who tries to root them out of their old ways.[10]

No doubt the motives of these American officials were complex, but, in part at least, it is likely that they found Ebtehaj's personality a hard one to live with. His 'overweening conceit, egocentricity, bad temper and intransigence' were frequently commented upon,[11] although neither conceit nor egotism was evident when, after he had left the Plan Organisation in 1959, he refused his successor's invitation to be present at the dedication ceremony of the Abadan to Ahwaz electric power transmission line – the first of the Khuzestan regional development projects to be completed – in case his presence would prove embarrassing. Making his excuses, he said 'Anyway ... it doesn't matter who started something, or who is in charge when it is finished, so long as the work gets done. The credit isn't important.'[12] Nonetheless, the personality traits required to stand against inefficiency and corruption were not those which inspired popularity among many Americans and still less, perhaps, among Iranians. 'Confidence in the thoroughness and competence of Ebtehaj' may have encouraged the favourable response of foreign investors such as the World Bank and international agencies, as the *Tehran Journal* reminded its readers in January 1959, but this favourable response merely led many Iranians to look upon him as the arch-servant of the West. The fact that he drew his authority 'not from family influence but from the authority of figures and facts, from the authority of technical, financial and legal advice and from hard work', may have given a fine example of how a modern administrator should operate, but it also seemed to undermine 'the individual and collective self-confidence' of his fellow countrymen.[13] His honesty and zeal may have made him internationally famous, but at home his enemies were merely incredulous that anyone with power over so much money could possibly be honest, and fostered the notion that he was somehow in league with the Shah and foreign firms in a system of 'kickbacks'.[14]

Ebtehaj's unrelenting determination to use current oil revenues to build his vision of a better future won him few friends. Ministers continually challenged the Plan Organisation's projects and lobbied for different ones of their own. Neither the Prime Minister nor the Shah was above interference, despite their avowed commitment to the Plan Organisation's independence of action. As early as October 1954, Ebtehaj referred to the 'impulsive tendencies' of the Shah and Prime Minister who were accustomed on the spur of the moment to issue instructions which ignored well-conceived plans – and this was in the first flush of enthusiasm for the newly-revived Plan Organisation, and for Ebtehaj himself.[15] Furthermore, the rivalry between the Plan Organisation and government ministries, and the 'impulsive tendencies' of the leadership, allowed private interests to flourish. Ebtehaj had pledged himself to end the interference in the Plan Organisation's operations of self-seeking local entrepreneurial groups, but he was unable, finally, to do so, given the support they received from government and the Court.[16]

Ebtehaj faced a constant struggle against vested and powerful interests, which he needed the Shah's authority to overcome. A classic instance was his struggle to secure 10,000 hectares of land for sugar cultivation in Khuzestan. Ebtehaj's own words perhaps best convey the story:

> In the case of the cane sugar project, D & R brought out a Puerto Rican expert, Dr Carlos E. Chardon, in April 1957, who had to carry out perhaps the most important job of selecting the land on which cane was to be produced. He did this and I was informed that a certain land of an area of 10,000 hectares, if handed over to D & R by a certain date, would make it possible for them to grow the kind of cane which would produce sugar. The time given to me to acquire this land was only a few months. I sent two of my senior colleagues to Khuzestan to acquire the 10,000 hectares. They returned to tell

me that the land was part of the villages owned by a sheikh [Khalaf] whose family had ruled the area for centuries and that Sheikh Khalaf begged them to buy the land elsewhere. In fact, he offered them a certain amount of money if they would abandon the idea of buying his land. Under a law, the Plan Organization was authorised to have the land evaluated by a committee of three people and deposit the amount as recognised by the committee as due to the landowner. This was done and the land was duly delivered to D & R before the deadline, which I believe was at the end of 1957. But meanwhile Sheikh Khalaf had started a campaign by appealing to all the authorities in Tehran, including the Imperial Court, the Prime Minister, the Speaker of the Majles and I received communications from all these authorities, particularly from the Shah who told me the Government owned millions of hectares of land in Khuzestan and why should Plan Organization have to pay 25 million Rials for this particular land. My reply to the Shah and others was that our consultants wanted these 10,000 hectares and that I could not demand that they carry out their obligations if I could not deliver to them the land that they had selected. I added that I thought the Shah should not waste his time and assured him that I would have paid, had I been required to do so, ten times as much as I had actually paid out for the 10,000 hectares. The military commander of the province of Khuzestan sent a telegram to the Shah saying he could not be held responsible for events if the land was not returned to its owner. I received a letter from my friend Mr Ala, who was then Minister of the Imperial Court, telling me that despite the importance of the cane sugar project the land should be restituted to its owner for political reasons. I answered the letter and said that the land had already been handed over to D & R and that in my opinion what the Plan Organization was doing in Khuzestan was in the best interest of Iran.[17]

By the end of 1958, opposition to Ebtehaj was mounting on all sides. Preparations for the 1959–60 budget finally brought matters to a head – 'in a complex situation involving calculations about American economic and military aid, pressure to increase military expenditures, the fostering of rival development projects in ministries, an expected deficit, an international loan tied to a balanced budget, Plan Organisation insistence that it receive its entire allotment from the oil revenues, and considerable personality conflict.'[18]

Ebtehaj became locked in a bitter feud with Prime Minister Manouchehr Eqbal and his government over the oil revenues: Eqbal had succeeded in cutting into them once already for the 1958–59 budget, and aimed to do so again for 1959–60, despite Ebtehaj's violent opposition and the fact that the World Bank loan's terms specified that there should be no further diversion of them.[19] The Plan Organisation thus faced considerable financial difficulty, and the question of expenditure priorities took on a new force. Ebtehaj was absolutely convinced that the requirements of economic development should take the highest priority, even over defence spending. This view increasingly irritated the Shah, for whom, especially post-Mossadeq, nothing was more important than the commitment to expansion of the armed forces, and the spending that entailed.[20] Very shortly before Ebtehaj's resignation, there was a serious clash over military expenditure. The occasion was a visit to the Plan Organisation by the American ex-Joint Chief of Staff, Admiral Radford, who was on an official mission to Iran and various other nations to assess armament needs. Farmanfarmaian was amongst those who attended the meeting between Ebtehaj and Radford:

> Admiral Radford started by saying that "I'm here to examine the military requirements of Iran and to talk to various authorities about it, and to look into Iranian development requirements, and talk to you and be briefed about what is going on". Once Admiral Radford had finished talking about his purpose to look into military need and military requirements, Ebtehaj made a fist and raised it and banged on the table so hard – I have never seen anything like it – and said, "Admiral Radford, Iran needs development, not military expenditure". And he proceeded on that theme with the greatest of gusto and fervor mixed with anger, if you wish. Ebtehaj said that the Iranian government doesn't understand these problems, that by any objective or rational examination of the Iranian situation, when there are people in the country of such low standards of living and the country at such low level of development, our first efforts must be guided to raising the standard of living, that no military or defense can be built on a weak economy ... Well, Admiral Radford's face turned completely red, of course, and he was deeply embarrassed, deeply embarrassed.[21]

While Ebtehaj was embarrassing the American military hierarchy, in January 1959 the conflict between the Plan Organisation and the ministries reached a new peak over a sudden announcement that the Ministry of Industry and Mines had signed a contract to erect a fertiliser plant in Shiraz – notwithstanding the clear understanding that all industrial development projects were to be carried out by the Plan Organisation, and that the Plan Organisation's own plans for a fertiliser plant in Ahwaz, Khuzestan, were already at an advanced stage.[22]

The Shiraz fertiliser plant became at one and the same time an expression of the conflict between the Plan Organisation and the ministries, a symbol of the personality clash between Ebtehaj and the politicians, and evidence of the Shah's resolution to curb the independence of the Plan Organisation. The contract seemed a direct challenge to the powers of the Plan Organisation. Ebtehaj was convinced that Iran could neither afford two fertiliser plants nor absorb their output. Moreover, the Shiraz project seemed to indicate a return to the chaotic days of contractor-led, turnkey-type projects. On investigation, it appeared about as bad a project as it could be. The large nitrogen fertiliser plant at Shiraz was to have the same capacity as the Ahwaz plant already designed by the Belgians for the Plan Organisation, but would cost 50 per cent more (its capital costs per ton in fact turned out to be among the highest in the world). It had been designed by the equipment suppliers, and sold to the Ministry of Industry and Mines without the benefit of competitive bidding. Its location at Shiraz was nowhere near any railway, and a considerable distance (some 100 kilometres) from the necessary natural gas sources.[23] This was all in complete contrast to the Ahwaz plant, the location for which was not only in the centre of the natural gas source which would provide the raw material and of the agricultural land on which the fertiliser would be used, but also of possibly the best road and railway communications in the country. In addition, the specifications for the plant had been carefully drawn up before being put out to international tender and the Belgian firm's bid had been judged the best on a competitive basis.[24]

Ebtehaj was quick to condemn the Shiraz project. At a private session of the Senate, convened to discuss it, he told senators that the 'decision of the Government, should it be true that a second plant was being erected . . . was sinful', and he spelled out in detail why this was the case.[25] His remarks caused a sensation. The senator representing Shiraz hotly defended the 'government's decision', saying that it was based on a policy of helping the people of the province of Fars. Ebtehaj's old mentor Ala, Minister of Court since he had resigned the Prime Ministership in 1957 on the grounds of ill-health, telephoned him to express surprise that he should have taken a stance so directly in contradiction of a decision taken by Cabinet. The Shah, at Ebtehaj's usual weekly meeting with him, told him that the Shiraz project was not intended to be competitive with the Ahwaz one – the plant's production would be for export only, and the contractors would be paying all the costs, re-couping these out of the proceeds of the exports. He suggested that Ebtehaj read the contract documents for himself.

Closer investigation merely confirmed Ebtehaj's conviction that the project was impossible. He discovered that although it was planned that the annual production of the plant, 100,000 tons of chemical fertiliser, would be exported, it was laid down that the government would pay the total cost of the plant in a foreign currency to be determined by the contractors, and that the Bank Melli would guarantee the payment of the amount in annual instalments through the issue to the contractors of promissory notes signed by government and countersigned by Bank Melli. This not only committed the country to a major foreign exchange outlay, but was in moral violation of a government pledge to the World Bank. Moreover, the expectation of being able to export 100,000 tons of chemical fertiliser annually was inconceivable for the foreseeable future in view of the lack of any road or rail communication between Shiraz and the Persian Gulf, and of the fact that the total capacity of the port of Bushehr was some 70,000 tons per year, all of which was already taken up by the normal traffic of imports and exports.[26]

While Ebtehaj was explaining to the Court exactly why the Shiraz project was unworkable, Prime Minister Eqbal made a statement in the *Majles* and then in the Senate that government had signed the Shiraz contract. He underlined the fact that the foreign consortium would erect the fertiliser plant and be re-paid out of the proceeds of the sale of its output abroad. He omitted to declare that the promissory notes were even then being signed at the Ministry of Finance. In the circumstances, the *Majles* and Senate supported government. And so, it appeared, did the Shah. Ebtehaj later recollected that according to Ala the Shah's reaction was 'one of resentment and indignation that I should condemn his Council of Ministers for having concluded a deal which in no way adversely affected Iran's interests'.[27] The fact that one of the Shah's mistresses had apparently been involved in negotiating the contract with the consortium concerned undoubtedly lent a delicate extra dimension to the affair,[28] and meant that Ebtehaj was moving in deep waters. Indeed, the Shah was so upset, Ala said, that he did not wish to receive Ebtehaj. The time had clearly come for Ebtehaj to test the extent to which he still had the Shah's backing – 'I forthwith addressed a letter to the Shah', he later recalled, 'tendering my resignation from the Plan Organisation and stating that it would be inappropriate for me to continue in my job since it was evident that I did not have his full confidence any more.'[29]

At first there was little reaction from the Shah, and he still refused to see Ebtehaj. But as the campaign against him gathered force, Ebtehaj, through Ala, insisted that the Shah should receive him. His position as head of the Plan Organisation required this consideration, at least. Finally he was granted an audience on 10 February 1959 – it was to be the last time he saw or spoke to the Shah for 18 years.[30] Ebtehaj spelled out once again his philosophy of economic and social development, and his ideas about the Plan Organisation and the use of Iran's oil revenues –

> I repeated what I had told him over the years that we had no right to spend the oil revenues for any purpose other than projects which would affect the daily lives of the Iranian people. I added that if we had to choose between military expenditure and development I would have no hesitation, as in the past, to say that development takes priority over military expenditure. I remarked that if we invested oil revenues honestly, competently and with dedication with the object of changing the conditions of living of our peoples, and the people of Iran came to realise and recognise that at long last they had men who were dedicated and determined to improve their conditions and were acting in complete good faith and honestly and sincerely, not only would the material conditions in Iran and in the way the millions of its people lived change, we would bring about a state of things when we would not have to depend on armed forces. The people of Iran would be behind us, a force far more important than the armed forces of a country.[31]

On 12 February, Ebtehaj learnt that the *Majles* was in secret session, debating a government bill which ceded the powers of the Plan Organisation's Managing Director to the Prime Minister. Later that day, Radio Tehran announced that such a bill had been presented by the Prime Minister and had been received with tumultuous applause. Ebtehaj knew that he had lost – the Shah had turned his back. On 14 February 1959, he wrote again to the Shah.

'MORE EUROPEAN THAN IRANIAN'?

Reminding him of his earlier letter of resignation, he confirmed his intention, as he clearly no longer had the Shah's confidence, of leaving his post as Managing Director of the Plan Organisation. He cleared out his office on the same day. Farmanfarmaian went to see him

> and saw some cardboard boxes on his desk in which he was collecting his things ... he said "I have just now written my letter of resignation. I don't know why they had to go to the Majles and change the law in order to get my resignation because I had submitted it several times before". And then Ebtehaj left.[32]

He never returned to the Plan Organisation.

In common with many other observers, Ebtehaj did not believe that the Shah had turned against him merely because of the one issue of the Shiraz fertiliser project.[33] 'I think', he recollected later, 'this was the result of a current that was building up and finally it came to a head.'[34] There were a variety of reasons for this. The growing number of enemies made by Ebtehaj in the government and administration was an obvious one – it became difficult and tiresome even for the Shah continually to support him in the face of widespread opposition.

Ebtehaj's opposition to military expenditure was another crucial factor, and the Shah must surely have been informed of his encounter with Admiral Radford. This incident apart – and American policy-makers at this time were not as enthusiastic about heavy Iranian military spending as they were later to become – Ebtehaj may well have been seen by Washington as an undesirably independent influence at a time when they were particularly sensitive about Iran's diplomatic and political situation. A coup in neighbouring Iraq in July 1958 had overthrown the pro-western monarchy there. Soviet criticisms of the Shah had subsequently become vocal. The American Ambassador to Tehran felt moved to describe the country, for the first time, as 'a valued ally' of the United States, and in March 1959 a bilateral United States–Iran defence pact was signed.[35]

Most significantly, perhaps, the Shah no longer wished to have a 'government within the government'. The transfer of the power and responsibilities of the head of the Plan Organisation to the Prime Minister, and the reduction of the status of the Plan Organisation which it implied, signalled that economic planning and development was being brought under the direct control of the Shah, since the power of the Prime Minister was in practice subordinated to that of the Shah. It was a reflection of the Shah's overall drive for centralisation of power, and evidence of his increasing self-confidence as a monarch. In supporting cabinet ministers against the Plan Organisation over the Shiraz project, the Shah was employing classic 'divide and rule' tactics in order to achieve his ends, which were to make sure that no one individual or group grew so powerful as to challenge his own position. His aim in this case seems to have been to contain the power of the Plan Organisation – an aim which could not be realised with Ebtehaj at its helm.[36]

It was a tribute to Ebtehaj that the Organisation he built up did not fall apart. Initially 'the bright young men' he brought into the Plan Organisation were devastated by his resignation, but the fact that Khosrow Hedayat, Ebtehaj's deputy, took over and no dramatic changes were made, meant that by mid-1959 they were less discouraged than they had been at first.[37] While Hedayat was no Ebtehaj, and 'essentially a politician ... firmly under the Prime Minister's thumb', he was said to be honest.[38] And while American Embassy officials noted a slackening of discipline, an increase in interference and petty politicking, and evidence that 'the bright young men' probably no longer enjoyed the same measure of autonomy and authority as they once used to, they remarked that the continued presence of Ebtehaj's acolytes in the Plan Organisation had 'probably curtailed the growth of inefficiency and graft' and assumed that 'as long as they continue to hold positions of responsibility the PO will still be morally and organizationally superior to most Ministries'.[39]

As for Ebtehaj himself, there were various opinions about what he would do next. Some expected him to feel very bitter towards the Shah and doubted that he would ever take another government job, others felt he would live in quiet withdrawal for a while but emerge in the future as Prime Minister.[40] Speculation was fuelled by his reaction to the usual overtures made by the Shah to restore friendly relations in such cases. He was made aware, informally, that if he wanted an ambassadorship, or to be a senator, or something similar, this would be arranged. Refusing to play the political game, he turned the offer down. Nor did he react positively to the message from the Court that the audience he had requested with the Shah had been granted. Rather than bowing to what was clearly a face-saving formula for rapprochement, he replied that he had made no such request but that if the Shah asked to see him he would be happy to comply.[41] Characteristically, it was not long before he provided his own answers to the speculation as to what he would do next by embarking once again on a career in banking. But this time he set about founding his own private commercial bank, and in January 1960, as the following chapter will relate, the Iranians' Bank opened its doors for business.

His new interest meant that Ebtehaj did not live in 'quiet withdrawal'. Putting together a project for a new bank meant consultations with old contacts and a range of officials in Tehran, and with his international banking friends. This gave him a platform for his views on economic planning and development, and for what was happening in Iran. It also allowed him to expound his thoughts and ideas on the West's foreign aid policy towards Third World countries, ideas he had held for some time, and which, as a result of his experience at the Bank Melli and the Plan Organisation, had crystallised into a specific thesis in favour of multilateral rather than bilateral aid. He was soon in political trouble.

Rather to his surprise, Ebtehaj found that even though he was now in the private sector, and no longer head of the Plan Organisation, he was sought out by foreign journalists and institutions. Towards the end of 1959, for example, he was interviewed for the American CBS network by Ed Murrow. Then, some months later, he was approached by a 'Panorama' team from British television, who, in anticipation of the Queen's visit to Iran in March 1961, wanted an interview. Ebtehaj told them that they had the wrong man – 'I said I am not an admirer and supporter of the Shah.' But it seemed that this was precisely the reason they had come to him. They intended to interview only two 'notables' – the Shah and Ebtehaj – and they had selected Ebtehaj because he was considered to be the only person who spoke his mind frankly and openly. They were not disappointed: in the interview, which was broadcast on 6 February 1961, Ebtehaj expressed his worries over the level of inflation in Iran and the lack of coordination in development planning, and criticised the Shah's regime for spending Iran's oil revenues and other resources on an army which was useless, and which Iran did not need.[42] Ebtehaj thus emerged as one of the most vocal and outspoken critics of the Shah's policies and, like most of the Iranian critics of this time, he blamed Washington for not forcing the Shah to change his ways.[43]

In September 1961, Ebtehaj attended the International Industrial Conference in San Francisco where he delivered a widely-publicised and controversial paper. It was a platform with which he was already familiar. In 1957 he had been present at the first of these

Conferences, which were sponsored by the Stanford Research Institute and the Time-Life Organisation, and had addressed the delegates on Iran's development effort. His contribution then, which had focused on Iran's attempt to devote its oil revenues to laying a groundwork for economic growth, with the goal of bringing about a free enterprise society, had been well received. Henry Luce, editor-in-chief of the Time-Life group of publications and Conference chairman, went so far as to take Ebtehaj's theme − 'It's Getting Late in Iran' − and make it the theme of the Conference generally. Ebtehaj had meant to imply his characteristic sense of urgency about Iran's development effort: with the pressure of Soviet Communism bearing down upon it across its long northern border, Iran was running out of time in which to raise living standards and transform itself into a modern economy while still maintaining the basic freedoms. Luce had broadened the scope, and asked 'How much time have we to create a rational, workable world economic order?'[44]

At the 1961 Conference, Ebtehaj's contribution, again on the subject of planning and development, took the debate a stage further. In speaking of the need for both government planning and a strong private sector in developing countries, he focused on the question of foreign aid − so badly needed by the recipients but such a source of potential difficulty − and he made a strong case for much greater multilateral assistance than had been given in the past. He had come to believe, he said, 'that appropriate international institutions are of singular importance and, in fact, indispensable to the achievement of rapid economic progress'. The financial assistance needed if underdeveloped countries were to achieve such progress had to be 'first, adequate in amount; second, nominal in cost; third, assured of continuity; fourth, reasonably long term; and finally, most important of all, under international supervision.' He argued that 'the bilateral, government-to-government approach of recent years, despite increasingly generous allocations of cash' suffered from inherent weaknesses −

> Under the present bilateral approach creditor governments are diverted from development projects by military and political considerations . . .
>
> Even if a recipient government became convinced in all good faith of the fairness of certain bilateral programs offered by another country, it would soon be condemned in the public mind. Opposition leaders will charge the government with

selling out to the imperialists, and the public will believe those charges ... Bilateral aid poisons the relationship between nations, frustrates the donor, and causes revulsion in the recipient.

Donor nations are obliged to channel aid through the receiving country's officials whether they be qualified, honest, efficient or otherwise. Where the recipient government is corrupt, the donor government appears, in the judgement of the public, to support corruption ...

The bilateral approach cannot bring about reform. Furthermore, government-to-government aid delays internal pressure toward reform by providing considerable material resources to corrupt regimes and by unwittingly fostering the fear that development aid will be stopped if the old regime is overthrown. Under bilateral programs the lending government cannot impose a creditor's normal discipline for fear of jeopardizing the entire fabric of international relations.

Ebtehaj then proceeded to illustrate his thesis by referring to the case he knew best: Iran —

I can think of no better summary of all the disadvantages and weaknesses of the bilateral system than the modern history of my own country. Not so very many years ago in Iran, the United States was loved and respected as no other country, and without having given a penny of aid. Now, after more than $1 billion of loans and grants, America is neither loved nor respected; she is distrusted by most people, and hated by many.

As an alternative to the bilateral approach, he advocated an international programme, 'with rules of development spending that apply to all countries equally and are openly administered under a board of directors that includes debtor as well as creditor nations'.[45]

The paper delivered by Ebtehaj in San Francisco was extraordinarily provocative, seeming overtly to criticise both Iran and the United States. He later maintained that he did not consciously set out to provoke. What he wanted was to express 'a deep feeling' that he had had for some time of 'criticism of the American Foreign Aid Policy', and he could not do so without reference to Iran, because 'Iran was ... an outstanding example of what was happening, that the U.S. was giving aid to Iran, military aid, political aid, financial aid, development aid, in order to maintain a regime in power which was not popular'. Moreover, he wanted to express his strong conviction that the channelling of multilateral aid to all developing countries, through an international agency, was 'the only salvation for the relationship between the haves and the have nots'.[46] By doing this, 'we can remove one of the major causes of world tension', he argued, for

> The Soviet Union would be invited to participate as a principal contributor of both capital and technical assistance. It could either join the agency and work within its rules, or remain outside, clearly labeled as the only industrialised power in the world that is unwilling to give aid without political strings. Here is a disarmament scheme which depends solely upon us, and which, in its very nature, prevents sabotage by duplicity.[47]

What in fact happened, however, was that his talk caused a huge stir. Ebtehaj was bombarded by the press and television. He was asked to take part in a television debate in San Francisco, and had to explain his ideas in detail. His paper was published and circulated. Inevitably there was a reaction from Iran.

Ebtehaj was aware that his remarks would not be well received in Iran, but was prepared to face the consequences. It was not long before he had some idea of what these consequences might be. Before returning home he attended the IMF/World Bank annual meeting in Vienna. Iran's delegation, headed by the Minister of Finance, Jahangir Amuzegar, was already there by the time he arrived and had been talking about the reaction in Tehran to the San Francisco episode. Ebtehaj's friends in the World Bank and IMF, warned him that he was likely to be arrested if he went back to Iran, and tried to dissuade him from doing so. 'Some even went so far as to offer me a job', Ebtehaj later recollected. But he was determined to go home and stand by his right to express his views. In Tehran, the same rumours were rife. Ebtehaj's wife, who was at the airport to meet him, warned him that it was common knowledge that he would be arrested.[48] Soon after, on 11 November 1961, not much more than a month after the San Francisco affair, he was arrested and thrown into gaol.

Not that the San Francisco talk was ever mentioned in connection with his detention. As no official charges were ever laid, Ebtehaj's arrest remained surrounded in mystery and confusion. According to the 'official' version given to the American Ambassador by the Prime Minister, he had been arrested because when he was summoned to the Civil Service Tribunal – presumably as a witness and presumably also with regard to Plan Organisation affairs – 'he was so rude and abusive that the examining magistrate arrested him on his own authority'. However, few believed such an ingenuous explanation. Nor was the explanation that he faced charges relating to the contract signed with the American D & R Corporation while he was head of the Plan Organisation much more convincing. Certainly Ebtehaj's interrogation by the Civil Service Tribunal focused on this contract as symptomatic of the fact that during his time at the Plan Organisation he had given contracts involving excessive expenditure and was generally guilty of waste. It was alleged, for example, that the D & R contract was concluded without the approval of government and the responsible *Majles* committee. In addition, the competence and qualifications of Lilienthal and Clapp were called into question, and various purchases by D & R were objected to. But while these charges were quickly refuted, Ebtehaj remained in detention. It appeared likely that the accusations were no more than the 'excuse' for his arrest – a reasonable enough excuse it might be supposed given the fact that the D & R contract had been concluded in an incredibly short space of time, too short to have allowed for its approval by the necessary authorities and strict observance of every provision of the laws and regulations governing the Plan Organisation and the Second Seven Year Plan. Unfortunately for his accusers, and to the embarrassment of the authorities, the D & R contract proved to have gone through all the necessary stages of approval and was watertight.[49]

Amidst the welter of speculation, one thing did seem clear. It simply was not plausible to anyone in Tehran that the arrest of so prominent a person as Ebtehaj could possibly have been carried out without clearance from a higher authority – presumably the Shah. And it was not long before both the Tehran and international press were relating his detention directly or indirectly to his open criticism of America's foreign aid policy, and the corruption and suppression of freedom within the Iranian government.[50] Ebtehaj himself was convinced that this was the reason.[51] It came also to be the view shared by many historians and observers. As one remarked, 'It would seem incontestable that His Majesty had resorted to imprisoning Ebtehaj not for mismanagement or corruption, but as chastisement for these aspersions against his regime, Iran, and the United States.'[52] Ebtehaj was imprisoned because his was a voice of criticism which was listened to outside Iran.

Although no formal charges were ever laid against him, the 62-year-old Ebtehaj remained in prison for seven months. That his

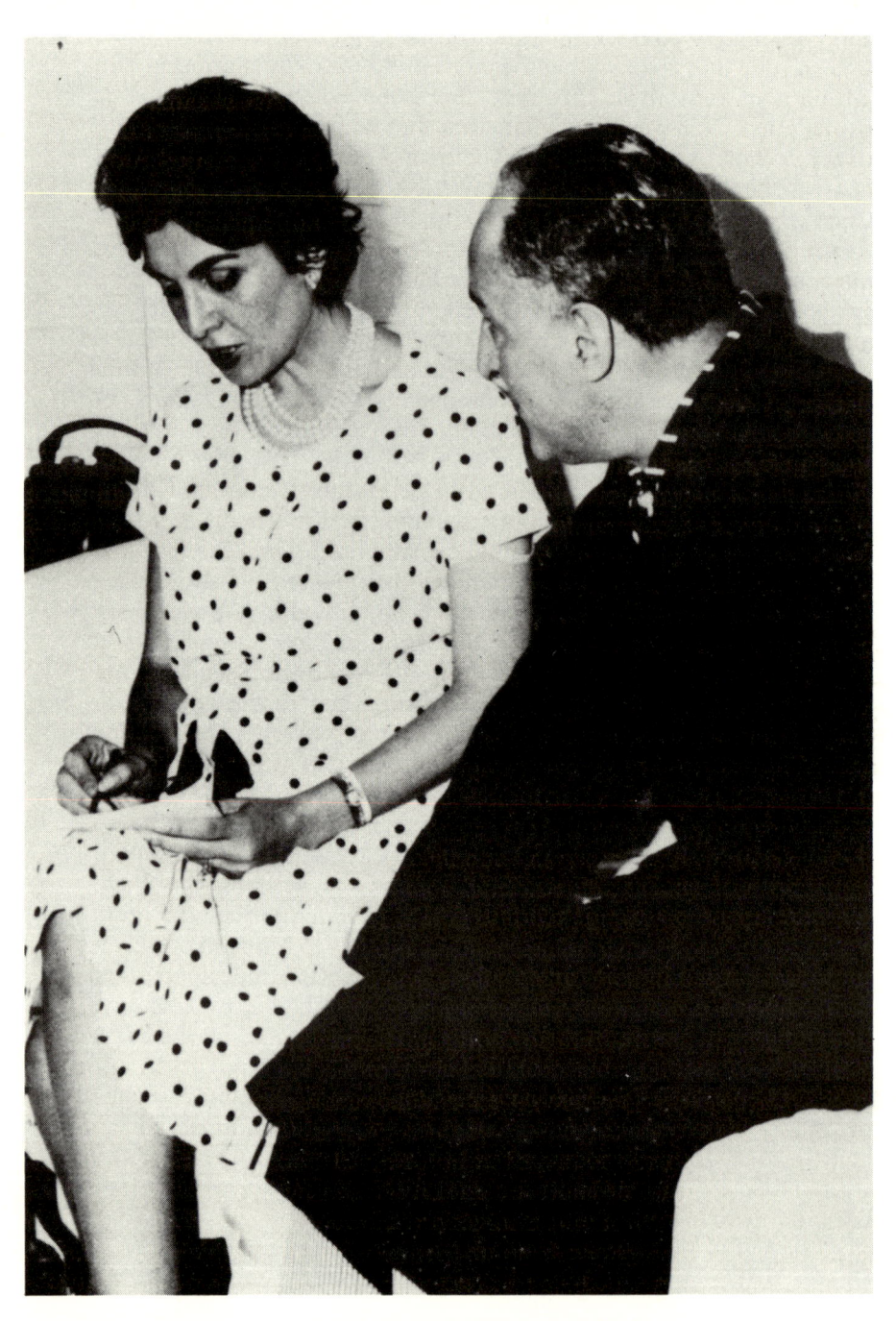

10. Ebtehaj being visited in the police hospital by his wife, Azar, in early 1962

detention was more of a face-saving exercise than anything else, especially once it became clear that the accusations of misconduct over the D & R contract provided insufficient grounds to warrant laying charges against him, seems certain. For one thing, it was not long before he was allowed various special privileges. At first he was kept in isolation, although his wife contrived to visit him each evening under the pretext of visiting another detainee and heavily veiled in a *chadour*.[53] After ten days, however, and within 24 hours of informing the prosecutor of the Civil Service Tribunal that if the affairs of the Iranians' Bank suffered from his forcible detention he would hold his detainers responsible, he was officially allowed to see his wife, his children, his brother and his lawyers. He was permitted to have whatever reading matter he wanted, and to receive letters. Taking advantage of the marginal relaxation in restrictions, he began to run his affairs, both banking and personal, from his cell, and then after developing hernia trouble, from the police hospital where he spent the rest of his period of internment.[54] This gave him an opportunity, albeit unofficial, to correspond with the outside world; he despatched letters, smuggled out of gaol by his wife, to all his friends and contacts in the West – to the editors of such newspapers and journals as the *Washington Post*, the *New York Times*, *Time*, and *The Economist*, and to individuals such as George McGhee in the American State Department, Eugene Black, Adlai Stevenson (then United States Ambassador to the United Nations), Walter Lippmann, Ed Murrow, Weldon Gibson of Stanford Research Institute, Henry Luce and others.[55]

Luce's immediate reply, expressing his 'profound admiration for you [Ebtehaj] as a man of courage and integrity' and his distress at Ebtehaj's detention was symptomatic of the reaction evoked overseas.[56] By early 1962, a groundswell of international protest was under way. In Britain, *The Economist* referred to the 'mystery' surrounding the imprisonment of 'this great Persian public servant . . . with unfaltering vision and energy'.[57] In the United States, not only did the press take up his case – the *Washington Post* ran a four-column feature reviewing his career and achievements, observing that he was 'considered by many to be Iran's No. 1 economist'; the *New York Times* also reported the drama, noting that Ebtehaj had been 'for years a symbol of incorruptibility in Iran'; *Time* magazine praised the 'unswerving honesty' of this 'highly successful Teheran banker with a reputation for hard work'[58] – but the Senate Foreign Relations Committee began an informal investigation into the reasons for his imprisonment.[59] Coincidentally, the Kennedy

Administration at this time began to exercise pressure on the Shah for reform over a wide spectrum of issues, initiating in March 1962 a plan designed to 'shift the shah's preoccupation from military security to economic progress'.[60] Meanwhile, a campaign was started on his behalf in the United Nations by its Secretary General, Dag Hammarskjöld, and by Adlai Stevenson.[61] Ebtehaj attributed his eventual release, in June 1962, to the fact that his cause was espoused in the West — particularly in the United States.

Public response within Iran, while more muted, must also have played a part, however, signalling to the Iranian government popular outrage at the imprisonment of a man widely known and respected for his integrity and honesty. Initial officially-inspired rumours that Ebtehaj was under investigation for corruption were greeted with incredulity. Tehran's English-language newspaper, *Kayhan International*, voiced the general feeling, observing that 'to suggest that he is guilty of corruption will only appear nonsensical to those who have known him well and worked with him'.[62] In view of Ebtehaj's unpopularity in Tehrani political and business circles for much of his career in public life, and the bad relations with the press which caused him to have sometimes as many as 60-odd libel writs against newspapers and journals on hand at any one time, it was paradoxical to find the press not only taking up cudgels in his defence but going so far as to review his career in such terms as the following —

> Ebtehaj was a powerful figure who guided the Iranian economy for many years in his capacity as Director of the Plan Organisation. . . . Some tremendous development projects were prepared during his office. It was again Mr Ebtehaj who fought against Dr Millspaugh and his unlimited powers and finally came out victorious. He was invited on several occasions by international development agencies to prepare their projects, but he turned them all down and preferred to remain in Iran and serve his country. . . . [*Asia*] regrets that while the greatest Iranian economist is sent to prison, the enemies of the State are free to roam as they please. "Is this the reward for dedicated service?"[63]

There were of course opposing views, but press comment was on balance not only favourable to Ebtehaj but at pains to point out the real achievements of the Plan Organisation under his leadership, his personal reputation for probity and the high regard in which he was held in international financial circles.[64]

As the clamour by the world's press and governments grew, the Iranian government recognised that something had to be done about its illustrious prisoner. In June 1962, Ebtehaj was offered release on bail. The bail was set, however, at 10.7 billion *rials* (over $140 million), a sum almost equal to the grand total of America's economic and military loans and grants to Iran in 1961, and four times the size of the D & R contract.[65] The *Washington Post* believed that the huge amount 'may set a world precedent'.[66]

Ebtehaj categorically refused to leave gaol though his wife raised pledges for the bail money in less than a week: he demanded either to be charged and prosecuted or declared innocent and released. Even when the bail demand was reduced to the equivalent of $35 million, and he was offered a letter affirming his innocence and wrongful arrest, he refused to be moved. Only when the issue of bail was dropped altogether did Ebtehaj agree to be liberated. However, in earnest of his undertaking not to leave the country, he posted a $140 million bond. Most of the collateral was contributed by sympathetic countrymen – many of them quite ordinary people who did not know Ebtehaj personally – in the form of land deeds, securities, and cash pledges.[67]

There was no more telling evidence of popular reaction to Ebtehaj's detention than an incident which took place shortly after his release. He went with his wife and a British friend to dine in a smart Tehran restaurant, filled with his peers – the kind of people whose egos he had trampled and who had in the past been highly critical of him. The restaurant was, as usual, very crowded and the Ebtehajs and their friend had to be led to a table at the far end of the room. As they passed by, everyone stood and bowed. It was a subtle, typically Iranian way of indicating disapproval of the Shah, and respect for Ebtehaj.[68]

8

THE PRIVATE CITIZEN

On his resignation from the Plan Organisation, Ebtehaj reverted, for the first time since 1936, to the role of private citizen. He remained, however, in the public eye. In 1964, the political counsellor at the American Embassy in Tehran commented that Ebtehaj had 'continued to this day to be Iran's most internationally respected economist and manager, perhaps the only person in this category' and that 'his experience with Iranian justice and politics have in no way quieted him or made him more amenable to compromising his convictions'.[1] The Americans, indeed, were sufficiently impressed by him to contemplate installing him as Prime Minister. He also, despite being by then in his sixties, established a successful bank and insurance company. Ebtehaj remained, in other words, a fireball of intellectual and physical energy.

Ebtehaj found plenty to criticise in Iran after his release from gaol. On the surface there seemed much cause for optimism. The second half of the 1960s saw greater political stability than had been experienced at any time since the War, and accelerating economic growth. Expansion was fuelled by the quadrupling of oil prices in 1973–74, an event in which the Shah himself took a leading role.[2] In the West, moreover, some saw the Shah as a great social reformer; his famous White Revolution was launched in 1962, a programme of land reform (to be paid for by the sale of government factories to the private sector) combined with such other measures as the nationalisation of forests, the enfranchisement of women, and the introduction of profit-sharing in industry.

Unfortunately the darker side of the Shah's regime – the side Ebtehaj had criticised in the 1950s and had been gaoled for criticising – also flourished. Especially after widespread anti-government demonstrations in 1963 – in which a charismatic *molla*, Ayatollah Ruhollah Khomeini, had played a prominent role – the state became increasingly repressive. SAVAK, the state security organisation set up by the Shah, with American help, in 1957, grew

THE PRIVATE CITIZEN

in power and became ever more brutal. The Pahlavi Foundation, nominally a charitable foundation, fostered official corruption. From the early 1970s, corruption was rampant and entrenched in nearly every part of the government. Iran's oil revenues were used to finance the Shah's grandiose schemes to make Iran the dominant military power in the Middle East, enjoying a 'special relationship' with the United States.

Until 1964, Ebtehaj was effectively muzzled in his criticism of official policies because the case which had put him in gaol was still outstanding. But he had by no means been forgotten by his friends outside Iran. On the contrary, the 1963 demonstrations and riots were a cogent reminder to many of his 1961 San Francisco speech, and the subsequent warning letters about the dangers of an explosion in Iran as a result of the widespread corruption and general discontent which he had sent from gaol to prominent American public figures. Ebtehaj remained convinced that the United States' government had the power to pressure the Shah into following improved policies. And, indeed, the Kennedy Admini stration was ready, as already mentioned, to urge the necessity for internal reform, although the pressure it was prepared to exercise to achieve this was not wholly consistent.[3] It is no great surprise, then, to learn that in 1963, when it looked as though revolution was imminent in Iran and the Shah's position in jeopardy, a rumour was circulating in Washington that the United States' Administration was contemplating the necessity for a change of regime and the setting up of a republic, and that Ebtehaj's name had been mentioned in this context. State Department officials, under Under-Secretary of State George McGhee, had, it appeared, been deputed to investigate and report on Iran's worsening political situation, and had come up with a number of recommendations, of which this was one.[4]

While the State Department may have been doing no more than preparing the ground for a total change of regime as one of several alternative possibilities should the situation in Iran deteriorate beyond control, it is illuminating that a few days after the riots of 5–7 June 1963, Ebtehaj was approached by an official at the United States Embassy in Tehran on behalf of Washington, and asked whether he would be prepared to become Prime Minister.[5] Ebtehaj agreed – but conditionally. He said that he would only be willing to take on the job if Iran's armed forces were reduced to the numbers required for internal security (the officers and NCOs thus released would, he envisaged, be employed in a vast technical training programme); if the Shah confined his role to that of a reigning monarch and ceased to interfere with government or have any contact with cabinet ministers except through the Prime Minister; and if Iran agreed to withdrawal from CENTO (successor to the Baghdad Pact), which he thought was a totally ineffectual organisation and no better than a 'talking shop', as a *quid pro quo* for demanding from the Soviet Union annulment of the contentious clause in the Irano-Soviet Treaty of 1921, still in force and a source of constant anxiety to Iran, which gave the Soviets the right in certain circumstances to use Iran as a base for military action.[6] Given America's regional strategy imperatives, and the fact that CENTO was an American creation, Ebtehaj must have been aware that there was little hope of his conditions being accepted. Indeed, he heard no more from the American Embassy on the subject.

Although the prospect of high public office at home was still-born, there was a distinct likelihood at this time that Ebtehaj might take up some sort of international appointment. His reputation outside Iran remained high. In the aftermath of his resignation from the Plan Organisation, he had had overtures from both the IMF and the World Bank to work in Washington, but had decided that any such move so soon after his resignation would only indicate that he had been kept in power by 'foreigners' and that he was still being protected by them.[7] However, he had kept in close touch with his friends in the West, and, until his imprisonment, he had continued to attend such gatherings as the SRI International Industrial Conferences and to meet his international banking contacts at the annual meetings of the IMF and World Bank, to which he received special invitations on a regular basis. During 1963, there were various rumours that a United Nations' appointment was in the offing, and it was the eventual offer of just such an international appointment that finally led to the dropping of the legal case against him.

At the end of December 1963, Ebtehaj received a telegram from Paul Hoffman, Chairman of the International Development Society in New York, asking him to participate in a conference on monetary stabilisation to be held in New York in March 1964. He decided to use the invitation to draw attention to the fact that, despite his release from gaol in 1962, officially the case had never been resolved. Through Hossein Ghods-Nakhai, Minister of Court and a close friend, Ebtehaj let the Shah know that he would not accept the invitation unless his name was formally cleared. According to Ghods-Nakhai, the Shah was amazed to hear that the case against Ebtehaj was still pending, but indicated that he could not interfere in the judicial process – a reaction which Ebtehaj found so implausible that he asked Ghods-Nakhai to speak to the Shah again.

At this point, the World Bank asked Ebtehaj to head a mission to Algeria to advise the Algerian government on economic development and on the establishment of a planning agency. Ebtehaj requested that Ghods-Nakhai pass this information on to the Shah, making a point of the fact that he could hardly accept such an appointment in the present circumstances. He warned that if the case against him was not finally dismissed he would inform the World Bank that he could not accept the offer because he was 'not a free man in his own country'. The Minister of Justice was approached in the same vein. The combined pressure had the desired effect: the Shah instructed the Ministry of Justice 'to carry out justice as soon as possible', the Minister of Justice expressed embarrassment about the whole affair and said it would be sorted out forthwith, and on 13 February 1964 Ebtehaj was informed officially that all charges (which, it will be recollected, were never formally laid) had been dropped. But this was not enough. Ebtehaj wanted a public declaration and he requested that the then Prime Minister, Asadollah Alam, make an announcement in the press that his name had been cleared. Finally, on 17 February, the Shah and Prime Minister having agreed, this was done.[8]

The news came too late for Ebtehaj to attend the International Development Conference on 17 March, but not too late for him to travel to Washington at the end of March to discuss the Algerian project with the World Bank. On the way, he stopped off in New York long enough to speak to the International Development Society, where he proceeded to demonstrate that his brush with the Shah and the Iranian authorities had done nothing to inhibit him from expressing his views as freely as ever. He plunged straight back into his favourite theme of the urgent necessity for the establishment of a new multilateral aid agency, along the lines of the World Bank but with broader responsibilities (including some of the short-run functions of the IMF), which would be able to impose the sort of stringent external conditions necessary if development planning in a country like Iran were ever to be made to work.[9]

Before deciding whether to head the World Bank mission to Algeria, Ebtehaj determined to have a look at the situation there for himself, visiting Algeria on his way back to Iran.[10] The upshot was that he decided to accept the World Bank appointment, though he was concerned that the Algerian government might be too wedded to a 'socialist' approach for his tastes.[11] As it turned out, some influential members of the Algerian government also had reservations about his appointment and Algeria requested the World Bank to cancel the proposed mission. Ebtehaj was not unhappy at the outcome, as he had secured official clearance of his name in Iran, freedom to travel overseas when he wished, and public restoration of his reputation in international financial circles.[12]

Other similar opportunities were to arise over the next few years, but like Algeria nothing came of them. Sometimes Ebtehaj was not sufficiently interested; sometimes, as in the case of the presidency of the newly-formed Asian Development Bank, his candidacy was unsuccessful for reasons which had more to do with Iran than with him: it was Iran that failed to get the appointment. Meanwhile, with his good name restored, Ebtehaj felt free again to say what he thought within Iran. In conversation with American Embassy officials, he reiterated his criticisms of the Shah's policies, and of United States' strategy in the Persian Gulf region which, he believed, encouraged the Shah's paranoia. He no longer had a personal relationship with the Shah: between 1959 and 1977 the two men never met, and although in 1965 the Shah agreed that Ebtehaj should be asked to run for the presidency of the Manila-based Asian Development Bank, this seemed to be more a ploy to get him out of the country than a sign of official favour.[13] Nonetheless, this did not stop him from making his views known to government through personal links. During the 1960s no fewer than six members of the Council of Ministers had been his employees at one time or another. He also had a good relationship with Amir Abbas Hoveyda, Prime Minister from January 1965 to August 1977 – a period of office longer by far than achieved by any other Prime Minister in twentieth-century Iran. Ebtehaj was one of the people used by Hoveyda as a 'sounding board', though given the Shah's increasingly dictatorial control over government from 1963 onwards this meant less than it might have done in earlier years.

It is certain, in any case, that the Shah would not have cared for the opinions Ebtehaj expressed through Hoveyda, for Ebtehaj was critical of practically every aspect of official policy in the 1960s and 1970s. Predictably, he continued to condemn the diversion of oil revenues from economic development to what he regarded as unnecessary military expenditure. He had little patience with the Shah's grandiose aspirations for Iran as a military power, and he grew ever more critical of American willingness to encourage them. At one stage, Hoveyda asked him for a written memorandum on the subject, and it seems very probable that Ebtehaj's observations were destined for the Shah.[14] The continued build-up of Iran's military arsenal demonstrated just how little notice the Shah took of such criticisms.

As was to be expected, Ebtehaj also had strong opinions about government economic policies. He condemned the politicisation of the Plan Organisation from the early 1960s, and was highly critical of the way in which the Third Plan, launched in September 1962, was managed. The Third Plan was actually a first attempt at 'comprehensive planning', and it laid a heavier stress upon industrialisation than the earlier Plans had done. The coincidence of the Third Plan with a period of considerable growth has been taken by some as a sign of the Plan's effectiveness, though one recent study has concluded 'that the good performance was less the result of good planning than of good fortune'.[15] Ebtehaj criticised the erosion of the Plan Organisation's autonomy: in his view, planning barely existed in Iran by 1963. The Plan Organisation followed government instructions and might just as well have been an adjunct of the Ministry of Finance. The Third Plan had become, he felt, essentially a 'seven-day' plan 'changed every week in accordance with the whims of the government', and under-resourced.[16] It was not a view he held in isolation. During 1962–3, a number of the Plan Organisation's more effective Iranian economists had resigned in frustration over the political pressures faced by the Plan.[17]

Primarily because of the shortcomings in the operations of the Plan Organisation, Ebtehaj was pessimistic about the state of Iran's economy in the mid-1960s, at a time when many other observers saw it as having turned the corner and being ready for 'take-off'. But he also perceived as a great weakness the tendency in Iran 'to proclaim decisions and enact legislation which sounded and appeared to be progressive and, at times, revolutionary', with little or no regard as to whether such decrees and laws were rational and enforceable.[18] Thus he did not share the general enthusiasm for the White Revolution, his reaction to the whole programme being clouded by his disagreement with two of its first principles – land reform and worker profit sharing – the effects of which he thought would be positively harmful to Iran's economic development. Again, his views ran counter to the general euphoria with which many people regarded these principles in particular, and, typically, they focused on the practical weaknesses and consequent dislocation inherent in introducing such policies before they had been properly thought through.

While Ebtehaj agreed wholeheartedly with those who were opposed to the archaic system of land tenure operating in Iran, he totally disagreed with the methods of dealing with this formulated in the Land Reform Bill of January 1962. Appalled at the Kennedy Administration's promises of virtually unlimited support for the land reform programme, he wrote, while still in prison, a memorandum encapsulating his objections, which he circulated to a number of his friends in the United States. Essentially, he was opposed to the principle of 'forced dispossession' as a method of changing the structure of land ownership. He saw this as a policy which, for the sake of short-term political expediency, would result in the creation of a large body of discontented and resentful landlords and a new class of peasant farmers, unable to stand on their own feet, and thoroughly disillusioned having had their expectations raised. He predicted that numerous economic and social difficulties would result – including a fall in productivity as large agricultural units were broken down into unviable small-holdings, the exacerbation of this as inheritance practices began to divide small into still smaller units, growing instability as the reality of land redistribution failed to live up to perceived expectations, and the myriad administrative complications likely to be encountered by the government machine as it attempted to create the mechanisms necessary to support the small farmer. But Ebtehaj was not merely destructive in his criticism. He put forward his own scheme for land reform in Iran – a scheme based on a system of land taxation related to its real or potential productive value, which he envisaged would create, for the first time, a market for the buying and selling of land. He argued that this market would develop as landowners were forced either to adjust themselves to the new tenure conditions or dispose of all or part of their land because they were not prepared to pay the tax due on it.[19]

Ebtehaj was just as strongly opposed to the idea of workers' equity participation in industry, which grew out of another of the basic principles on which the White Revolution was founded, profit sharing. Like land reform, it was something the Shah had been thinking about for some years. He had discussed the possibility with Ebtehaj not long after the latter took over the Plan Organisation in 1954, convinced that the government-owned industrial plants which the Plan Organisation ran should pave the way. Ebtehaj thought the idea unworkable, not least because it would seriously reduce the already low level of new private investment and thus increase the need for a high level of public investment, but as the Shah had been unwilling to dismiss the idea out of hand, he undertook to ask George Fry & Associates, the firm of American consultants already advising the Plan Organisation on the management and organisational problems of the government-owned industries, to submit a report on the subject. After thorough investigation, this firm came to the same conclusion as Ebtehaj, and the idea was dropped.[20] Some six years later, it reappeared as one of the initial six principles of the White Revolution. As Ebtehaj had predicted it proved both extremely difficult to implement, and a source of dissatisfaction to both industrialists and workers. In 1975, implementation was finally given the force of law, owners of manufacturing companies being legally required to sell 49 per cent of their shares to their employees and the public. The effect was to aggravate an already unsettled situation so far as private sector investment was concerned. Reflecting the industrial community's alarm that this presaged closer government monitoring, intervention and higher taxes, there began an unprecedented flight of capital out of the country.[21]

Many historians would now concur, especially in the light of the February Revolution of 1979, that the White Revolution was badly flawed. While land reform resulted in land titles changing hands and an increase in the number of independent farmers, together with a greater degree of mechanisation and some other progressive developments, the process produced, as Ebtehaj had feared, as many problems as it solved.[22] A new and disaffected 'landless' class of peasants was created, who had little option but to look to the towns for work. They drifted mostly towards the large cities – Tehran, Esfahan and Tabriz – where there was a rising demand for unskilled labour in the construction industry. These cities lacked the infrastructure to cope with such an influx, however, and problems of traffic congestion, water shortages and homelessness multiplied. Economic growth, as so often, exacerbated income inequalities. The rich grew richer, the poor stayed poor, and the central regions, especially Tehran, profited at the expense of the rest of the country.[23]

Ebtehaj could not, however, make a living by being a professional Cassandra, and, after leaving the Plan Organisation, earning his living became a matter of urgency. Ebtehaj had always been financially dependent on his salary. Equally, he had never been able to live on it, even while he was at the Plan Organisation where he was perhaps the highest paid government official in the country, and consequently he had accumulated considerable debts.[24] His financial affairs were not improved by the Shah's displeasure. To make matters worse, he and his family were told by their landlords, the Pahlavi Foundation, to vacate forthwith the villa they were renting in the grounds of the Darband Hotel while their own home was being built. Ebtehaj requested two or three months' grace since the family's new house was not ready for occupation, only to find the next day that both electricity and water had been cut off, and a load of rubbish from the Hotel had been dumped outside their door. The family had to move at once, despite the fact that their house had neither doors nor windows and was quite unfit for occupation.[25]

The decision to return to commercial banking – a career Ebtehaj had left in 1936 – was a sudden and rather surprising one. Having rejected the idea of representing a government in which he had no confidence, and doubting the wisdom for the time being of accepting an overseas appointment, Ebtehaj found himself temporarily at a loss as to what to do next.[26] Then, as he himself recounts it, he was going through the newspapers one day when

> I came across a report in a weekly publication called *Ferdowsi* which said that I intended to establish a private bank. This came to me as an inspiration. I had never thought that I would have to work in the private sector for my living. Therefore I made up my mind that I would try to establish a private bank.[27]

Having made the decision, he lost no time in moving into action. There were two basic essentials – to get a group together to finance the venture, and to get authorisation from the central bank (still, in 1959, the Bank Melli) for its establishment. Despite having no experience in setting up a private bank, Ebtehaj was clearly regarded as a good risk, and before the year was out, he was successful on both counts. The Iranians' Bank opened its doors for business on 31 January 1960, less than a year after his resignation from the Plan Organisation, with Ebtehaj as its Chairman and President. Apart from his salary 'which was very respectable compared with the norm ruling in the country', he was accorded 35 per cent of the profits.[28] He also took a 30 per cent equity stake in the venture.

What he lacked in experience, Ebtehaj more than made up for in the breadth of his contacts. The friends he approached in Tehran welcomed the idea of a new, serious, commercial bank in the private sector and agreed to put up the necessary money.[29] One of them, moreover, gave Ebtehaj a room in his flat in one of Tehran's main thoroughfares, which he was able to use as an office while he put the project together. Not being sure of the correct procedures, and in particular how far he could properly go in negotiating terms with his shareholders, Ebtehaj turned naturally to his banking friends overseas for advice. He went to Paris to see Eugene Black, who was still President of the World Bank, and, on discussing with him some of the rather generous terms and conditions agreed, was pleased to discover that Black thought they were perfectly appropriate. This boosted his confidence when the project for the new bank went before the Control Board at the Bank Melli for authorisation and the terms from which the Chairman and President of the new bank would benefit were declared to be 'over-generous', and permitted him to argue his case that the bank's sponsors had entered into the project, and had decided to accord certain privileges to the bank's founder, of their own free will.[30]

On 19 September 1959, the Bank Control Board gave Ebtehaj's new private commercial bank formal authorisation, but not before Ebtehaj had had to make one concession. He had initially decided that his bank should be known as *Bank-e Mellat* (Bank of the Nation), but this did not meet with approval. It was too similar to the name of the Bank Melli. Instead, Ebtehaj settled on *Bank-e Iranian* – Iranians' Bank.

The day after acquiring the necessary authorisation, Ebtehaj left for the annual IMF meeting in the United States. He intended to use the opportunity to establish correspondence arrangements for Iranians' Bank with various American and European banks, and hopefully lines of credit also.[31] A measure of his reputation, both on a personal level and as a banker, was the offer from Chase Manhattan Bank of a $1 million line of credit (to be increased if it was not sufficient) – this to a bank, not yet formally registered, whose entire capital was little more than $1 million. It was, to say the least, an unusual vote of confidence. Moreover, Chase's example meant that Ebtehaj was able to obtain a further $750,000 credit from the Irving Trust Company, and a similar facility from Morgan Guaranty (which, however, he never used).[32]

Iranians' Bank was initially capitalised at 80 million *rials* (£380,952) – only half of which was called up – and by 1962 its total assets only amounted to some 662 million *rials*, so that it was by no means a large enterprise. Moreover, although the capital was eventually increased in a number of stages to 1000 million *rials*, it remained one of the smallest banks in Iran. Despite its small size, however, Iranians' Bank acquired a high reputation, with its shares frequently being quoted more highly than any other bank shares on the Tehran Stock Exchange. Predictably, Ebtehaj employed all his institution-building skills in the Bank's creation, including the construction as its head office of a ten-storey building in central Tehran which was a model of its kind.[33] He was determined that the Bank's name should not only be synonymous with efficiency, but with 'honest conduct, honest management'.

Ebtehaj was, as only to be expected, a hard-working and energetic head of the Bank, who maintained a firm grasp of every aspect of its business. His management style proved to be effective, for notwithstanding its small size and the fact that initially it did not receive the level of support and encouragement usually given by the central bank to private commercial banks, Iranians' Bank prospered.[34] By the 1970s it was profiting from the fast growth in the Iranian economy: it had acquired some important business clients, and such notables as Prime Minister Hoveyda had given it the seal of their approval by opening personal accounts.[35] Furthermore, the Bank found a particular market niche by being the first in Iran to introduce a trust department and trustee service to undertake such business as looking after the property and affairs of people who had to leave town or spend time abroad, executing wills for customers and acting as executors in the event of death.

A feeling that the growth of Iranians' Bank was being constrained by limited resources, the increasingly restrictive business environment, and the fact that all his competitors seemed to be taking on foreign partners, led Ebtehaj in 1965 to plan an association with a 'first class' foreign bank despite his basic disapproval of such a course. He first approached the Chase Manhattan Bank 'because I knew its Chairman, David Rockefeller, who was an old friend of mine'. Chase was the leading American bank in Iran, and had an important relationship with the National Iranian Oil Company, a share in the Industrial and Mining Development Bank, as well as many private clients. These operations were managed from a representative office in Tehran. Rockefeller initially expressed interest, but eighteen months went by without any action on Chase's side. Finally, Ebtehaj wrote to Rockefeller announcing his intention to look elsewhere unless Chase was prepared to come to a definite decision: the response was that this was impossible for the moment. It was only when one of its American rivals expressed interest that Chase was belatedly stirred into action, and then Rockefeller made it clear that in view of their long friendship he expected Ebtehaj to form an association with Chase. Chase's chagrin was confirmed when Ebtehaj also received admonitory letters from Eugene Black, now retired from the World Bank and a member of Chase's board of directors. But by now it was too late. Ebtehaj replied to both men that he had waited a long time for Chase to make up its mind, had given clear warning of his intention to look elsewhere, and was now committed to his current negotiations. Chase eventually became directly involved in Iran through a joint venture private bank established in conjunction with the state-owned Industrial Credit Bank in 1975.[36]

Unable to get any firm decision from Chase, Ebtehaj's next approach had been to First National City Bank (hereafter referred to by its current name, Citibank), and again contact was made on the 'old boy network'. At the IMF annual meeting in Rio de Janeiro in 1967, Ebtehaj met an old friend from his IMF days in Washington, John Exter, who was now with Citibank, and asked him whether he thought Citibank might be interested in an association with his Iranians' Bank. Exter promptly introduced him to Al Costanzo, the man in charge of Citibank's foreign operations, who happened to be heading the Citibank delegation in Rio, and over lunch Ebtehaj 'told Costanzo that my bank was probably the smallest bank in the world with practically no branches and very insignificant deposits, that the only thing I had to offer was my reputation'. But reputation was, according to Costanzo, all that really mattered, and he knew Ebtehaj's reputation well. In less than thirty minutes the two men had agreed in principle to an association between Citibank and Iranians' Bank.[37]

The speed with which Costanzo had come to this decision impressed Ebtehaj mightily, but the detailed negotiations were to take a further 18 months – twice the time it had taken him to establish Iranians' Bank in the first place. The discussions proved to be both prolonged and tough. Ebtehaj took time to grow accustomed to the idea of Citibank, the style of whose executives was quite different from that of his friends at Chase. For its part, Citibank had to swallow, with more than a little difficulty, the unpleasant pill of acquiring not only a minority interest but a partner whose management style would be more independent than was normally tolerated. Citibank's usual policy when moving into new areas was to establish an institutional presence through extending its own branch network. Where this was not possible, acquisition of at least majority control of a local bank was the preferred policy. However, Citibank wanted to enter an apparently promising market – and Ebtehaj looked as good an entrée to Iran as it could have wished for.[38]

Finally, in November 1968, the negotiations came to a fruitful conclusion and, at a celebratory gathering in New York, the agreement between the two banks was signed. Under its terms Citibank purchased a 35 per cent shareholding in Iranians' Bank (the maximum foreign shareholding at that time allowed by Iranian law), spending something over $1 million in the process, mostly on a new share issue which increased the capital base of Iranians' Bank. In addition Citibank initially supplied two of its own men to join Iranians' Bank on secondment, while at the management level, it was represented on the Iranians' Board by its permanent representative in the Middle East.[39]

The relationship with Citibank was never altogether comfortable. Citibank had the reputation of having an aggressive style,[40] a reputation with which Ebtehaj was in many ways perfectly happy as Iranians' Bank needed this sort of boost. But an aspect of this was the assumption that when entering into an overseas' joint venture Citibank would be 'in the driving seat'. Ebtehaj, on the other hand, had never had any intention of handing over the effective management of his bank and becoming a mere figurehead. As time went by, the regional management of Citibank increasingly tried to press Iranians' Bank into the more usual mould of Citibank subsidiaries, with the result that relations between them and Ebtehaj were often strained. Things were not helped when, in the early 1970s, Citibank, in company with many other western banks anxious to get a share of Iran's burgeoning oil revenues, opened its own agency in Tehran.[41] Ebtehaj resented the independent business – mostly off-shore dealing and lending – transacted by the agency, arguing that all such business should go through Iranians' Bank. His concern and irritation were justified it seemed: complaints from other foreign banks that Citibank's agency had broken the rules laid down for such representative agencies and was conducting a full banking service and making unauthorised loans led to its investigation by the Bank Markazi (Central Bank) and the dramatic curtailment in its activities.[42]

Despite the daunting task of establishing a new bank and then running it in harness with Citibank, life as a private citizen left Ebtehaj with more time for his family. After some 25 years of marriage to his wife, Ebtehaj caused a considerable scandal in Tehran by falling in love with another woman – Azarnoosh Sani, a close friend of his younger brother and sister-in-law – and divorcing Maryam.[43] In September 1956, he married Azar. Having had no children by Maryam, Ebtehaj found himself suddenly with a ready-made family of two step-children, Alireza and Elaha, and then with two children of his own – a daughter, Shahrsad, born in January 1958, and a son, Davar, in April 1961. As shrewd and ambitious as she was beautiful, Azar was as unusual an example of her nationality and mileu as Ebtehaj himself. She was both university-educated and – as an assistant professor of dentistry at Tehran University – a professional working woman. Nor was she content to be a typical Iranian wife. She not only continued to teach at the University but took a close and active interest in Iranians' Bank, both as a shareholder and a director (she had been a member of the board from the start, the first woman in Iran to be elected to such a position). She also developed business interests of her own – opening the first bowling alley in the country – and proved to be, in many ways, more adept in this arena than Ebtehaj himself: two very different personalities, she was the 'business woman' while he was the 'statesman'. When Ebtehaj was detained in 1961, it was Azar who took his place at Iranians' Bank. Although she knew nothing about the mechanics of banking, she was able to ensure that business continued as usual and that, despite the fall in the price of its shares (from 12 *rials* to 4 *rials*) which followed the news of Ebtehaj's arrest, the Bank did not collapse.[44]

Ebtehaj had taken nothing with him when he left Maryam, except his tennis racket, his golf clubs and his books. As a result, he and Azar started with very little. Fortunately, Azar owned a piece of land in the foothills of the mountains north of Tehran, near the Darband Hotel, on which they could build, and it was while they were waiting for their new home to be ready that they rented a villa from the Pahlavi Foundation. She also owned a house in the centre of Tehran, but sold this in order to raise capital for Iranians' Bank.

In 1974, Ebtehaj – then aged 75 – added insurance to his banking interests by founding, in association with one of the largest American insurance groups operating outside the United States (American International Group, later known as American International Underwriters), the Iran America International Insurance Company. The initiative had come from the American group. Looking for a way of getting into Iran, they had approached Ebtehaj and asked whether he would be interested in joining them. He leapt at the chance, 'because I wanted to have an insurance company that would go into life insurance'. It was the sort of challenge Ebtehaj relished. For years he had been told by 'all the so-called experts' that life insurance would never be accepted in Iran because of the fatalism inherent in the country's Islamic culture – the notion that as God was in control there was no point in any individual making provision.[45] The established insurance companies did very little life insurance business in the 1960s and early 1970s.[46] Ebtehaj was determined to prove the experts wrong, and the Iran America International Insurance Company was the first to go into life insurance in a big way. Ebtehaj's enthusiasm for life insurance proved justified. His Insurance Company was a success from the start, both in terms of subscription to its equity and of its business. His faith in the future of life insurance in Iran also led him to retain his shares in the Company after he retired as Chairman in 1979, although after the Revolution, banks and insurance companies were nationalised without compensation to Iranian shareholders.

In contrast, Ebtehaj's interest in Iranians' Bank was not maintained throughout the 1970s. As the Bank's capitalisation increased after 1969, in the wake of Citibank's involvement, he found it more and more difficult to maintain his 30 per cent shareholding. Each new issue meant having to negotiate a loan from Citibank to meet his commitment. Eventually he gave up the struggle, and reduced his interest by half to 15 per cent, which meant that, together, Citibank and Ebtehaj had a 50 per cent holding in the Bank – not a majority. While the remainder of the equity was widely dispersed, there was no particular problem, but in the mid-1970s Ebtehaj became aware that someone was buying up large quantities of Iranians' Bank shares, at the enormously inflated rate of 300 per cent over par value. It was plain that this man, Hozhabr Yazdani – a very wealthy businessman, who apparently had unlimited credit facilities within the banking system, and the backing of the head of SAVAK, General Nassiri – was intent on acquiring a majority holding in order to make a financial killing.[47] When Ebtehaj found out that Yazdani already held more than 25 per cent of the Bank's shares, he was determined to try and prevent any possibility of him acquiring a majority. But when Yazdani was approached, he gave Ebtehaj a clear alternative: he offered either to buy Ebtehaj out completely, or to sell Ebtehaj his shareholding at the current Stock Exchange rate. It was no real choice since he knew perfectly well that Ebtehaj had no means of buying him out.

In an effort to protect the Bank, and prevent it being taken over, Ebtehaj proposed to Al Costanzo, now Deputy Chairman of Citibank, that Citibank give him a 'soft loan' with which to purchase an additional five per cent of Iranians' Bank shares at the market price, the principal of the loan together with interest at a nominal rate being repayable out of the dividend revenues of the shares bought by him. This would bring the combined holdings of Citibank and

Ebtehaj to 55 per cent – a comfortable majority. Furthermore, recognising the natural concern within Citibank about the future of its relationship with Iranians' Bank given his advancing years, Ebtehaj sought to ensure continuity in the management of the Bank, and in the Ebtehaj/Citibank relationship, suggesting that his step-son, Alireza Arouzi, an Oxford graduate who was Deputy Minister of Commerce in the government, should join the Bank to be trained and groomed for the job of President. He also undertook to have his younger son, Davar, trained in banking in the United States, so that he too could join Iranians' Bank, eventually to succeed Alireza.[48]

Costanzo agreed to recommend to his Board that Ebtehaj be granted the 'soft loan'. There was a strong feeling in Citibank that Ebtehaj should be supported. On the other hand, Citibank's arrangement with Ebtehaj remained virtually unique and in clear contrast to its usual practice of entering into associations on a majority-interest basis only – a principle which by 1977 was, if anything, more firmly held to than ever. Thus, although Ebtehaj's loan was agreed at senior management level, agreement was conditional on there being no dissentient voice. And there was a dissentient voice. In the middle of the negotiations, there was a management reshuffle, and the new executive vice-president for the Middle East and Africa region, George J. Clerk, objected. He voiced his disapproval of the minority relationship with Iranians' Bank, and vetoed any idea of a non-commercial loan to Ebtehaj.[49]

When Ebtehaj heard that he would not get the loan he wanted, his immediate response was to inform the Citibank representative in Tehran of his intention to sell his remaining shares in Iranians' Bank as soon as he received an acceptable offer. The decision reflected his lack of confidence in the future of the Bank if majority control were to pass into the hands of a third party. It also, however, had much to do with the way in which Citibank's rejection of his loan application was communicated to him. Having heard no word from New York for some months, the news was eventually passed on to him in a curiously roundabout fashion by a Citibank representative in Abu Dhabi. Already frustrated with Citibank because of an accumulation of small irritations, Ebtehaj saw this as the last straw. It was not long before he received from Yazdani an offer for his shares too good to refuse. Deeply depressed at the turn of events, and the prospect of abandoning the Bank which he had founded and nurtured, Ebtehaj decided to take a vacation. He went abroad, to France, leaving all the negotiations for the sale of his shares to his wife (who was also selling her shareholding), and returning only when the deal was ready to be concluded.

As it happened, there were still some obstacles to overcome. The Bank Markazi objected to the proposed sale on the grounds that it would make the purchaser the majority shareholder of Iranians' Bank. Ebtehaj interpreted this as meaning that 'the establishment' was out to obstruct the deal. He took his case to Prime Minister Hoveyda, pointing out that a number of private banks were owned by one or a very small number of shareholders. Within days of providing Hoveyda with written evidence of this fact, he learned that the Central Bank had been told to drop its objection. The next hurdle came when Ebtehaj was informed that the Tehran Stock Exchange was unable to accept the operation because the sale price of the shares was too high for the Exchange to accept. Again Ebtehaj entered the fray and won his case. According to Hoveyda, no longer Prime Minister by this time but still, as Minister of Court, close to the Shah, it was the Shah himself who had ordered his ministers to allow the sale to proceed without further difficulties.[50] This gesture led to the first meeting between Ebtehaj and the Shah for 18 years.

The offer made to Ebtehaj for his shares was, in his own words, 'fantastic'. He was able to pay off, with the Central Bank's approval, his debts to Citibank, together with his various other debts within Iran, and still retain a considerable profit. His own inclination was to invest this in Iranian government bonds, which carried interest at around 11 per cent as against an average interest of something like five per cent available in European money markets, but his wife persuaded him to transfer it overseas. In view of all the difficulties which had arisen over the sale of the shares, and convinced that the authorities might yet find some way of depriving them of the money, she felt that it would be safer to transfer the funds out of the country. By the end of 1977, with the knowledge and approval of the Central Bank, this had been done.[51] Planning to spend, in future, at least six months of every year in Europe, the Ebtehajs left Iran in May of 1978. Fortuitously, they were still in Europe at the time of the February 1979 Revolution.

Fortuitously, too, Citibank had sold out its 35 per cent holding in Iranians' Bank by 1979, retaining only a nominal interest. Far from denoting any particular foreknowledge of events to come, the decision to sell was a direct reaction to the loss of Ebtehaj, lack of confidence in the new majority shareholder, and the fact that it was able to sell at the top of the market. In fact, neither Citibank nor Ebtehaj had any special foresight in selling their interests in Iranians' Bank. On the contrary, Citibank's latest 'country risk analysis' on Iran had been very enthusiastic about future prospects and had recommended increasing Citibank exposure there very substantially.[52] Moreover, despite the warnings Ebtehaj had been expressing for years about the dangers of the policies pursued by the Shah, he himself had no immediate forebodings – otherwise he would undoubtedly have sold out his shares in the Iran America International Insurance Company as well. He later explicitly admitted that he, like most of Iran's élite, was utterly unprepared for the suddenness and speed with which the events culminating in the Islamic Revolution took place:

> I admit ... that while I predicted an explosion, which I believed the U.S. and the British Governments acting together could have prevented, I had no idea that it would be carried out by the Mullas. Corruption on the highest possible scale, universal discontent, and the appearance on the scene of a leader with a remarkable degree of self-confidence on the one hand, and the Shah's inherent weakness combined with a fatal illness and a U.S. Administration utterly incapable and incompetent created the ideal conditions for the debacle.[53]

Some ascribe the Ebtehajs' good timing to his wife's shrewdness. In the view of one close associate, 'she outguessed all the experts and managed to get the Ebtehajs out of Iran before Khomeini returned'.[54]

In the aftermath of the Revolution, the Ebtehaj home was taken over by the revolutionary guards and its contents confiscated. Ebtehaj and his wife, described as leading industrialists and contractors, also featured in a list, published in all the Tehran newspapers, of people who had transferred large sums of money out of the country during 1978–79 – the implication being that this had been done illegally. Ebtehaj at once contacted all the authorities concerned, including Ayatollah Khomeini, to protest in the strongest terms that neither he nor his wife had sent any money out of the country since 1977 – and then the transaction had been undertaken through the Central Bank in accordance with all the necessary regulations – nor had either of them ever been industrialists or contractors. He also sent an open letter to the revolutionary authorities, which was published in the two leading Tehran newspapers, *Ettelaat* and *Kayhan*. The only reply he received was from the Prime Minister's office, and it merely informed him that his

11. Abol Hassan and Azar Ebtehaj in 1988

letter refuting the charges against him had been referred to the competent authorities for investigation.[55]

It seems probable that Ebtehaj's connections with American business through Iranians' Bank and his Insurance Company would have been enough to condemn him in the eyes of the new Islamic Republic proclaimed after the fall of the Shah's regime. It was a considerable irony that he should find himself condemned by the new government after his years of vocal criticism of American policy in Iran, and of the excesses of the Shah's regime. Unable to return to Iran, the Ebtehajs settled at first in Cannes in the south of France before moving to London in 1984.

PART FIVE

PLANNING AND POWER

9

EBTEHAJ IN PERSPECTIVE

Ebtehaj's ideas and work focused on a central issue facing twentieth-century Iran — how the revenues from the oil industry were to be utilised. His view was that Iran's enormous economic and social backwardness could only be overcome by the rational allocation of oil revenues to the promotion of economic growth, which over time would raise the living standards of all of the Iranian people. This process, he believed, had to be taken out of the hands of those subject to short-term considerations, and conducted by professionally competent and disinterested administrators. During the 1940s and 1950s, both at the Bank Melli and at the Plan Organisation, he sought to implement this strategy by building modern efficient bureaucracies, recruiting and training staff, and devising and putting into practice his concept of planned economic development. Ebtchaj's views, however, never won more than partial acceptance in Iran. The Pahlavi shahs, father and son, succumbed to the delusions of dictatorial power, diverting the oil revenues to costly prestige projects, overblown armies, and the pockets of those around them. Their post-1979 successors, the *mollas*, have in turn regarded Iran's oil as a useful resource in their mission to spread Islam, and, more specifically, to overthrow the 'Godless' regime of their neighbour, Iraq.

Ebtehaj has sometimes been cast as an alien element in Iranian society. This would provide a convenient explanation for the failure of his ideas to take hold, but in fact any such interpretation is open to many objections. His ideas grew out of his own experiences, and were the product of his time and place. Ebtehaj's nationalism was a reaction to the political and economic realities of early twentieth-century Iran, a disintegrating society subject to foreign political interference, where even the state bank was British-owned and disinclined to appoint Iranians to management positions. Ebtehaj's belief in planning, too, was less an espousal of a concept which became fashionable world-wide after 1945, than a rational man's reaction to a political system which seemed set to squander Iran's new wealth. Ebtehaj was not simply an importer of western or foreign ideas and concepts into Iran, although he was inevitably influenced by what was happening elsewhere.

It is true that Ebtehaj pursued his ideas with a vigour and determination matched by few of his contemporaries. British diplomats and the various ill-informed westerners who were apt to characterise all Iranians as devious, dishonest opium-smokers concluded that he must be 'more European than Iranian', but again this is an over-simplification. The influences of Ebtehaj's family and upbringing on his character are plain. He inherited the moral strength and probity of his father. The benefit of a foreign education in his teens gave him a more cosmopolitan outlook than many of his peers. People of Ebtehaj's character and calibre are unusual in any society, and he is best seen as a representative of that small minority to be found in each generation of any country who become outstanding public servants, entrepreneurs or political leaders. 'If Ebtehaj was in America', concluded Khodadad Farmanfarmaian, 'he would have been either Secretary of the Treasury or . . . I don't know, maybe he wasn't that much of a politician, but at least he would have operated the biggest corporations in America.'[1] Far from being 'more European than Iranian', plausible comparisons can be made between Ebtehaj's character and that of his near contemporary, Ayatollah Khomeini (who was born in 1902): the same determination, even ruthlessness, and the same incorruptibility were there despite the enormous ideological gulf which separated the two men.

Why was Ebtehaj able to achieve so much at the Bank Melli and the Plan Organisation, notwithstanding the opposition and obstacles he faced? The immediate answer lies in his own abilities, and in his possession of the professional skills which Iran so patently lacked. A man who would ignore a tank sent to overawe him by an irate Prime Minister, and who was prepared to speak out against an increasingly brutal regime, was someone not easily stopped.

Yet power in Iran (or elsewhere) rarely flows automatically to those best qualified to exercise it. Ebtehaj reached and remained in power because of the support of influential patrons. In the 1930s it was men such as Ali Akbar Davar and Hossein Ala. In the 1940s and 1950s it was Ahmad Qavam and, crucially, the Shah. Ebtehaj could not have obtained and exercised authority without this patronage, given the nature of the Iranian political system, but his dependence upon it was also a critical weakness. His hopes of rational planning rested on the power of irrational politicians and individual reformers.

Herein lies the explanation for Ebtehaj's eventual 'failure', or more specifically his exclusion from official influence in Iran after 1959. Lacking political understanding or a personal political power base – except the respect of other like-minded administrators – his position in the 1940s and 1950s had depended on the Shah. And the Shah was a man who, especially after the traumas of the Mossadeq years, became increasingly autocratic, and drawn into policies of grandeur and megalomania which were anathema to Ebtehaj. By the 1960s, the Shah wanted to hear not the uncomfortable home truths offered by Ebtehaj, but the flattery of sycophants.[2]

Aspects of Ebtehaj's own character did little to strengthen his position. In any political system there will be conflict between politicians and those seeking to take a long-term view. But Ebtehaj's abrasive personality and absolute conviction that he was right led him into acrimonious clashes with anyone who opposed him – his own staff, government ministers, American admirals, or the Shah:

> he often took such a hard position on things, you know . . . he would scream . . . he would raise his hands, he would bang on the table . . . He used foul language sometimes with certain senior persons which was not in good taste, but it was out of sheer exasperation. When he got mad, God forbid, we heard him at the other end of the building.[3]

Such behaviour, however justified, made powerful enemies.

Beyond the question of personality, however, Ebtehaj's hopes that planning could be kept away from politics were always unlikely to succeed over the long term. Planning could not exist as an island of rationality and probity in a murky ocean of special interests, pressure groups and corruption. The independence of the Plan Organisation created in 1949 was already compromised when the First Plan was interrupted by the nationalisation of the oil industry, the cessation of oil revenues and the economic crisis of the Mossadeq years. In the period 1954 to 1959 Ebtehaj came closest to creating a 'government within a government', but he failed to establish the *modus vivendi* between the Plan Organisation and other ministries necessary if tensions were not to arise. In retrospect, it is apparent that a greater attempt should have been made to work with other government departments, despite the incompetence and corruption in them which Ebtehaj accurately diagnosed.

Ebtehaj's positive impact on Iran's development is undeniable. The struggle in the 1940s to raise Iran's international status despite the humiliation of the wartime Allied occupation; the accumulation of gold and foreign exchange during the war years designed to provide resources for post-war growth; the 'institution-building' at Bank Melli and the Plan Organisation; these were all concrete achievements which stand in sharp contrast to – for example – the destructive xenophobia of Mossadeq, who remains a far better known figure in the United States and Europe.

Furthermore, Ebtehaj's role as the pioneer of planned economic development in Iran cannot be disputed. The plans with which he was associated were not technically or mathematically sophisticated, although Ebtehaj did implement considerable improvements over time in controls and administrative structures. Nor were the First and Second Plans original in content or strategy compared with those of such other non-socialist developing countries of the period as Turkey or India. A more novel aspect of the Ebtehaj design was the concept of a wholly autonomous planning agency: in the political circumstances of Iran this may not have been an ideal solution, but at the time it was possibly the only way to ensure that economic development did not become a matter of all words and no action. It was certainly a thoroughly understandable response to the problems of dealing with the 'soggy mess' of the government machine. The most striking feature of Ebtehaj, however, was not his policies, but that he got so far with implementing them despite all the obstacles he faced in Iran. His vision of the urgency of the need for development in his country stands out as a beacon of light amidst the petty politics, intrigues and corruption of Pahlavi Iran.

It is easy to belittle the economic achievements of the first two Iranian Plans. Both of them experienced shortfalls between estimated and actual expenditure. The First Plan ended in chaos, while the Second ended in the severe recession of the early 1960s. The wide-ranging economic and social goals look hollow and overblown given the failure of the planners to state firm policy priorities. Yet, for all these problems, the early plans left behind physical monuments which changed the face of Iran and the lives of its people:

> Many projects were developed. Both long-term types of projects as well as short-term. Roads, railways, ports were

built. A whole program of fertilizer, pesticide [*sic*] was carried out very successfully. Mechanization of farming and distribution and maintenance of tractors. Cities received electricity, sewage systems, water supplies. . . . Many industries such as cement, textiles, sugar, etc were established. And of course, this expenditure by the public sector began to generate activity in the private sector. . . . And we begin to get, about this time, the emergence of a whole new group of entrepreneurs in the private sector.[4]

The economic growth of the 1950s under the plans was certainly an improvement on the costly and sometimes madcap projects launched by Reza Shah in the 1930s.

The physical achievements of the plans cannot be disputed: what can and has been disputed is the wisdom of the overall strategy. Ebtehaj's faith in the benefits that economic growth would bring, his views on the merits of industrialisation and his willingness to seek foreign technical assistance might all be questioned by development theorists of the 1980s, as well as lay him open to accusations of being one of those who sought to modernise and westernise Iran at too fast a pace for its own society. The problems which followed from some aspects of the planning policies in the 1950s are also apparent. Ebtehaj was always a man in a hurry, and some things happened too quickly. The preference for large dams in Khuzestan, for example, and the corresponding neglect of secondary and tertiary irrigation systems looks, in retrospect, a misallocation of resources, although it has to be said that Ebtehaj was not in control of the Plan Organisation for long enough to monitor implementation and see the whole Khuzestan regional development project through to a rational conclusion.

Yet Ebtehaj's policies deserve more than to be dismissed as part of an out-dated development strategy. He cannot be included in the same category as the inflated and incompetent planning bureaucracies that emerged in many Third World countries. He was no supporter of the kind of extensive state regulation and public ownership which stifled the heavy industrial sector in, for example, India from the 1950s. He may not have been an exponent of the free market economies of the 1980s – and the effectiveness of such policies in promoting economic development remains far from proven – but he certainly sought to encourage rather than constrain private sector initiative.

Ebtehaj and his fellow planners in the 1950s also recognised that there was more to economic development than growth rates. The 'social improvement' scheme was just one illustration of this recognition. The constraints on the Plan Organisation were, however, formidable. Some western commentators perceived the character of Iranian culture to be the biggest constraint: its individualistic nature and apparent endemic corruption seemed to spell doom for Ebtehaj's kind of planning. While undoubtedly there is validity in such cultural explanations, it was not a line of thought which Ebtehaj himself espoused. Rather he was convinced that 'the Persians have a readiness to accept new ideas more readily than most other nations' and that 'what was wrong in Iran was not the new ideas that people resented and disliked, it was the manner in which these were carried out that caused the resentment'.[5] He argued – surely rightly – that petty corruption was not so much a permanent feature of the Iranian character as a reflection of the traditional way in which business and politics had been organised. His strategy of paying his staff adequate salaries so that they were not dependent on influence and favour certainly seemed to go some way towards curbing graft.

The constraints facing Ebtehaj were more concrete than the national character of his fellow Iranians. They included the products of economic backwardness, such as the severe shortage of trained personnel to implement his policies and of skilled manpower for the industrial sector. The central government's weakness in rural areas and the absence of nationwide media also hindered the implementation of the plans. The nature of the Iranian government bureaucracy meant that it took an enormous effort to build and operate an effective planning agency, let alone to try and influence wider aspects of Iranian social and economic life. As Khodadad Farmanfarmaian later recalled,

> the whole apparatus of taxation [and] fiscal policy was an important factor over which we had no control. Taxation and fiscal policy and administration was ancient and entrenched and we could not influence it much. Regardless of what we did – and God knows our efforts were very valiant and we persisted over the years, we never gave it up – but we never really succeeded in breaking into that bastion which was called the Ministry of Finance. The old practices continued, the old ways continued . . . if our policy and reform suggestions were accepted, they would have improved income distribution, even in the early period.[6]

EBTEHAJ IN PERSPECTIVE

There was a limit to what anyone, even Ebtehaj, could achieve in such a situation.

The United States emerges as a further, albeit somewhat shadowy, constraint on Ebtehaj's policies. There is now almost an epidemic of books critical of American foreign policy in Iran after 1945, from the fateful support given to Britain against Mossadeq and the sponsorship of the 1953 coup, to the May 1972 Nixon–Kissinger commitment to full uncritical support for the Shah and the chaotic policies pursued in 1978–79.[7] This study adds to the picture of misguided and sometimes mischievous United States' policies. There was a suspected American role in Ebtehaj's removal from both Bank Melli in 1950 and the Plan Organisation in 1959. His hopes of using Iran's oil revenues to promote development were not always fully supported by American officials, some of whom clearly disliked him and found him difficult to deal with. In 1963, despite misgivings about the regime in Iran, the Kennedy Administration would not support Ebtehaj once he had made it clear that in his view development had to take priority over military spending. Ebtehaj may have over-estimated the influence of the United States over the Shah, but the picture which emerges of United States foreign policy in Iran is nonetheless unflattering.

What is surprising, given this range of constraints, is not how little Ebtehaj achieved, but how much. It is also vital to distinguish between the Ebtehaj era of the 1950s, and what happened in the Shah's Iran in later years, and especially after the huge oil price rises of the early 1970s. The responsibility for 'the grandiose economic and atomic energy development plans, the massive imports of food and consumer goods, the rapidly rising rate of inflation, the spreading corruption, the shortage of electricity, the infrastructural "bottlenecks", the decline of agricultural productivity, the maldistribution of wealth, etc'[8] could not be laid at Ebtehaj's door. Ebtehaj explicitly opposed the two features of the Shah's Iran which were, above all, to lead the regime to disaster – official corruption and escalating military spending. His stand against these two evils lay behind his resignation from the Plan Organisation and his subsequent imprisonment.

Much happened in Iran after Ebtehaj's resignation in 1959, and it would be idle to speculate whether if he had remained in power as the country's economic supremo the Islamic Revolution might have been prevented. The social stresses of modernisation in Iran would have been acute under any administration, and the Shah's flawed character and increasing reluctance to allow any one member of the government, administration or armed forces to become too powerful would have been ever harder to control. Nevertheless, Ebtehaj must surely be seen not as a precursor of, but as offering an alternative to, the fateful path actually taken by the Iranian regime in the 1960s and 1970s. While seeking modernisation and even (by some definitions) westernisation, his policies were of a different kind from those eventually espoused by the Shah. In place of grandiose prestige projects, he offered rational planning designed to use Iran's oil revenues to promote economic and social development. In place of an inflated military establishment and the illusion of Great Power status, he offered a small army defending a strong (albeit pro-western) economy – a Middle Eastern Japan. In place of corruption and abuse of power, he offered rectitude, public service and professional competence. It was not a package that would have won the approval of Ayatollah Khomeini, nor of the left-wing opponents of the government. Yet it might have kept for the Shah the respect of many of his people and, conceivably, have saved the Pahlavi dynasty.

REFERENCES

INTRODUCTION

1. *New York Times*, 21 March 1962.
2. For the economy of Iran at the beginning of the twentieth century, see generally, J. Bharier, *Economic Development in Iran 1900–1970* (London, 1971), Chapter 1: for the history of the late nineteenth and twentieth centuries, see, for example, E. Abrahamian, *Iran Between Two Revolutions* (Princeton, 1982); P. Avery, *Modern Iran* (London, 1965); F. Kazemzadeh, *Russia and Britain in Persia, 1864–1914: A Study in Imperialism* (New Haven, 1968); N. Keddie, *Roots of Revolution* (London, 1981).
3. A. Banani, *The Modernisation of Iran 1921–1941* (Stanford, 1961), p.3; Banani's book is one of the best surveys of Reza Shah's era.
4. Abrahamian, *Iran*, p.530.
5. Fred Halliday, *The Making of the Second World War* (2nd edn. London, 1986), pp.90–5; Halliday lists 14 Third World Revolutions between 1974 and 1980.
6. Ibid, p 94.
7. Figures for Iran's oil revenues to 1945 can be found in Bharier, *Economic*, p.158, and, from 1946 to 1980, in Geoffrey Jones, *Banking and Oil* (Cambridge, 1987), Appendix 11.2.
8. R. Kapuscinski, *Shah of Shahs* (London, 1986), pp.67–78; for relations between government and the clergy during the Pahlavi era, see Sharough Akhavi, *Religion and Politics in Contemporary Iran* (New York, 1980); for a summary of the thoughts of contemporary Shiite thinkers, see the chapter by Yann Richard in N. Keddie, *Roots*.
9. Memorandum by John Murray, 22 Aug. 1951, Foreign Office Correspondence Series, Public Record Office (hereafter FO) 371/91462.
10. U.S. Central Intelligence Digest, 1955, United States Department of State (hereafter USSD).
11. Hossein Razavi and Firouz Vakil, *The Political Environment of Economic Planning in Iran, 1971–1983* (Boulder, Colorado, 1984).
12. Ibid, p.25. See also, Kamran Mofid, *Development Planning in Iran* (Wisbech, Cambs., 1987), p.47. Although Ebtehaj has been largely neglected by students of development planning, he is beginning to attact the attention of political scientists; see, for example, J.A. Bill, *The Eagle and the Lion. The Tragedy of American–Iranian Relations* (London, 1988).
13. Robert Graham, *Iran: The Illusion of Power* (London, 1978), p.49.
14. There are as many variations on this theme as there are authors. For a sustained attack on the Pahlavi 'pseudo-modernists' pursuing superficial notions of western modernisation, see Homa Katouzian, *The Political Economy of Modern Iran* (London, 1981). British and American diplomats active in Iran in the 1970s have – retrospectively – attributed the Revolution to the regime's over-hasty modernisation policies; see, for instance, Jack C. Miklos, *The Iranian Revolution and Modernization: Way Stations to Anarchy* (Washington, 1983) and Sir Anthony Parsons, *The Pride and the Fall* (London, 1984). On a more sophisticated level, see Abrahamian, *Iran*, p.427 for the view 'that the revolution came because the shah modernized the socioeconomic level . . . but failed to modernize on another level – the political level'.

199

15. M.H. Pesaran, 'Economic Development and Revolutionary Upheavals in Iran', in H. Afshar (ed), *Iran: A Revolution in Turmoil* (London, 1985), p.18.
16. A.H. Ebtehaj, 'A Program for Economic Growth', Address given to the International Industrial Conference, San Francisco, Sept. 1961: see also, reports in the *Washington Post*, 4 Jan. 1962, and *Kayhan International*, 16 Nov. 1961.
17. G.B. Baldwin, *Planning and Development in Iran* (Baltimore, 1967), p.197. And see, Mofid, *Development*, pp.45–6.
18. A.H. Ebtehaj to George McGhee, Under-Secretary of State, U.S. State Department, 10 Dec. 1961.

CHAPTER ONE

1. For the history of this period see, for example, P. Avery, *Modern Iran* (London, 1965); R.L. Greaves, *Persia and the Defence of India 1884–1892* (London, 1959); F. Kazemzadeh, *Russia and Britain in Persia 1864–1914* (New Haven, 1968); D. McLean, *Britain and Her Buffer State* (London, 1979); M.E. Yapp, '1900–21: The Last Years of the Qajar Dynasty', in H. Amirsadeghi (ed.), *Twentieth Century Iran* (London, 1977).
2. G. Jones, *Banking and Empire in Iran* (Cambridge, 1986), pp.9–12.
3. N.R. Keddie, *Religion and Rebellion in Iran: The Tobacco Protest of 1891–92* (London, Cass, 1966).
4. The standard contemporary work on the Constitutional Revolution is E.G. Browne, *The Persian Revolution of 1905–1909* (Cambridge, 1910; repr. Cass, 1966). See also, R. McDaniel, *The Shuster Mission and the Persian Constitutional Revolution* (Minneapolis, 1974).
5. Recorded Interview with Christopher Cook (hereafter, Cook Interview), August 1985: much of the personal information on Ebtehaj's early years comes from this source, but where possible it has been double-checked.
6. E. Abrahamian, *Iran Between Two Revolutions* (Princeton, 1982), pp.111–12.
7. M. Donohue, *With the Persian Expedition* (London, 1919), p.127, quoted by Abrahamian, *Iran*, p.112.
8. The silver *kran* was the standard monetary unit in Iran until 1932 when it was superseded by the *rial*, one *rial* being equivalent to one *kran*. In this book the sterling figures are given in brackets and are equivalents at contemporary exchange rates.
9. Interview with A.H. Ebtehaj, Sept. 1986.
10. R.W. Ferrier, *The History of the British Petroleum Industry*, Vol 1: *The Developing Years 1901–1932* (Cambridge, 1982); G. Jones, *The State and the Emergence of the British Oil Industry* (London, 1981), Chapter 5.
11. Frances Bostock and Geoffrey Jones, 'British Business in Iran, 1860s–1970s' in R. Davenport-Hines and G. Jones (eds), *British Business in Asia Since 1860* (Cambridge, 1988), p.35.
12. Jones, *Banking and Empire*, pp.18–31.
13. Jones, *State*, Chapter 6; Ferrier, *History*, Vol. 1.
14. Jones, *Banking and Empire*, Chapter 6.
15. *Ibid*, p.285.
16. Staff Record, attached to Tehran Confidential Letter of 30 Oct. 1934, BBME Archives, Hongkong Bank Group, hereafter referred to as BBME.
17. For the Reza Shah period generally, see Amin Banani, *The Modernization of Iran 1921–1941* (Stanford, 1961); Abrahamian, *Iran*; N.R. Keddie, *Roots of Revolution* (London, 1981); W. Knapp, '1921–1941: The Period of Riza Shah', in Amirsadeghi (ed), *Twentieth*; D. Wilber, *Riza Shah Pahlavi: The Resurrection and Reconstruction of Iran* (New York, 1975); R. Cottam, *Nationalism in Iran* (Pittsburgh, 1964); L.P. Elwell-Sutton, *Modern Iran* (London, 1941). For economic aspects of the

REFERENCES

industrialisation programme, see especially, J. Bharier, *Economic Development in Iran 1900–1970* (London, 1971); W.M. Floor, *Industrialisation in Iran 1900–1941* (Centre for Middle Eastern and Islamic Studies, University of Durham, Occasional Papers No 23, 1984).
18. Jones, *Banking and Empire*, pp.217–27.
19. Ibid, p.211.
20. Tehran Confidential Letters to London, 26 April 1932 and 22 July 1933, BBME.
21. Tehran Confidential Letter to London, 26 April 1932; E. Wilkinson to Sir Hugh Barnes, 19 April 1934, BBME.
22. For cancellation of the concession, see P.J. Beck, 'The Anglo-Persian Oil Dispute 1932–3', *Journal of Contemporary History* (1975).
23. Tehran Confidential Letter to London, 26 April 1932; London Confidential Letter to Tehran, 27 May 1932, BBME.
24. Jones, *Banking and Empire*, p.285.

CHAPTER TWO

1. R. Oakshott to F. Hale, 4 July 1936, X51/33, BBME, reporting a conversation with Ebtehaj.
2. C. Phelps Grant, 'Iran. Test of Relations Between Great and Small Nations', *Foreign Policy Report* (New York, Foreign Policy Association Inc), Vol XX, No.3, 15 April 1945; A.K.S. Lambton, 'Persia' in *Royal Central Asian Society Journal*, Vol 31, Jan. 1944. See also, E. Abrahamian, *Iran Between Two Revolutions* (Princeton, 1982); A. Banani, *The Modernization of Iran 1921–1941* (Stanford, 1961); W. Knapp, '1921–1941: The Period of Riza Shah' in H. Amirsadeghi (ed), *Twentieth Century Iran* (London, 1977).
3. Memorandum of Conversation between U.S. Under Secretary of State, Sumner Welles, and the British Chargé in Washington, 23 Sept. 1941, *U.S. Foreign Relations* (1941), Vol III, p.462.
4. A. Saikal, *The Rise and Fall of the Shah* (London, 1980), p.26. For this period, see also, G. Lenczowski, *Russia and the West in Iran 1918–1948* (Ithaca, 1949).
5. P. Avery, *Modern Iran* (London, 1965), pp.359, 370.
6. G. Baldwin, *Planning and Development in Iran* (Baltimore, 1967), p.4.
7. Avery, *Modern Iran*, pp.359–61; J. Thorpe, 'The Mission of Arthur C. Millspaugh to Iran, 1943–1945' (unpublished PhD Thesis, University of Wisconsin, 1973), p.19.
8. G. Jones, *Banking and Empire in Iran* (Cambridge, 1986), p.300; see also, Habib Ladjevardi, *Labor Unions and Autocracy in Iran* (Syracuse, N.Y., 1985).
9. Memorandum by A.H. Ebtehaj, 10 Oct. 1986; Cook Interview, pp.30–1; Jones, *Banking*, pp.239, 286.
10. H. Seymour to A. Eden, 24 April 1937, FO 371/20831: Seymour reported that Ala had been appointed Director General of the Department of Commerce; and was President of the Council for the supervision of state-owned companies since these now came under the Department of Commerce.
11. Cook Interview, pp.37–8: Ebtehaj described Ala as a very courageous man who later stood up to Gromyko in the Security Council and defended Iran 'like a brave lion'. He was also one of only a handful of people, including Mossadeq, to oppose Reza Shah's accession to the monarchy. British officials, however, while admiring Ala's acumen, habitually referred to his lack of courage.
12. H. Seymour to A. Eden, 24 April 1937, FO 371/20831; P.B. Olsen and P.N. Rasmussen, 'An Attempt at Planning in a Traditional State – Iran' in E.E. Hagen (ed), *Planning Economic Development* (Holmewood, Illinois, 1963), p.224, fn.3; Cook Interview, pp.35–6,
13. Cook Interview, pp.40–1: it was not long before Ala also gave up his job as Minister

of Commerce (the Department had been created a Ministry in October 1937). He was on bad terms with the Minister of Finance, and he was totally out of sympathy with the direction the economy was taking: N. Butler to Viscount Halifax, 22 April 1938, FO 371/21889.
14. Cook Interview, pp.41–2. For the Legation view of Farzin's ability, see Legation Personalities List, 16 May 1938, FO 371/24582.
15. H. Seymour to Lord Halifax, 10 May 1939, enclosing the Legation's Annual Economic Report for 1938, FO 371/23256; J. Bharier, *Economic Development in Iran 1900–1970* (London, 1971), p.241; Interview with Mr Aqa Khan Bakhtiar (a member of the Bank Rahni staff in the early 1940s and later, in the early 1950s, President of that bank), 30 April 1987.
16. Interview with Mr Aqa Khan Bakhtiar, 30 April 1987; Cook Interview, pp.43–8.
17. Despatch #422, L.G. Dreyfus, U.S. Embassy Tehran to U.S. Secretary of State, 4 Jan. 1943, USSD 891.516/157.
18. A.C. Millspaugh, *The American Task in Persia* (New York, 1925); D.N. Wilber, *Riza Shah Pahlevi; The Resurrection and Reconstruction of Iran* (New York, 1975).
19. M. Agah, 'Some Aspects of the Economic Development of Modern Iran' (unpublished DPhil Thesis, Oxford, 1958), p.52.
20. Jones, *Banking*, pp.226–7.
21. Agah, 'Some Aspects', pp.52–3.
22. L. Binder, *Iran: Political Development in a Changing Society* (Berkeley, 1962), p.267.
23. Memorandum by A.H. Ebtehaj, 10 Oct. 1986.
24. Cook Interview, pp.95, 99.
25. Report by Col. G. Wheeler, 28 Oct. 1949, enclosed with Sir John Le Rougetel to E. Bevin, 1 Nov. 1949, FO 371/75467.
26. Memorandum by A.H. Ebtehaj, 10 July 1986: since Ebtehaj's appointment by Prime Minister Qavam as Governor of Bank Melli did not take place until December 1942, more than a year after Reza Shah's abdication, he was in no position to have transferred the Shah's assets out of the country in any event.
27. Ibid.
28. N.S. Roberts to G.H. Pinsent, H.M. Treasury, 14 Dec. 1945, FO 371/52692.
29. For example, Despatch #67, U.S. Embassy Tehran to State Department, 9 Aug. 1955, USSD 788.00/8-955.
30. L. Payne to F. Ayrton, 10 May 1948, X51/57, BBME.
31. Cook Interview, pp.136–8, 141–2: Ebtehaj says he was offered the Prime Ministership in 1944 by the Shah through his Aide, General Yazdanpanah. The Embassy Financial Counsellor thought it very probable that he had been offered the Finance Ministry – Report by E.N.R. Trentham, 3 July 1944, enclosed in D.N. Lascelles to A. Eden, 9 July 1944, FO 371/40167. In 1946, the Shah mentioned Ebtehaj to the U.S. Ambassador as possible Prime Minister if Qavam resigned – Telegram #885, U.S. Embassy Tehran to State Department, 24 June 1946, USSD. In both 1950 and 1951, there was, according to the U.S. authorities, talk in Tehran of Ebtehaj becoming Prime Minister – Note #D-289, U.S. Embassy Tehran, 20 May 1950, USSD; Sir Oliver Franks, Washington, to FO, 27 March 1951, FO 371/ 91454. In February 1950, the Shah made it plain to both the British Ambassador and Chargé that the appointment of Ebtehaj as Prime Minister was in his mind: Sir John Le Rougetel to C.R. Attlee, 1 Feb. 1950, and V. Lawford to E. Bevin, 21 Feb. 1950, FO 371/82310.
32. A.C. Millspaugh, *Americans in Persia* (Washington, 1976 edn.), p.95.
33. Ibid.
34. Cook Interview, pp.43–9, 67: the Russians prevented the transport of wheat supplies to Tehran – presumably the surplus crop was diverted to the Soviet Union.
35. Memorandum by A.H. Ebtehaj, 10 Oct. 1986.
36. Memoranda by A.H. Ebtehaj, 10 Oct. 1986; Cook Interview, p.100.
37. Interview with Dr Eprime Eshag, 21 May 1987; Conversation with Mr Mehdi Samii, 28 Sept. 1987; Cook Interview, pp.102, 138–41; V. Walter to F. Hale, 2 July 1946,

REFERENCES

X51/52, BBME. A more positively anti-Ebtehaj view of the union affair is to be found in Anvar Khamenei, *Forsat-e Bozorg Az Dast Rafteh* (Great Opportunity Lost) (Tehran, 1363 edn.[1984]), Vol 2, p.327: Khamenei (like Eshag, a member of the Tudeh Party) maintains that before Eshag joined Bank Melli this institution was Ebtehaj's 'impregnable castle' – Eshag, with his demand for a union, was the first person to oppose Ebtehaj's unpopular and oppressive dictatorship within the Bank.

38. Interview with Dr Cyrus Ghani, 15 June 1987; Interview with Dr Khodadad Farmanfarmaian, 17 March 1987.
39. V. Walter to F. Hale, 8 Feb. 1943; 15 Feb. 1943, enclosing letter from A.C. Millspaugh to Prime Minister Qavam of 11 Feb., X51/45; V. Walter to F. Hale, 12 April 1943, X51/46; BBME.
40. Information from A.H. Ebtehaj; and see K. Farmanfarmaian, 'Report on Formation and Development of Economic Bureau 1336–1342', *Ford Foundation* (Tehran, May 1963), p.3.
41. For Ebtehaj's opinion, Cook Interview, p.181; for Millspaugh's opinion, Millspaugh, *Americans*, p.95.
42. Report #G.4143, U.S. Embassy Tehran to Office of Strategic Services, Washington (hereafter OSS), 6 July 1944, OSS RG226.83177, USSD.
43. Thorpe, 'Millspaugh', pp.247, 249, 253–5.
44. Ibid, pp.259, 290; and see generally pp.289 ff; Thorpe makes it plain that Millspaugh's relations with many of his own team members were far from satisfactory and that there were fundamental disagreements over many issues. See also Millspaugh, *Americans*, pp.127 ff.
45. Report #G.6565, U.S. Embassy Tehran to OSS, 4 Nov. 1944, OSS RG226.L48889, USSD: many years later, Ebtehaj met the then Under-Secretary of the U.S. Treasury in the Carter Administration (later President of the Federal Reserve Bank) – a man who had been a member of Millspaugh's expanded team in the 1940s – who said that he had entirely endorsed Ebtehaj's position in his controversy with Millspaugh.
46. Thorpe, 'Millspaugh', pp.304–5; Jones, *Banking*, p.309.
47. Extracts from Millspaugh's letter to Prime Minister Qavam re Ebtehaj, enclosed with Tehran Confidential Letter, 25 January 1945, X51/48, BBME.
48. Thorpe, 'Millspaugh', p.219, mentions Millspaugh's 'constant illness' and his continuing suspicions of intrigues against him by fellow Mission members. Some years after Millspaugh's departure from Tehran, Allahyar Saleh told Ebtehaj that when he was in the United States in 1942, just prior to becoming Minister of Justice and then Minister of Finance in Qavam's government, a former U.S. Minister to Iran, Hoffman, had informed him about Millspaugh's time in a mental hospital.
49. Cook Interview, p.121.
50. W.A.B. Iliff to Sir Reader Bullard, 30 September 1943, FO 371/35057.
51. Telegrams from Sir Reader Bullard to FO, 22 Nov. and 20 Dec. 1943, FO 371/35057.
52. Cook Interview, pp.116–18; Jones, *Banking*, pp.305–7, 320 ff.
53. Bank Melli Iran Annual Report of the Executive Board for 1327 (1948–9), p.8; Agah, 'Some Aspects', pp.59–61; Bharier, *Economic*, pp.79–81.
54. Interview with A.H. Ebtehaj, Nov. 1986. An article on Iran in *The Economist*, 31 March 1951, referred to 'the fear of inflation such as was caused by the incursion of the Allied occupiers during the war' as inhibiting 'all those who are ignorant of modern currency practices' and causing them to cling to a fixed ceiling for the note issue and the provision of 100 per cent cover. The article goes on to mention that an 'ex-director [sic. Ebtehaj] of the bank of issue, which is a well-run organisation, tried to establish elasticity to meet the expansion and contraction of business in a fast-developing economy', but he was shouted down'. See also, BMI Annual Reports of the Executive Board for 1327 (1948–9) and 1328 (1949–30).
55. Survey of Economy of Iran, 8 Dec. 1947, FO 371/68725B; BMI Annual Report of

PLANNING AND POWER IN IRAN

the Executive Board for 1328 (1949-50), p.12.
56. Report #G.7186, U.S. Embassy Tehran to OSS, 23 Feb. 1945, OSS RG226. 116991, USSD.

CHAPTER THREE

1. W.A.B. Iliff to Sir David Waley, 20 March 1943, FO 371/35051.
2. See OV10/13, Bank of England Archives, generally for Bank of England views.
3. See, for instance, Sir Wilfred Eady to Sir Orme Sargent, 13 Oct. 1947, FO 371/62017; Telegram FO to HM Ambassador Tehran, 53, 19 Jan. 1949, FO 371/75487; J. Wiley, U.S. Ambassador Tehran to Secretary of State, 7 July 1949, *U.S. Foreign Relations*, 1949, VI, pp.536-9; J.D. Somerville, U.S. Chargé Tehran to Secretary of State, 3 and 14 Feb. 1949, in Ibid, pp.477-8, 479.
4. *New York Herald Tribune*, 27 March 1947.
5. Note #A-309 by James Somerville, U.S. Embassy Tehran, 10 Dec. 1949, USSD.
6. C.W. Baxter, FO, to H.E. Mohammad Ali Moghaddam, 17 Oct. 1940, OV6/278, Bank of England. See generally, R.F. Mikesell, 'Sterling Area Currencies of the Middle East,' *Middle East Journal*, 2, 1948.
7. G. Jones, *Banking and Empire in Iran* (Cambridge, 1986), pp.300-1; see also J. Thorpe, 'The Mission of Arthur C. Millspaugh to Iran, 1943-1945' (Unpublished PhD Thesis, Wisconsin, 1973), p.24; *U.S. Foreign Relations*, 1942, IV, p.199.
8. Jones, *Banking*, pp.302-5; see also J. Bharier, *Economic Development in Iran 1900-1970* (London, 1971), p.80, Table 6.
9. Memorandum by W.A.B. Iliff, Financial Counsellor H.M. Legation Tehran, on Anglo-Persian Agreement, 30 May 1942, FO 371/31405; Jones, *Banking*, pp. 302-5.
10. See, for instance, FO to HM Embassy Washington, 8 April 1942, and FO to HM Legation Tehran, 9 April 1942, FO 371/31403.
11. See Cyrus Ghani, *Iran and the West: A Critical Bibliography* (London, 1987), p.57: reviewing Sir Reader Bullard's *Britain and the Middle East* (London, 1951), Ghani graphically describes the lack of sympathy between Bullard and the Iranian authorities, saying 'based on his writings and public utterances, it is evident that [Bullard] never liked Iran or the Iranians and he was in turn the least popular British Ambassador since 1919.... He is venomous towards Reza Shah ... and towards anyone who casts doubt on the purity of British motives in Persia.' On this interpretation, Ebtehaj was unlikely to have got far with Bullard if he dealt with him direct.
12. *U.S. Foreign Relations*, 1942, IV, p.301.
13. Cook Interview, pp.76-8, 83-8, 109-10.
14. Jones, *Banking*, pp.303-4; Memorandum by W.A.B. Iliff, 30 May 1942, FO 371/31405.
15. At first a three-man commission was proposed, the membership of which – Ebtehaj, V. Walter of the Imperial Bank and A.H. Hajir, Minister of Commerce – was described by Iliff as collectively 'a workmanlike body to be trusted to bring in a sane report' – Telegram, Sir Reader Bullard to FO, 16 August 1942, transmitting message from W.A.B. Iliff to HM Treasury, OV6/278, Bank of England. However, in the event, a four-man commission was appointed, its members being Ebtehaj, Hajir, Ala (still Governor of the Bank Melli), and Dr Ali Amini – V. Walter to F. Hale, 31 August 1942, X51/45, BBME.
16. V. Walter to F. Hale, 19 Oct. 1942, X51/45, BBME; Cook Interview, pp.111-13.
17. *US Foreign Relations*, 1942, IV, pp.155ff; Cook Interview, pp.112.
18. See Telegram CS/12560, General Wilson to War Office, 13 Nov. 1942, FO 371/31407, for plans to take over the banks. In April 1942, before the Financial Agreement was signed, several contingency plans were discussed to solve the

REFERENCES

currency problems, including the printing of notes by the British authorities, the importation of currency notes from Iraq or India, the blocking of Iran's Sterling balances, and the cutting off of essential supplies: see Telegram 484, FO to British Legation Tehran, 9 April 1942, FO 371/31403.

19. The original Financial Agreement bill before the *Majles* was withdrawn, and the new amended one presented for ratification. Cook Interview, pp.87–93; Jones, *Banking*, p.304.
20. Note by C.W. St James Turner on Tehran 61, Persian Claim for Gold, January 1943, OV6/278, Bank of England.
21. Telegram, FO to HM Legation Tehran, 18 June 1945; Telegram, Sir Reader Bullard to FO, 21 July 1945; Sir Reader Bullard to E. Bevin, Report on Persian Affairs for July, August, September 1945, 7 Nov. 1945; FO 371/45454.
22. Sir Reader Bullard to A. Eden, 6 April 1943, Review of Events in Persia in January, February, March 1943, FO 371/35117. For the American Agreement, see also, Secretary of State to U.S. Minister Tehran, 16 Feb. 1943, *U.S. Foreign Relations*, 1943, IV, pp.568–9. For the terms of the Soviet Agreement, signed 27 March 1943, see X51/46, BBME.
23. Hossein Makki, *Tarikh-e Bist Saleh-e Iran* (Iran's History of the Past Twenty Years) (Tehran, 1364 edn.[1985]), Vol. 8, p.298: while Makki admits that Iran was the only country able to secure an arrangement with the British during the 1940s which involved selling *rials* for Sterling convertible into gold, he mistakenly maintains that it was thanks to the Soviets that Iran was able to do this. The Agreement with Britain was in fact concluded well before any talks with the U.S.S.R. on this subject took place.
24. See W.A.B. Iliff to FO, 3 Nov. 1946, FO 371/52695.
25. *Bank Melli Bulletin*, XII, 69; Middle East Financial Conference Resolutions, enclosed with V. Walter to F. Hale, 28 May 1944, X51/47, BBME.
26. D.W. Lascelles to A. Eden, 9 July 1944, enclosing Report on the Financial Situation by E.N.R. Trentham, 3 July 1944, FO 371/40167; Sir Reader Bullard to A. Eden, 6 July 1944, Review of Events in Persia in April, May, June 1944, FO 371/40187.
27. V. Walter to F. Hale, 7 May 1944, X51/47, BBME.
28. Thorpe, 'Millspaugh', p.289.
29. Translation of letter from A.H. Ebtehaj to *Iran* newspaper, 14 Dec. 1944, enclosed in Tehran Confidential Letter to London, 25 Jan. 1945, X51/48, BBME.
30. Interview with A.H. Ebtejah; also Cook Interview, p.237.
31. Thorpe, 'Millspaugh', p.290, quoting Millspaugh's letter to US Chargé, 8 June 1944.
32. Thorpe, 'Millspaugh', pp.263, 292.
33. Lord Keynes to Sir David Waley, 30 May 1944, in D. Moggridge (ed), *The Collected Writings of J.M. Keynes*, Vol XXVI, *Activities 1941–46: Bretton Woods and Reparations* (London, 1980), pp.41–2.
34. Ibid, pp.197, 226; see also, E.565, Summary of Discussions at Bretton Woods, 3 Aug. 1944, FO 371/40919, and IBRD Articles of Agreement, FO 371/40920.
35. Telegram from Acting Secretary of State, Stettinius, to U.S. Chargé Tehran, 31 July 1944, *U.S. Foreign Relations*, 1944, V, pp.422–3.
36. Ibid; Thorpe, 'Millspaugh', pp.291–3; Barry Rubin, *Paved With Good Intentions* (New York, 1980), p.23; J.A. Bill, *The Eagle and The Lion* (London, 1988), p.46.
37. Note by A.H. Ebtehaj on pp.422–3, *U.S. Foreign Relations*, 1944, V; Memorandum by A.H. Ebtehaj, 16 Aug. 1986; C. Hull, *The Memoirs of Cordell Hull* (London, 1948), Vol. 2, p.1508.
38. Thorpe, 'Millspaugh', pp.292–3.
39. Cook Interview, p.123.
40. E.S. Mason & R.E. Asher, *The World Bank Since Bretton Woods* (Washington, 1973), pp.171–3; and also W. Diamond, 'Activities of the International Bank in the Middle East', *Middle East Journal*, III, 1949; for details of Iran's proposed loan

PLANNING AND POWER IN IRAN

application and other loan applications to the World Bank, see Bank Melli, 'Report of Executive Board for 1325 (1946– 47)' – the World Bank's first loans were, apart from one to Chile, all to European countries involved in post-war reconstruction.
41. L.S. Pressnell, 'The End of the Sterling Area', *The Three Banks Review*, (1979), pp.11–13; A. Cairncross, *Years of Recovery* (London, 1985), pp.88–120.
42. Mikesell, 'Sterling Area', p.169; Pressnell, 'The End', pp.11–13.
43. Telegram, FO to H.M. Embassy Tehran, 23 Feb. 1946, FO 371/52692.
44. Telegram, Sir Reader Bullard to FO, 28 Feb. 1946, FO 371/52692.
45. Telegram, Sir John Le Rougetel to FO, with message from W.A.B. Iliff, 24 Oct. 1946, FO 371/52695.
46. Telegram, Sir John Le Rougetel to FO, with message from W.A.B. Iliff, 3 Nov. 1946, FO 371/52695.
47. Sir John Le Rougetel to E. Bevin, 26 Nov. 1946, FO 371/52696: a Minute by L.F.L. Pyman, 16 Dec. 1946, on this despatch said: 'The reason the Treasury do not want these arrangements published is that Persia has had to be given exceptionally favourable treatment and the Treasury do not wish to encourage others to apply for the same treatment.'.
48. Telegram, W.A.B. Iliff to N.S. Roberts, 9 July 1947, FO 371/62017.
49. Cairncross, *Years of Recovery*, pp.121–64.
50. Brief by K. Anderson for HM Minister of State for Economic Affairs, for Financial Negotiations with Persia, 14 Sept. 1950, FO 371/82342; see also, Note by P.S. Beale, 1 Oct. 1947; Note for Minister, 16 Oct. 1947; Telegram 38, Sir John Le Rougetel to FO, 20 Dec. 1947; and *passim*; OV10/13, Bank of England.
51. P.S. Beale to Miss F.M. Loughnane, HM Treasury, 1 Oct. 1947, OV10/13, Bank of England.
52. Sir Wilfred Eady to Sir Orme Sargent, 13 Oct. 1947, FO 371/62017; Brief by K. Anderson, 14 Sept. 1950, FO 371/82342.
53. Sir Wilfred Eady to A.H. Ebtehaj, 7 Nov. 1947, OV10/13, Bank of England.
54. Memorandum by A.H. Ebtehaj, 16 Aug. 1986.
55. D.S. & P.G. Franck, 'The Middle East Economy in 1949', *Middle East Journal*, IV, 1950, p.221.
56. Telegram #3135, U.S. Embassy Tehran to Secretary of State Washington, 11 Feb. 1953, USSD.
57. Note #A–309 by James Somerville, U.S. Embassy Tehran, 10 Dec. 1949, USSD .
58. G. Lenczowski, *The Middle East in World Affairs* (London, 1980 edn), p.188; R.K. Ramazani, 'Iran and the United States: An Experiment in Enduring Friendship', *Middle East Journal*, 30, 1976, pp.324–5.
59. R. Cottam, *Nationalism in Iran*, (Pittsburgh, 1979 edn), p.208; Rubin, *Paved*, pp.41–2, 44–5.

CHAPTER FOUR

1. There is an extensive literature on the clash between the Iranian government and the Anglo-Iranian Oil Company. See especially R.W. Ferrier, *The History of the British Petroleum Company* Vol.1, *The Developing Years 1901–1932* (Cambridge, 1982), Chapter 13; P.J. Beck, 'The Anglo-Persian Oil Dispute 1932–33', *Journal of Contemporary History* (1975); R.B. Stobaugh, 'The Evolution of Iranian Oil Policy, 1925–1975', in G. Lenczowski (ed), *Iran Under the Pahlavis* (Stanford, 1978); R.W. Ferrier, 'The Development of the Iranian Oil Industry', in H. Amirsadeghi (ed), *Twentieth Century Iran* (London, 1977); L.P. Elwell-Sutton, *Persian Oil, A Study in Power Politics* (London, 1955).
2. See, for instance, V. Walter to F. Hale, 8 Feb. 1943, X51/45, BBME.
3. Memorandum by L.C. Payne, Chief Manager Imperial Bank, on his interview with A.H. Ebtehaj, 1 May 1948, X51/57, BBME.

REFERENCES

4. N.S. Roberts, H.M. Commercial Counsellor Tehran, to N.E. Young, H.M. Treasury, 27 Jan. 1948, OV10/13, Bank of England. Memorandum by L.C. Payne, 1 May 1948, X51/57; Draft Banking Law, enclosed in L.C. Payne to F. Ayrton, 22 Sept. 1948, X51/59; BBME.
5. Note by C.E. Loombe, 10 March 1948, OV10/13, Bank of England.
6. D. Merrett, *ANZ Bank: An Official History* (Sydney, 1985), pp.72–3.
7. Reported by P.S. Beale in Notes for the Governor, 2 Oct. 1947, in OV10/13, Bank of England.
8. Ibid.
9. H.A. Siepmann to N.E. Young, H.M. Treasury, 10 Feb. 1948, OV10/13, Bank of England.
10. P.S. Beale, Notes for the Governor, 2 Oct. 1947, OV10/13, Bank of England.
11. Minute by H.A. Siepmann on Ibid.
12. Telegram from Sir John Le Rougetel to FO, 40, 22 Oct. 1946, with message from Iliff about a discussion with Lord Kennet, FO 371/52695; See also, Notes on Lord Kennet's Visit to Iran and Iraq, 16 Nov. 1946, SG Box 100/24, BBME.
13. V. Walter to F. Hale, 22 Jan. 1947, X51/54; Memorandum by L.C. Payne, 1 May 1948, X51/57; BBME.
14. V. Walter to F. Ayrton, 7 January 1940, reporting conversation between A.H. Ebtehaj and H. Musker, X51/41, BBME.
15. V. Walter to F. Hale, 12 Jan. 1942, X51/44, BBME.
16. G. Jones, *Banking and Empire in Iran* (Cambridge, 1986), p.307.
17. Ibid, p.308.
18. Ibid, pp.320–1.
19. V. Walter to F. Hale, 15 Jan. and 18 Feb. 1946, X51/51, BBME.
20. V. Walter to F. Hale, 18 Feb. 1946, X51/51, BBME. Minute by W.A.B. Iliff, 4 Aug. 1946, FO 371/52694.
21. V. Walter to F. Hale, 18 Feb. 1946, X51/51, BBME.
22. Minute by W.A.B. Iliff, 4 Aug. 1946, FO 372/52694.
23. Jones, *Banking and Empire*, pp.321–2.
24. Ibid, p.322.
25. Ibid, pp.323–5.
26. Memorandum by A.H. Ebtehaj, March 1987; the records of the Imperial Bank – BBME Archives – confirm the details of the Dehlavi affair.
27. Quoted in Jones, *Banking and Empire*, p.324.
28. Note by C.E. Loombe, 9 Oct. 1947, OV10/13, Bank of England.
29. Jones, *Banking and Empire*, pp.326–9. The reason for the high level of 55% for deposits to be handed over to Bank Melli was the imperative need to safeguard Iran's bank of issue from the spectre of bankruptcy.
30. Minute by A. Leavett, 7 Nov. 1949, FO 371/75489.
31. Ibid; and Memorandum by the Governor of the Bank of England, enclosed with C.F. Cobbold to Sir Henry Wilson Smith, 12 Oct. 1949, FO 371/75489.
32. Jones, *Banking and Empire*, pp.331–2.
33. Sir John Le Rougetel to M.R. Wright, 27 June 1949, FO 371/75489.
34. H. Musker to F. Hale, 16 Sept. 1945, reporting a conversation between N.S. Roberts, IIM Commercial Counsellor Tehran, and M. Bader, Minister of Finance, X51/50, BBME.
35. V. Walter to F. Hale, 12 March 1946, X51/51, BBME.
36. R. Rountree, Deputy Director of Office of Greek, Turkish and Iranian Affairs, U.S. State Department, to J. Jernegan, Director, 23 March 1950, *U.S. Foreign Relations*, 1950, V, p.492.
37. Translation of article in *Seda-ye Mardom*, 14 December 1949, X51/63, BBME.
38. Memorandum by A.H. Ebtehaj, 16 Aug. 1986.
39. Despatch #D-40, U.S. Embassy Tehran to State Department, 24 July 1950, Report of Conversation with Prime Minister Razmara regarding A.H. Ebtehaj, U33D.

40. Ebtehaj had warned the Shah, through Ala, that Taghi Nasr's appointment would end in disaster. His reservations proved justified when in September 1950, Taghi Nasr deserted his post as head of Iran's delegation to the IMF meeting in Paris at which he was to have explained his policy of restoring multiple exchange rates: Memorandum by John Murray, 22 Aug. 1951, FO 371/91462. He later surfaced in the United States.
41. See for instance, despatch EP 1102/1, 29 Dec. 1949, FO 371/82333, regarding a conversation at the home of Prince Abdor Reza at which both the British and American Ambassadors were present. In addition, Ebtehaj later recalled details of a conversation in the United States between a friend of his and Gerry Dooher, a former U.S. Embassy official in Iran, in which Dooher 'snapped his fingers' and said 'I fired Ebtehaj': Memorandum by A.H. Ebtehaj, 16 Aug. 1986; Dooher's wheelings and dealings in Tehran are corroborated by R.L. Schott who was also in the U.S. Embassy at the time: Letter to Frances Bostock, 9 April 1986.
42. Memorandum by A.H. Ebtehaj, 16 Aug. 1986.
43. Ibid.

CHAPTER FIVE

1. For details on the progress towards economic planning in various countries, see B. Higgins, *Economic Development* (London, 1959), pp. 706, 726, 731, 749, 751. For Egypt, see R. Mabro and S. Radwan, *The Industrialisation of Egypt 1939–1973* (Oxford, 1976), p.65. For Iran see especially: G.B. Baldwin, *Planning and Development in Iran* (Baltimore, 1967); and also, L. Binder, *Iran: Political Development in a Changing Society* (Berkeley, California, 1962), pp.308–9; P.B. Olsen and P.N. Rasmussen, 'An Attempt at Planning in a Traditional State: Iran', in E.E. Hagen (ed), *Planning Economic Development* (Holmewood, Illinois, 1963); H. Mehner, 'Development and Planning in Iran after World War 1', in G. Lenczowski (ed), *Iran Under the Pahlavis* (Stanford, 1978); H. Razavi and F. Vakil, *The Political Environment of Economic Planning in Iran, 1971–1983* (Boulder, Colorado, 1984), Chapter 2; S. Rezazadeh Shafaq, 'The Iranian Seven Year Development Plan', and J. Lotz, 'Problems and Proposals', *The Middle East Journal*, IV, 1950, pp.100–5; Jahangir Amouzegar, 'Capital Formation and Development Finance', in E. Yar-Shater (ed), *Iran Faces the Seventies* (New York, 1971). For the Colonial Development Corporation in the British Empire, see D.J. Morgan, *The Official History of Colonial Development* (London, 1980), Vol 2, Chapter 6; Vol 4, Chapters 5 and 6.
2. Cook Interview, pp.36, 255–71.
3. Quoted in Baldwin, *Planning*, p.25, fn. 3. Baldwin's information came from Bank Melli Bulletin, No. 75, April/May 1945, pp.1–12.
4. Cook Interview, pp.38, 266.
5. Baldwin, *Planning*, p.25, fn. 3.
6. Ibid, pp.24–5.
7. Ibid, p.25.
8. Mehner, 'Development', p.168. Mehner does not mention Ebtehaj, referring only to 'officials', but he cites the Bank Melli as his source, and that meant Ebtehaj. Baldwin, *Planning*, makes it quite plain that the initiative was all Ebtehaj's at this stage.
9. Cook Interview, p.277.
10. H.L. Farquhar to FO, 9 April 1946, FO 371/52763.
11. Translation of Qavam's statement, quoted in Ibid.
12. Baldwin, *Planning*, p.25.
13. *New York Herald Tribune*, 12 March 1947.
14. Interview of Dr Khodadad Farmanfarmaian by Habib Ladjevardi, *Iranian Oral*

REFERENCES

History Project, Harvard University Center for Middle Eastern Studies, November 1982 (hereafter, Harvard Project: Farmanfarmaian Interview), Tape 3, p.25. The view that economic growth would automatically lead to higher living standards and, especially, social equity, has been largely disproven by the experience of many developing countries in the 1960s and 1970s. This has led to a refocusing of attention in development planning towards problems of poverty and unemployment, and the view that success in dealing with social problems of this kind would have a favourable impact on growth. Ebtehaj's views, of course, were formulated at a time when mainstream development thinking concentrated on generating economic growth. See, for example, M.S. Ahluwalia, N.G. Carter and H.B. Chenery, 'Growth and Development in Developing Countries', *Journal of Development Economics*, (1979), and Gary S. Fields, 'Who Benefits from Economic Development? – A Re-examination of Brazilian Growth in the 1960s', *American Economic Review* (1979).

15. A. Gerschenkron, *Economic Backwardness in Historical Perspective* (New York, 1962).
16. A.H. Ebtehaj, 'A Program for Economic Growth', paper delivered at *International Industrial Conference*, Stanford Research Institute, San Francisco, Sept. 1961.
17. Baldwin, *Planning*, pp.25–6.
18. Minute by D.A. Greenhill, 9 May 1946, E. 3678; and draft letter FO to HM Ambassador Tehran, 20 May 1946, FO 371/52763. See also, Minute by R.A. Clinton-Thomas, 31 Dec. 1948, FO 371/68709.
19. Dean Acheson to W. Byrnes, 1 Oct. 1946, in *U.S. Foreign Relations*, 1946, VII, p.520, Minute by R.A. Clinton-Thomas, 31 Dec. 1948, FO 371/68709.
20. Olsen and Rasmussen, 'An Attempt', p.224; Baldwin, *Planning*, p.26.
21. Minute by C. Gandy, 6 Dec. 1946, E. 11741, FO 371/52696.
22. See, for instance, Ibid; and C.W. Baxter to J.H. Le Rougetel, 22 Jan. 1947, FO 371/62003.
23. Telegram from J.H. Le Rougetel to FO, 28 March 1947, FO 371/62001.
24. Information from A.H. Ebtehaj; Note by W.A.B. Iliff, enclosed with J.H. Le Rougetel to E. Bevin, 24 Nov. 1946, FO 371/52696.
25. J.H. Le Rougetel to E. Bevin, 31 Dec. 1946, FO 371/62003.
26. Summary of the Morrison Knudsen Report on the Persian Development Programme, shown confidentially to the British Commercial Counsellor by his American colleague, and copy enclosed with Board of Trade to Miss Waterlow, 24 Sept. 1947, FO 371/62003.
27. C. Van H. Engert's Report on Conversations with A.H. Ebtehaj, Dec. 1948, enclosed in Sir J. Troutbeck to B. Burrows, 22 Feb. 1949, FO 371/75483.
28. J.H. Le Rougetel to M.R. Wright, 17 March 1948, FO 371/68712.
29. Baldwin, *Planning*, p.28. Max Weston Thornburg, who was to be the leader of the OCI mission to Iran in 1949, described Naficy's Report as 'the best summary statement of its kind that I have seen in any of the countries I have studied' – Memorandum by Thornburg, 12 March 1948, enclosed in J.H. Le Rougetel to M.R. Wright, 17 March 1948, FO 371/68712.
30. Summary of Preliminary Report of Persian Seven-Year Plan, by Dr. Mosharef Naficy, Chairman of the Supreme Planning Board, enclosed with J.H. Le Rougetel to E. Bevin, 28 Jan. 1948, FO 371/68711.
31. J.H. Le Rougetel to E. Bevin, 28 Jan. 1948, FO 371/68711.
32. Note for C.E. Loombe, Bank of England, from FO, 27 Feb. 1948, OV10/13, Bank of England.
33. Summary of Naficy Report, in J.H. Le Rougetel to E. Bevin, 28 Jan. 1948, FO 371/68711; and C.E. Loombe's preliminary analysis of the Naficy Report for H.A. Siepmann, 3 March 1948, OV10/13, Bank of England.
34. E.A. Bayne, *Persian Kingship in Transition* (New York, 1968), p.115.
35. Naficy Report, E. 2672, 4 Feb. 1948, FO 371/68711; M.J. Cresswell to E. Bevin, 12

May 1948, FO 371/68712.
36. Baldwin, *Planning*, pp.28–9.
37. A. Vaidyanathan, 'The Indian Economy since Independence (1947–70)', in D. Kumar (ed), *The Cambridge Economic History of India* (Cambridge, 1983), Vol 2, p.950.
38. Harvard Project: Farmanfarmaian Interview, Tape 3, p.14.
39. Ibid.
40. Ibid, Tape 10, p.9; Tape 4, p.19.
41. J.H. Le Rougetel to E. Bevin, 1 Dec. 1948, FO 371/68714A; Baldwin, *Planning*, p.29.
42. J.H. Le Rougetel to E. Bevin, 1 Dec. 1948, FO 371/68714A.
43. Interview with A.H. Ebtehaj, Dec. 1986.
44. J.H. Le Rougetel to M.R. Wright, 17 March 1948, FO 371/68712.
45. J.H. Le Rougetel to E. Bevin, 1 Dec. 1948, FO 371/68714A. See Baldwin, *Planning*, for the extent of Thornburg's involvement. Ebtehaj disputes the fact that Thornburg was as closely involved in the 1946–48 period as Baldwin suggests – Interviews with A.H. Ebtehaj.
46. Interview with A.H. Ebtehaj, Dec. 1986.
47. Baldwin, *Planning*, p.51; Report by H.R. Stewart on OCI Tour of Central Persia, 30 Nov. 1948, FO 371/68714A.
48. Interview with A.H. Ebtehaj, Dec. 1986.
49. H.R. Stewart's Report, 30 Nov. 1948, FO 371/68714A; for Lotz's views on the Plan, see J. Lotz, 'Problems and Proposals'.
50. C. Van H. Engert's Report on Conversations with A.H. Ebtehaj, in Sir J. Troutbeck to B. Burrows, 22 Feb. 1949, FO 371/75483.
51. Baldwin, *Planning*, pp.30–1.
52. Cook Interview, pp.286–7.
53. Talk to Iran–America Society, 16 July 1958, transcript enclosed with Despatch #79, US Embassy Tehran to State Department, 29 July 1958, USSD 888.00 Seven Year/7–2958 HBS.
54. Enabling Bill for Plan, Sept. 1948, enclosed in J.H. Le Rougetel to E. Bevin, 1 Dec. 1948, FO 371/68714A.
55. N.S. Roberts to N.E. Young, 22 Oct. 1947, enclosing Memorandum of his conversation in London with Mr Pineo on 20 Sept. 1947, OV10/13, Bank of England.
56. Ibid; and Minute by L.F.L. Pyman, 15 Sept. 1948, E.12379, FO 371/ 68731, from which the quotation comes. For the World Bank and Iran at this time, see Edward S. Mason and Robert E. Asher, *The World Bank Since Bretton Woods* (Washington, 1973), pp.171–3.
57. N.S. Roberts to N.E. Young, 22 Oct. 1947, OV10/13, Bank of England.
58. For example, when he was in Washington in Oct. 1948 for the annual IMF meeting. In conversations with Cornelius Van Engert in Tehran, Dec. 1948 – see Engert's Report in Sir J. Troutbeck to B. Burrows, 22 Feb. 1949, FO 371/75483.
59. For the World Bank's view on individual project finance, see, for instance, W.A.B. Iliff's remarks in confidence to H.M. Ambassador Washington, Sir Oliver Franks, reported in Telegram 430, 21 Jan. 1949, FO 371/75482. Iliff was by this time a senior member of the World Bank's Loan Department.
60. Telegram from Acting Secretary of State, Washington to U.S. Embassy Tehran, 28 Sept. 1949, in *U.S. Foreign Relations*, 1949, VI, p.562; see also, George McGhee, *Envoy to the Middle World: Adventures in Diplomacy* (New York, 1983), p.75.
61. Telegram from Acting Secretary of State, Washington to U.S. Embassy Tehran, 9 Nov. 1949, in *U.S. Foreign Relations*, 1949, VI, p.567. Military aid at this time, when Iran's armed forces were still suffering from wartime debilitation, was not the controversial issue it was later to become, nor contemplated on anything like the same scale.
62. Notes on Development Schemes in the Middle East, Iran, for discussion with the

REFERENCES

President of the World Bank, 25 April 1949, E.5211, FO 371/75085.
63. Memorandum on the Financial Aspect of Persia's Development Programme, by H.M. Commercial Counsellor Tehran, 15 Sept. 1947, FO 371/62003.
64. Baldwin, *Planning*, pp.31–3.
65. Sir Francis Shepherd to K.G. Younger, 9 Sept. 1950, and Minutes: especially Minute by L. Barnett, 6 Oct. 1950, FO 371/82334.
66. Ibid.
67. J. Bharier, *Economic Development in Iran 1900–1970* (London, 1971), p.81.
68. Cook Interview, pp.309–10.
69. Ibid, pp.315.
70. Ibid, pp.318–22, 311–15.
71. Telegram #175, U.S. Embassy Tehran to State Department, 21 July 1950, USSD.
72. Ibid.
73. Cook Interview, pp.324–5.
74. Ibid, pp.326–46 and interviews with A.H. Ebtehaj.
75. On Mossadeq, see, for instance, S. Zabih, *The Mossadegh Era* (Chicago, 1982); Farhad Diba, *Mohammad Mossadegh, A Political Biography* (London, 1986). On American policy towards Mossadeq and its consequences, see Barry Rubin, *Paved With Good Intentions* (New York, 1980), Chapter 3; Kermit Roosevelt, *Countercoup – The Struggle for the Control of Iran* (New York, 1979); Dean Acheson, *Present At the Creation* (New York, 1969), Chapter 52, pp.499–511, and Chapter 71, pp.679–85. Bill, James A. and Louis Wm. Roger (eds), *Musaddiq, Iranian Nationalism, and Oil* (London, 1988).
76. Cook Interview, pp.355–62. The Chairman of the Joint Oil Committee was Sepahbodi, and he related this story to Ebtehaj in Washington soon after it happened.
77. W.R. Louis, *The British Empire in the Middle East 1945–1951* (Oxford, 1984), pp.651–3, 689. Sir Francis Shepherd, British Ambassador in Tehran between 1950 and 1952, regularly referred to Mossadeq as a 'lunatic'.
78. For similar views on Mossadeq, see R.W. Cottam, *Nationalism in Iran* (Pittsburgh, 1964), pp.270–2. It should be noted, however, that Ebtehaj had little respect for the Anglo-Iranian Oil Company either and was critical of its policies in Iran. He later recalled his opinion of William Fraser, the Chairman of the Company at the time of nationalisation: 'Fraser . . . was a person who was not capable of understanding the feelings that the people of Iran had towards his company. When I met him for the first time in London in 1947 and he asked me to lunch with him and a number of his directors, I expressed my sentiments regarding the attitude of his company towards Iran. At that time Iran was receiving 20% of the company's net profits. I told Fraser that Iranians did not even know how this insignificant 20% of the net profits of the company was arrived at and I suggested that we name a British firm of auditors to carry out an audit to assure us that Iran's interests under the existing concession were protected. His answer was "over my dead body".' – Note by A.H. Ebtehaj, enclosed in A.H. Ebtehaj to F. Bostock, 19 Dec. 1986; Cook Interview, pp.353–4.
79. Telegram #870, U.S. Embassy Tehran to State Department, 10 Oct. 1953, USSD.
80. Cook Interview, pp.367–8; Memorandum by A.H. Ebtehaj, 22 Aug. 1986.
81. Memorandum by A.H. Ebtehaj, 22 Aug. 1986.
82. Cook Interview, pp.368–72; Memorandum by A.H. Ebtehaj, 22 Aug. 1986.

CHAPTER SIX

1. H. Razavi and F. Vakil, *The Political Environment of Economic Planning in Iran, 1971–1983* (Boulder, Colorado, 1984), pp.20–1; G.B. Baldwin, *Planning and Development in Iran* (Baltimore, 1967), pp.197–8; E.A. Bayne, *Persian Kingship in Transition* (New York, 1968), pp.144–5; Farhad Daftary, 'Development

Planning in Iran: A Historical Survey', *Iranian Studies*, (1973); Kamran Mofid, *Development Planning in Iran* (Wisbech, Cambs, 1988).
2. Baldwin, *Planning*, p.40.
3. Telegram from Sir George Binney, United Steel Companies, to A.H. Ebtehaj, 10 Dec. 1954, and other telegraphic correspondence in the same month between the United Steel Companies, the FO and HM's Tehran Embassy, FO 371/110025.
4. A. Michaelis, 'The Middle East Economy in 1950', *Middle East Journal*, 5, 1951, p.227. See also, R.L. Greaves, '1942–1976: The Reign of Muhammad Riza Shah', in H. Amirsadeghi (ed), *Twentieth Century Iran* (London, 1977), pp.68–9; and, generally, Baldwin, *Planning*, pp.31–5.
5. These were predictable reactions; see, for instance, T. Cuyler Young, cited by Greaves, '1942–1976', p.69; J. Amuzegar, *Technical Assistance in Theory and Practice: The Case of Iran* (New York, 1966), pp.101–2.
6. Amuzegar, *Technical Assistance*, pp.103–5. For a description of the Point Four programme in Iran from the point of view of one of its directors, see W.E. Warne, *Mission for Peace* (Indianapolis, 1956).
7. Telegrams #549 and #825, U.S. Embassy Tehran to Secretary of State, Washington, 4 Sept. and 7 Oct. 1954, USSD; Record of Meeting at HM Treasury on 19 Nov. 1954, at which Hector Prud'homme reported on his visit to Tehran, 22 Nov. 1954, OV10/18, Bank of England; British Embassy Economic Reports for Sept. and Nov. 1954, FO 371/110003. For details on past and prospective U.S. aid, see Report by Mr Milner on his visit to Iran in Nov. 1954, OV10/18, Bank of England: having allocated some $20 to $24 million a year to Iran under Point Four aid from 1951 on, the U.S. Aid programme in the fiscal year 1954–55 was planned to amount to $127 million (including Point Four aid of $21.5 million); $42 million of this was to be grant aid and $85 million in the form of loans – including Export–Import (EXIM) Bank credits of $53 million for approved development projects, and loans for budget and trade support.
8. Despatch #570, Enclosure 1, re Ebtehaj's Press Conference on 12 June 1955, U.S. Embassy Tehran to State Department, 22 June 1955, USSD 888.00/6-2255.
9. A.H. Ebtehaj to H. Prud'homme, 1 Dec. 1954, enclosed in J.L.B. Titchener to FO, 15 Dec. 1954, FO 371/110004. See also, Despatch #780, U.S. Embassy Tehran to State Department, 14 March 1956, USSD 888.00/3-1456.
10. See, Frances Bostock and Geoffrey Jones, 'British Business in Iran, 1860s–1970s', in Richard Davenport-Hines and Geoffrey Jones (eds), *British Business in Asia Since 1860* (Cambridge, 1988), 57, 61–2.
11. Razavi and Vakil, *Political Environment*, p 21.
12. Baldwin, *Planning*, pp.197–8. The phrase 'a government within a government' appears more than once in U.S. State Department documents: see, for example, Airgram #A–1635, W.E. Warne, U.S. Embassy Tehran to Foreign Operations Administration (FOA), 7 March 1955, USSD.
13. Harvard Project: Farmanfarmaian Interview, Tape 4, pp.1–2.
14. D.E. Lilienthal, *The Road to Change 1955–1959*, Vol IV of *The Journals of David E. Lilienthal* (New York, 1969), p.180.
15. Notes by A.H. Ebtehaj on USSD documents, 24 Oct. 1986.
16. Memorandum by A.H. Ebtehaj, 22 Aug. 1986.
17. Sir Roger Stevens to A. Eden, 22 Feb. 1955, FO 371/114823.
18. Harvard Project: Farmanfarmaian Interview, Tape 3, pp.14–16.
19. Sir Roger Stevens to A. Eden, 22 Feb. 1955, FO 371/114823; see also, Airgram #A–1635, W.E. Warne, U.S. Embassy Tehran to FOA, 7 March 1955, USSD.
20. Despatch #583, U.S. Embassy Tehran to State Department, 21 Feb. 1959, USSD 888.00 Seven Year/2–2159.
21. R. Cottam, *Nationalism in Iran* (Pittsburgh, 1964), p.290.
22. Sir Roger Stevens to A. Eden, 22 Feb. 1955, FO 371/114823.
23. Account of a conversation between Shapur Reporter, *The Times* correspondent, Tehran, and A.H. Ebtehaj, enclosed with Sir Roger Stevens to L.A.C. Fry, 15

REFERENCES

March 1955, FO 371/114823.
24. Minute by L.A.C. Fry, 19 Feb. 1955; Telegram Sir Roger Stevens to FO, 21 March 1955, FO 371/114810. See also, *The Economist*, 25 June 1955, p.1135 (the author of this article, according to the FO, was Elizabeth Monroe).
25. Harvard Project: Farmanfarmaian Interview, Tape 3, pp.27-8.
26. Telegrams Sir Roger Stevens to FO, 21 March 1955 and 6 April 1955, FO 371/114810.
27. Memorandum by A.H. Ebtehaj, 24 Oct. 1986; Telegram #2425, U.S. Embassy Tehran to Secretary of State, 14 June 1955, USSD.
28. Despatch #363, U.S. Embassy Tehran to State Department, 16 Nov. 1955, and enclosures, USSD D.351986.
29. Despatch #435, U.S. Embassy Tehran to State Department, 6 Dec. 1955, USSD 788.00/12-655; Despatch #780, U.S. Embassy Tehran to State Department, 14 March 1956, USSD 888.00/3-1456.
30. Notes by A.H. Ebtehaj on PRO documents, 24 Oct. 1986; Eugene Black to F. Bostock, May 1986 – Mr Black commented that Ebtehaj's appointment to the Plan Organisation and his management of it 'were of utmost importance to us in our dealing with Iran'. See also, Proceedings of the 180th Board Meeting of the World Bank, 11 Oct. 1956.
31. H. Prud'homme to A.H. Ebtehaj, 25 May 1983.
32. Ibid; see also Telegram from HM Ambassador Washington to FO, 26 April 1955, FO 371/114823.
33. Telegram HM Ambassador Washington to FO, 26 April 1955, FO 371/114823; Telegram HM Ambassador Washington to FO, 27 May 1955, FO 371/114824.
34. H. Prud'homme to A.H. Ebtehaj, 25 May 1983; Despatch #363, U.S. Embassy Tehran to State Department, 16 Nov. 1955, USSD D.351986. See also Memorandum by A.H. Ebtehaj, 24 Oct. 1986: in Ebtehaj's view, Binger performed an outstanding job.
35. H. Prud'homme to A.E. Ebtehaj, 25 May 1983.
36. Khodadad Farmanfarmaian, 'Formation and Development of Economic Bureau 1336-1342 (1959-1963)', Report submitted to *The Ford Foundation* (Tehran, 1963), pp.3-5, 11, 114 ff; see also, Plan Organisation, Division of Economic Affairs, *Review of the Second Seven Year Plan Program* (Tehran, 1960).
37. Despatch #876, U.S. Embassy Tehran to State Department, 26 April 1958, USSD 888.00/4-2658 HBS.
38. Ibid; and Despatch #24, U.S. Embassy Tehran to State Department, 9 July 1958, USSD 888.00/7-958; Memorandum by IBRD on Iranian Plan Organisation and Foreign Engineering Personnel, supplied by H. Prud'homme, SOA(55)13, Annex 1, FO 371/114824. See also, Plan Organisation, *Review*.
39. Despatch #876, U.S. Embassy Tehran to State Department, 26 April 1958, USSD 888.00/4-2658 HBS.
40. See, for instance, Despatch #53, U.S. Embassy Tehran to State Department, describing the Plan Organisation in the Isfahan Consular District, 9 June 1958, USSD 888.00 Seven Year/6-958.
41. Eric J. Hooglund, *Land and Revolution in Iran 1960 1980* (Austin, Texas, 1982), pp.45-6.
42. Despatch #24, U.S. Embassy Tehran to State Department, 9 July 1958, USSD 888.00/7-958.
43. Despatch #583, U.S. Embassy Tehran to State Department, 21 Feb. 1959, USSD 888.00 Seven Year/2-2159. Ebtehaj would never have described himself as an economist, but rather as an administrator and organiser.
44. Memorandum by A.H. Ebtehaj, 22 Aug. 1986.
45. Ibid.
46. Despatch #887, U.S. Embassy Tehran to State Department, 18 April 1956, USSD 888.00 Seven Year/4-1856.
47. Despatch #887, U.S. Embassy Tehran to State Department, 18 April 1956, USSD

888.00 Seven Year/4–1856; Razavi and Vakil, *Political Environment*, pp.22–4; J. Bharier, *Economic Development in Iran 1900–1970* (London, 1971), p.91. Eighteen months after the start of the Second Plan, a 20% increase in the total expenditure allocation was approved, bringing this to 84 billion *rials* (about $1105 million); in 1958, there was a complete reappraisal, and a revised Plan was presented based on actual expenditures at the half-way stage and estimated expenditures for the second half: see Despatch #1130, U.S. Embassy Tehran to State Department, 23 June 1958, USSD 888.00 Seven Year/6–2358; Despatch #24, U.S. Embassy Tehran to State Department, 9 July 1958, USSD 888.00/7–958; Bharier, *Economic Development*, pp.92–3; B. Olson and P.N. Rasmussen, 'An Attempt at Planning in a Traditional State: Iran', in E.E. Hagen (ed), *Planning Economic Development* (Holmewood, Illinois, 1963), p.232.
48. Razavi and Vakil, *Political Environment*, pp.24–5; see also, Baldwin, *Planning*, p.40, which suggests that the inflationary pressures and overheating of the economy towards the end of the 1950s, resulting in the need to resort to the IMF's 'stiff medicine' and the consequent recession, were caused by a major boom in private investment which generated such excesses as rising prices and falling exchange reserves. A combination of factors was responsible for the private investment boom – the unprecedentedly high level of government expenditure outside the Plan, the Plan's own large development expenditure, the availability of liberal bank credit, and easy access to foreign exchange.
49. Bharier, *Economic Development*, pp.42–5, 49–56, 58–9; C. Issawi, 'The Economy: An Assessment of Performance', in E. Yar-Shater (ed), *Iran Faces The Seventies* (New York, 1971), pp.46–50; C. Issawi, 'The Iranian Economy 1925–1975: Fifty Years of Economic Development', in G. Lenczowski (ed), *Iran Under the Pahlavis* (Stanford, 1978), pp.140–1; Homa Katouzian, *The Political Economy of Modern Iran* (London, 1981), pp.229, 255–7. Bharier estimates that Gross Domestic Fixed Capital Formation (GDFCF) rose from some 18.1 billion *rials* at current market prices in 1953 to 71.5 billion *rials* in 1959. GDFCF was 34.1 billion *rials* in 1955. After falling between 1960 and 1963 – to 56.3 billion *rials* in the latter year – it shot up to 100.9 billion *rials* in 1965: see Table 5, pp.50–1. See also, Jahangir Amouzegar, *Iran: An Economic Profile* (Washington, 1977). For comparative growth statistics for each decade 1950–1980, see Lloyd G. Reynolds, *Economic Growth in the Third World: An Introduction* (New Haven, 1986), p.79: between 1960 and 1970, Reynolds gives Iran a 6.7% rate of growth of real GDP per capita – South Korea and Taiwan had 6.4%, Turkey 3.4% and India 1.2%.
50. Jahangir Amuzegar, 'Capital Formation and Development Finance', in Yar-Shater (ed), *Iran Faces the Seventies*.
51. Interview with Dr Reza Moghaddam, 25 March 1987.
52. For example, R.K. Ramazani, 'Who Lost America? The Case of Iran', *The Middle East Journal*, 36, No. 1, 1982.
53. Harvard Project: Farmanfarmaian Interview, Tape 2, pp.18–19: Farmanfarmaian was involved in drawing up the Third Plan, and remained in the Plan Organisation after Ebtehaj had resigned.
54. Derived from Enclosure 1, Report on Plan Organisation Development Budget 1337–1341 (1958–9 to 1961–2) in Despatch #1130, U.S. Embassy Tehran to State Department, 23 June 1958, USSD 888.00 Seven Year/6–2358.
55. Despatch #442, U.S. Embassy Tehran to State Department, 28 Nov. 1956, USSD 888.00 Seven Year/11–2856 HBS.
56. Memorandum by A.H. Ebtehaj, 16 Aug. 1986. The promise of $40 million came directly from John Foster Dulles when he visited Iran in 1956.
57. Transcript of 180th Board Meeting of World Bank, 11 Oct. 1956. Non-specific ('program') loans had been made to European countries and Australia before 1957, but the 1957 loan to Iran was the first to a developing country: see Edward S. Mason and Robert E. Asher, *The World Bank Since Bretton Woods* (Washington, 1973), pp.264, 274.

REFERENCES

58. Memorandum by A.H. Ebtehaj, 16 Aug. 1986. Black's willingness to back Ebtehaj, and take the World Bank in new directions in so doing (viz. the Technical Bureau and the $75 million loan), provides a salutary counter-balance to the picture of him as one of the World Bank's more conservative Presidents: see, for instance, Cheryl Payer, *The World Bank: A Critical Analysis* (New York, 1982), pp.24–5.
59. Transcript of 180th Board Meeting of World Bank, 11 Oct. 1956.
60. Ibid.
61. Telegram #976, U.S. Embassy Tehran to State Department, 27 Dec. 1956, USSD 888.00 Seven Year/12–2756 HBS. One difficulty, which, apart from the opposition of many deputies, delayed approval, was the firm pledge of oil revenues allocated to the Plan Organisation insisted on by the World Bank since the agreement for EXIM Bank's $53 million line of credit, granted to Iran in 1954 (of which only $19 million had been spent by 1956), contained a 'negative pledge' clause pertaining to oil revenues as a whole. EXIM Bank had to be persuaded to accept payment out of those oil revenues not allocated to the Plan Organisation, and eventually was – Telegram #1293, State Department to U.S. Embassy Tehran, 10 Jan. 1957, USSD 888.00 Seven Year/1–857.
62. Farmanfarmaian, Report to *Ford Foundation*, op.cit, pp.98, 90ff. Some of these loans spilled over into the Third Plan period – the foreign loan revenue utilised during the Second Plan period was about $320 million in all: see figures in Bharier, *Economic Development*, pp.93–4, Tables 4 and 5.
63. 'Iran: Dez Multipurpose Project', in J.A. King, *Economic Development Projects and their Appraisal: Cases and Principles from the Experience of the World Bank* (Baltimore, 1967), p.210, and ff. For details of the loans raised, see Farmanfarmaian, Report to *Ford Foundation*, pp.90ff.
64. King, *Economic*, p.219; Payer, *World Bank*, pp.272–3.
65. Memorandum by A.H. Ebtehaj, 16 Aug. 1986.
66. Olsen and Rasmussen, 'An Attempt', p.232; Baldwin, *Planning*, pp.114–17.
67. Bharier, *Economic Development*, pp.93–4; Olsen and Rasmussen, 'An Attempt' pp.234–5.
68. Private Briefing for U.S. Embassy Staff by Plan Organisation, reported in Despatch #90, U.S. Embassy Tehran to State Department, 23 July 1957, USSD 888.00/7–2257.
69. Memorandum by A.H. Ebtehaj, 3 Nov. 1986.
70. Ibid; Despatch #565, U.S. Embassy Tehran to State Department, 14 Jan. 1957, USSD 888.00 Seven Year/1–1457.
71. Despatch #876, U.S. Embassy Tehran to State Department, 26 April 1958, USSD 888.00/4–2658.
72. Development & Resources Corporation, 'The Unified Development of the Resources of the Khuzestan Region', *Report to Plan Organisation* (Iran, March 1959), pp.1–8.
73. See Reports by Major G.W. Binnie of Paiforce, and Lt. Col. E.W.C. Noel, on schemes for the development of Khuzestan, in 1944 (the damming of rivers, various forms of irrigation, power generation, schemes for regenerating the manufacture of sugar from cane, etc, were covered), FO 371/40212. See also R.W. Bullard to Sir Olaf Caroe, Government of India, 18 Aug. 1944, re possibility of financial assistance for these schemes, FO 371/40212; and FO Minute, 10 Sept. 1946, re 1942 loan to Khuzestan Agricultural Society and the current status of that Society, E.9104, FO 371/52785.
74. G.R. Clapp, 'Iran: A TVA for the Khuzestan Region', *The Middle East Journal*, 11, 1957, p.2; Memorandum by A.H. Ebtehaj, 21 July 1986.
75. See, for instance, Paper on Economic and Social Development in the Middle East, 11 April 1949, prepared by FO for the first meeting of the Working Party of the new Government Economic Development Committee, E.4719, FO 371/75084; also FO 371/75083–92 *passim*. See also, F. Bochenski and W. Diamond, 'TVAs in the Middle East', in *The Middle East Journal*, IV, 1950, pp.52–82.

PLANNING AND POWER IN IRAN

76. In 1945, as Governor of the Bank Melli, Ebtehaj had had discussions in London about the possibility of finding a group to harness the waters of the Karun and develop the region. The Karun Irrigation Scheme was described as a 'pet scheme of his' – see comments of Colonel George Bridges, enclosed with J.L.B. Titchener to L.A.C. Fry, 11 Jan. 1955, FO 371/114850.
77. Notes by A.H. Ebtehaj on PRO documents, July 1986. Lilienthal, *Road to Change*, pp.3–4, 26. Black had already suggested to Lilienthal in June 1955 that Iran might well prove to be an area requiring D & R's help.
78. Lilienthal, *Road to Change*, p.26.
79. Memoranda by A.H. Ebtehaj, 10 July 1986.
80. Ibid, 21 July 1986.
81. Lilienthal, *Road to Change*, pp.77–9; Clapp, 'Iran', pp.2–3; Ebtehaj, Memoranda.
82. Clapp, 'Iran', pp.2, 5; Lilienthal, *Road to Change*, pp.79–83.
83. Clapp, 'Iran', p.6.
84. D. & R. Report to Plan Organisation, p.13. For the whole unified programme see this Report; also, comments by F.R.C. Bagley, 'A Bright Future after Oil: Dams and Agro-Industry in Khuzistan', in *The Middle East Journal*, 30, 1976; Clapp, 'Iran'; Olsen and Rasmussen, 'An Attempt'; and others.
85. Olsen and Rasmussen, 'An Attempt'.
86. Ibid; Razavi and Vakil, *Political Environment*; Amuzegar, *Economic Profile*; Despatch #876, U.S. Embassy Tehran to State Department, 26 April 1958, USSD 888.00/4–2658 HBS.
87. Baldwin, *Planning*, pp.104–110, 114–20. See also, Joseph Kane, *Development Banking* (Lexington, 1975), pp.109–110; Mason and Asher, *World Bank*, p.369.
88. Note by A.H. Ebtehaj, April 1987.
89. Baldwin, *Planning*, pp.146–7.
90. Cook Interview, pp.56–9; Memorandum by A.H. Ebtehaj, 24 March 1987; H. Prud'homme to A.H. Ebtehaj, 25 May 1983.
91. R. Graham, *Iran: The Illusion of Power* (London, 1978), p.196; Baldwin, *Planning*, p.197.
92. Razavi and Vakil, *Political Environment*, p.41.
93. Despatch #887, U.S. Embassy Tehran to State Department, 18 April 1956, USSD 888.00 Seven Year/4–1856.
94. Despatch #90, U.S. Embassy Tehran to State Department, 23 July 1957, USSD 888.00/7–2257; Despatch #876, U.S. Embassy to State Department, 26 April 1958, USSD 888.00/4–2658 HBS.
95. Baldwin, *Planning*, p.46.
96. Ibid, p.198.

CHAPTER SEVEN

1. Despatch #583, U.S. Embassy Tehran to State Department, 21 Feb. 1959, USSD 888.00 Seven Year/2–2159 HBS.
2. P. Avery, *Modern Iran* (London, 1965), p.93.
3. R.K. Ramazani, 'Who Lost America? The Case of Iran', *The Middle East Journal*, 36, 1, 1982, p.17.
4. E.A. Bayne, *Persian Kingship in Transition* (New York, 1968), pp.188–9: the Shah's remark was made to Bayne himself in the 1960s.
5. See, for instance, R. Cottam, *Nationalism in Iran* (Pittsburgh, 1964), p.289; Despatch #583, U.S. Embassy Tehran to State Department, 21 Feb. 1959, USSD 888.00 Seven Year/2–2159 HBS; Sir Roger Stevens to C.A.E. Shuckburgh, 7 July 1955, FO 371/114810, quoting the Shah; Minute by D. Logan, 6 May 1952, FO 371/98729; Memorandum by A.H. Ebtehaj, 18 Nov. 1986.
6. Sir Roger Stevens to C.A.E. Shuckburgh, 7 July 1955, FO 371/114810.

REFERENCES

7. A.C. Millspaugh, *Americans in Persia* (New York, 1976 edn), p.95: while these comments are Millspaugh's, they are amply backed by similar remarks from British and American diplomats.
8. In order of quotation, the sources are D.A.H. Wright to P. Broad, 21 Sept. 1955, FO 371/114825; Note by James Somerville, Airgram #A-309 U.S. Embassy Tehran to State Department, 10 Dec. 1949, USSD; Note on Persian Political Personalities enclosed in A.D.M. Ross to Sir Patrick Scrivener, 16 May 1952, FO 371/98729.
9. See, notably, *Bamshad*, 22 Jan. 1959, in which the editor, Ismail Poorvali, hitherto a consistent critic of Ebtehaj, leapt to his defence on hearing a rumour that he had resigned from the Plan Organisation under pressure. Poorvali described Ebtehaj as 'a respected figure in his own field' with 'certain outstanding qualities', who had served his country to 'an outstanding degree': translation of this editorial is attached to Despatch #503, U.S. Embassy Tehran to State Department, 24 Jan. 1959, USSD 788.00/1-2459.
10. D.E. Lilienthal, *The Road to Change 1955-1959*, Vol IV of *The Journals of David E. Lilienthal* (New York, 1969), p.131; see also, p.324.
11. Memorandum of a Conversation between L.P. Ralston, J. Fried and E.R. Freeman, State Department, 6 Oct. 1955, USSD.
12. Lilienthal, *Road to Change*, p.350: quoting, directly, Khosrow Hedayat, Ebtehaj's successor at the Plan Organisation.
13. *Tehran Journal*, 18 Jan. 1959.
14. Despatch #583, U.S. Embassy Tehran to State Department, 21 Feb. 1959, USSD 888.00 Seven Year/2-2159 HBS.
15. Telegram #825, U.S. Embassy Tehran to State Department, re a conversation with Ebtehaj, 7 Oct. 1954, USSD.
16. A. Saikal, *The Rise and Fall of the Shah 1941-1979* (Princeton, 1980), p.61; Avery, *Modern Iran*, pp.473-4, 476-7.
17. Memorandum by A.H. Ebtehaj, 2 Sept. 1987.
18. L. Binder, *Iran: Political Development in a Changing Society* (Berkeley & Los Angeles, 1982), p.124.
19. Despatch #583, U.S. Embassy Tehran to State Department, 21 Feb. 1959, USSD 888.00 Seven Year/2-2159 HBS.
20. E. Abrahamian, *Iran Between Two Revolutions* (Princeton, 1982), pp.420, 435-6: the annual military budget was increased from $80 million in 1953 to nearly $183 million in 1963 (at 1960 prices and exchange rates).
21. Harvard Project: Farmanfarmaian Interview, Tape 4, pp.10 11; Dr Cyrus Ghani was also present at the meeting, and describes events in similar terms - Interview, 30 March 1987.
22. Memorandum by A.H. Ebtehaj, 26 Sept. 1986; see also, Despatch #503, U.S. Embassy to State Department, 24 Jan. 1959, USSD 788.00/1-2459.
23. G.B. Baldwin, *Planning and Development in Iran* (Baltimore, 1967), p.113, and generally pp.112-14.
24. Ibid; and Memorandum by A.H. Ebtehaj, 26 Sept. 1986.
25. Memorandum by A.H. Ebtehaj, 26 Sept. 1986 Ebtehaj's remarks were widely publicised as having included such words as 'treachery': in fact, however, the word he actually used was the Persian word 'jenayat' (criminal), not 'khianat' (treachery) - in the Persian script the two words are only distinguished by the placing of the dots above and below certain letters - Notes by A.H. Ebtehaj on Despatch #583, U.S. Embassy to State Department, 21 Feb. 1959, USSD 888.00 Seven Year/2-2159 HBS.
26. Memorandum by A.H. Ebtehaj, 26 Sept. 1986.
27. Ibid: Ebtehaj was told later that the statements made by Eqbal to the *Majles* and Senate were drafted by the Minister for Industry and Mines, Sharif-Emami, who had signed the Shiraz contract, and merely read out by Eqbal, Baldwin, *Planning*, p.113, indicates that Sharif-Emami spear-headed the mounting animosity to

to Ebtehaj within government.
28. Interview with Dr C. Ghani, 30 March 1987.
29. Memorandum by A.H. Ebtehaj, 26 Sept. 1986. Ebtehaj's wife recollects that after Ebtehaj gave his letter of resignation to Ala, Minister of Court, to hand to the Shah, Ala promptly telephoned her saying that the language used was far too strong and would have to be tempered. Mrs Ebtehaj asked him to return the letter, promising to get Ebtehaj to tone down the language. Under protest, Ebtehaj complied and the redrafted letter was sent back to Ala. Again it was returned: the wording was still unsuitable. This time, however, Ebtehaj dug his heels in and absolutely refused to moderate the language any further. Interview with Azar Ebtehaj, 10 Nov. 1987.
30. Memorandum by A.H. Ebtehaj, 26 Sept. 1986; American documents state that the Shah in fact refused Ebtehaj's resignation, but only on condition that he did not oppose the Shiraz project – see Despatch #503, U.S. Embassy to State Department, Jan. 1959, USSD 788.00/1-2459 – but according to Ebtehaj, he got no response at all to his letter from the Shah.
31. Memorandum by A.H. Ebtehaj, 26 Sept. 1986; see also, Telegram #1536 from Ambassador Wailes, U.S. Embassy Tehran to State Department, 12 Feb. 1959, USSD.
32. Harvard Project: Farmanfarmaian Interview, Tape 4, p.15.
33. For instance, Despatch #583, U.S. Embassy to State Department, 21 Feb. 1959, USSD 888.00 Seven Year/2-2159 HBS; Binder, *Iran: Political*, pp.124, 310; Saikal, *Rise and Fall*, p.61; Interview with Dr C. Ghani, 30 March 1987.
34. Cook Interview, p.675. An indication that Ebtehaj's relations with the Shah had already started deteriorating by the beginning of 1958 is afforded by the following anecdote about Mrs Ebtehaj and Princess Ashraf's fur coat. When visiting a well-known society dressmaker in Tehran in mid-1957, Mrs Ebtehaj noticed a mink coat hanging up and asked whose it was. On being told that it was for sale and, though technically secondhand, it was to all intents and purposes new, she expressed a wish to buy it. However, being somewhat superstitious and not wanting to have a coat with an unlucky history, she insisted on knowing to whom it had belonged. The owner of the mink was in fact Princess Ashraf, who did not want her name mentioned. However, on being told that the would-be purchaser was Mrs Ebtehaj, a close friend, Princess Ashraf allowed her name to be revealed. Mrs Ebtehaj then bought the coat. For two or three months all was well. Then, out of the blue, a messenger from Princess Ashraf arrived at the Ebtehaj home to ask for the coat back. At first Mrs Ebtehaj assumed there was some misunderstanding, but Princess Ashraf refused to speak to her on the telephone and it became clear that she was no longer in favour. She returned the mink – and never received a refund. Interview with Azar Ebtehaj, 10 Nov. 1987. The story is corroborated by Dr Cyrus Ghani, Interview of 30 March 1987, though the details vary.
35. Barry Rubin, *Paved With Good Intentions* (New York, 1980), pp.101-2.
36. Interview with Dr C. Ghani, 30 March 1987; Saikal, *Rise and Fall*, pp. 61-2. See also, Binder, *Iran: Political*, pp.309 ff, in which Binder discusses economic development in the context of the conflict between the traditional and rationalising tendencies in the transitional political system of Iran, and how the Shah used it to maintain his position and increase his power. M. Zonis, *The Political Elite of Iran* (Princeton, 1971), pp.91-2: Zonis discusses the Shah's divide-and-rule tactics in the context of the unease induced in him by the rise to prominence of exceptional individuals, and his tendency to dismiss such individuals from office or isolate them from political currents. Zonis mentions a number of people who had such treatment meted out to them, including Ebtehaj (forced to resign from the Plan Organisation and subsequently imprisoned) and Ayatollah Khomeini (forced into exile in 1964). And see, especially, J.A. Bill, *The Eagle and the Lion* (London, 1988), pp.121-3.
37. Despatch #908, U.S. Embassy to State Department, 6 June 1959, USSD 888.00 Seven Year/6-659.
38. Despatch #583, U.S. Embassy to State Department, 21 Feb. 1959, USSD 888.00

REFERENCES

Seven Year/2–2159 HBS.
39. Despatch #908, U.S. Embassy to State Department, 6 June 1959, USSD 888.00 Seven Year/6–659.
40. Views expressed in Despatch #583, U.S. Embassy to State Department, 21 Feb. 1959, USSD 888.00 Seven Year/2–2159 HBS and Despatch #611, U.S. Embassy to State Department, 28 Feb. 1959 (relating the opinion of an Iranian informant), USSD 888.00 Seven Year/2–285.
41. Interviews with Azar Ebtehaj, 10 and 18 Nov. 1987. Mrs Ebtehaj recollects that Princess Ashraf's then husband, Ahmad Shafiq, came to see Ebtehaj soon after his resignation, offering, on the Shah's behalf, a choice of this sort of government appointment. With regard to the audience with the Shah, rumours were apparently so rife in Tehran about Ebtehaj's alleged refusal to attend that the Shah, much offended, was constrained to write a note to Prime Minister Eqbal, on the lines of 'Some people claim that I wanted to see them but they refused'.
42. Cook Interview, pp.694–5; the CBS Interview was included in a Report, 'Iran: Brittle Ally', broadcast on 18 Dec. 1959, and we are grateful to CBS for supplying us with the transcript; the Panorama interviewer was James Mossman, and we are grateful to the BBC for permitting us to consult the transcript.
43. Rubin, *Paved*, pp.104–5. Ebtehaj's inability to compromise his views and criticisms was total, and his wife often went to considerable lengths in her efforts to win over people he had alienated and temper his more 'rash' actions. When Iranians' Bank opened, for instance, Ebtehaj absolutely refused to have the customary pictures of the Shah in the banking hall and offices, despite the remonstrances of SAVAK and his wife's anxious persuasion. The first thing his wife did when he was imprisoned, was to order a set of photographs and have them hung all over the bank: Interview with Azar Ebtehaj, 10 Nov. 1987.
44. A.H. Ebtehaj, 'It's Getting Late in Iran', and H.R. Luce, 'America's Unfinished Business', in J. Daniel (ed), *Private Investment: The Key to International Industrial Development* (New York, 1958).
45. A.H. Ebtehaj, 'A Program for Economic Growth', Paper delivered at *International Industrial Conference*, Stanford Research Institute, San Francisco, Sept. 1961. See also, Zonis, *Political Elite*, pp.68–9; and Bill, *The Eagle*, pp.129–30.
46. Cook Interview, pp.684–5.
47. Ebtehaj, 'A Program'.
48. Cook Interview, pp.684–90.
49. Despatch #280, U.S. Embassy Tehran to State Department, 9 Dec. 1961, USSD 788.00/12 96; Cook Interview, pp.746–62.
50. *Peygham-e Emruz*, 15 Nov. 1961; *Kayhan International*, 16 Nov. 1961; *Time*, 26 Jan. 1962; *The Washington Post*, 7 Jan. 1962; *The Economist*, 5 May 1962.
51. See, for instance, *The Washington Post*, 7 Jan. 1962 – Ebtehaj wrote to Warren Unna of *The Washington Post* from prison.
52. Zonis, *Political Elite*, p.69. See also, W. Forbis, *Fall of the Peacock Throne: The Story of Iran* (New York, 1980), pp.253–4; and Avery, *Modern Iran*, p.494.
53. Interview with Azar Ebtehaj, 18 Nov. 1987. Mrs Ebtehaj was largely responsible for ensuring that her husband's treatment in gaol was as good as it could be under the circumstances. She laid positive siege to the prison authorities on his behalf. Obviating any possibility of an unfortunate 'accident', she forbade him to eat or drink anything provided by the prison. Instead, she insisted on bringing him his meals twice a day – a regimen which was crucial in view of his recurrent stomach problems. When he was ill, she made sure that he received proper medical attention, but refused to allow him to be operated on in the prison hospital (which had no proper facilities). She also persuaded the prison authorities to provide Ebtehaj, always a very fastidious man, with a makeshift shower which made life a little less unbearable. In fact it was largely due to his wife's efforts that Ebtehaj, already suffering from both stomach ulcers and hernia problems when he went to gaol, survived his period of detention.

54. Cook Interview, pp.753–60.
55. For example, A.H. Ebtehaj to George McGhee, 10 Dec. 1961; to Alfred Friendly, *The Washington Post*, 17 Feb. 1962; to Henry Luce, 17 Dec. 1961.
56. H.R. Luce to A.H. Ebtehaj, 23 Dec. 1961, Time–Life Organisation Archives.
57. *The Economist*, 5 May 1962.
58. *The Washington Post*, 4 Jan. 1962; *The New York Times*, 4 Jan. and 21 March 1962; *Time*, 26 Jan. 1962.
59. *Time*, 22 June 1962.
60. Rubin, *Paved*, p.107.
61. Cook Interview, p.755; *Time*, 22 June, 1962; Weldon Gibson of the Stanford Research Institute organised a petition for his release on the West Coast of America, and similar petitions were organised elsewhere in the United States.
62. *Kayhan International*, 15 Nov. 1961; see also Press Review, 28 Nov. 1961, quoting *Setare-ye Tehran*.
63. *Kayhan International*, 14 Nov. 1961, Press Review quoting the daily newspaper, *Asia*.
64. Despatch #280, U.S. Embassy Tehran to State Department, 9 Dec. 1961, USSD 788.00/12–96.
65. *Kayhan International*, 7 June 1962.
66. *The Washington Post*, 14 June 1962; the bail amount reported here is in fact a little higher than in *Kayhan*.
67. Interview with Manouchehr Kazemi, 25 Oct. 1985.
68. Interview with Peter Avery, 2 April 1986 – Avery was the 'British friend' in question.

CHAPTER EIGHT

1. Airgram #A–448, U.S. Embassy Tehran to State Department, 19 Feb. 1964, USSD.
2. For details of Iran's social, economic and political history during the 1960s and 1970s, see the following in particular – E. Abrahamian, *Iran Between Two Revolutions* (Princeton, 1982), pp.419 ff; M.H. Pesaran, 'Economic Development and Revolutionary Upheavals in Iran', in H. Afshar (ed), *Iran: A Revolution in Turmoil* (London, 1985); M.H. Pesaran, 'The System of Dependent Capitalism in Pre- and Post-Revolutionary Iran', *International Journal of Middle East Studies*, 14, (1982); R.K. Ramazani, 'Who Lost America? The Case of Iran', *The Middle East Journal*, 36, 1 (1982); R. Graham, *Iran: The Illusion of Power* (London, 1978).
3. Abrahamian, *Iran Between*, pp.422–4. It was owing to the Kennedy Administration's pressure that in 1961 the Shah had had to appoint Dr Ali Amini, a man who had won the confidence of the State Department but whom he himself disliked and distrusted, as Prime Minister to liberalise the government and carry out a programme of economic reform. However, Amini failed to elicit American support when he clashed with the Shah over the need to cut the military budget. The United States, not for the last time, backed the Shah, and Amini had to resign after only 14 months.
4. Memorandum by A.H. Ebtehaj, 8 Oct. 1987. In April 1964, when Ebtehaj was in New York, en route for Washington and talks with George Wood, new President of the World Bank, a young Iranian, Bahram Saleh told him of State Department documents he had come across while researching his dissertation which referred to a 'task force' set up to report on Iran. Among the proposals considered, had been one postulating the setting up of a republic in Iran, and mentioning Ebtehaj as a possible leader. His story later changed – he had been told, he said, about the 'task force' by David Lilienthal. It seems likely that this may have been part of the contingent plans Washington had had since the early 1960s to get a reform

REFERENCES

government into power in Iran. In Nov. 1987, Habib Ladjevardi asked Mr Sharif-Emami, Prime Minister for some nine months in 1960–61, for his recollections on this point. Sharif-Emami said that during an audience he had had with the Shah, when the talk was about America's role in Iran, the Shah had given him a 'small booklet' to read. The next day, before he had a chance to do more than glance through it, the Shah, through Ala, had asked for it back. The booklet, which may have been published by 'one of the [U.S.] universities [as someone's doctoral thesis] or by another American institution, . . . discussed the possibility of a change of regime in Iran'. Ebtehaj's name was mentioned in the booklet, though whether it was mentioned in connection with his becoming president, Sharif-Emami has no precise recollection. What he does definitely remember, however, is that it was at this time that the Shah's attitude towards Ebtehaj, 'which had been very favourable up to that time, suddenly changed 180 degrees'. – Letter from Habib Ladjevardi, 18 Nov. 1987. Sharif-Emami's story seems to suggest that Ebtehaj's name may have come up in Washington when the Kennedy Administration was looking for someone to head a reform government in Iran. Dr Ali Amini, who followed Sharif-Emami as Prime Minister, was in fact Washington's choice. Whether or not there was any basis for the rumour either in 1963 or earlier mentioning Ebtehaj's name in connection with a change of regime, it is inconceivable, according to Khodadad Farmanfarmaian, that Ebtehaj would ever have consented to any such scheme as it would have been entirely against his principles.

5. Memorandum by A.H. Ebtehaj, 8 Oct. 1987; the authors have in their possession the copy of a letter to Ebtehaj from the U.S. official concerned, dated 4 Nov. 1987, which guardedly confirms this story.
6. The article of the Irano-Soviet Treaty of 1921 which Ebtehaj was so anxious to see cancelled as a *quid pro quo* for withdrawing Iran from CENTO became highly topical during 1987 in the context of the Iran–Iraq Gulf war – See *Economist Foreign Report*, 8 Oct. 1987.
7. Interview with Azar Ebtehaj, 18 Nov. 1987.
8. Airgram #A–448, U.S. Embassy Tehran to State Department, 19 Feb. 1964, USSD.
9. Airgram #A–548, U.S. Embassy Tehran to State Department, 11 April 1964, USSD.
10. Airgram #A–539, U.S. Embassy Tehran to State Department, 6 April 1964, USSD.
11. Airgram #A–628, U.S. Embassy Tehran to State Department, 14 May 1964, USSD.
12. Airgram #A–22, U.S. Embassy Tehran to State Department, 15 July 1964, USSD.
13. Note to U.S. Ambassador Tehran from First Secretary (Theodore Eliot), 23 Feb. 1966, USSD.
14. Interview with A.H. Ebtehaj, 21 Jan. 1986.
15. Hossein Razavi and Firouz Vakil, *The Political Environment of Economic Planning in Iran, 1971–1983* (Boulder, Colorado, 1984), p.29.
16. Memorandum of Conversations between A.H. Ebtehaj and U.S. Embassy officials, 13 April 1963 and 17 Oct. 1963, USSD.
17. Khodadad Farmanfarmaian was a case in point: see his 'Report on Formation and Development of Economic Bureau, 1336–1342 (1957–1963)', *Ford Foundation*, 20 May 1963, p.23; see also, Memorandum of a Conversation between A.H. Ebtehaj and U.S. Embassy officials, 13 April 1963, USSD.
18. Memorandum by A.H. Ebtehaj, 3 Nov. 1986.
19. Memorandum by A.H. Ebtehaj on Land Reform, Feb. 1962, attached to Memorandum of Conversation between A.H. Ebtehaj and U.S. Embassy officials, 13 April 1963, USSD; Airgram #A–457, U.S. Embassy Tehran to State Department, 19 Jan. 1963, USSD 888.16/1–1963, Memorandum by A.H. Ebtehaj, 16 Aug. 1986. For historical surveys and appraisals of land reform in Iran, see,

especially, A.K.S. Lambton, *The Persian Land Reform 1962–1966* (Oxford, 1969); N.R. Keddie, 'Historical Obstacles to Agrarian Change in Iran', *Claremont Oriental Studies*, 8, 1960; 'The Iranian Village Before and After Land Reform', *Journal of Contemporary History*, 3, 1968, pp.69–91.
20. Memorandum by A.H. Ebtehaj, 16 Aug. 1986.
21. Pesaran, 'Economic Development', p.34; Graham, *Iran: Illusion*, pp.94–5.
22. The latest study of the land reforms is Eric J. Hooglund's, *Land and Revolution in Iran 1960–1980* (Austin, Texas, 1982). Hooglund argues that the Shah's land reforms were primarily political in purpose, and in particular they were designed to extend Tehran's control over the countryside. He notes the limited impact of the reforms on land tenure. For the majority of peasants, Hooglund observes, 'extreme poverty coupled with economic insecurity remained their lot', (p.98).
23. Abrahamian, *Iran Between*, pp.426–35, 446–9.
24. Memorandum by A.H. Ebtehaj, 21 July 1986: known for his scrupulous honesty, Ebtehaj clearly did not resort to the usual Iranian methods of supplementing an income inadequate for his life-style.
25. Cook Interview, pp.692–3. Interview with Azar Ebtehaj, 10 Nov. 1987.
26. Interview with Azar Ebtehaj, 18 Nov. 1987. Mrs Ebtehaj, who still had family estates in Mazandaran (Land Reform had not yet been introduced), suggested that they might take up farming or even sell the lands and buy a factory or productive unit in Tehran. Neither suggestion met with her husband's approval – he knew, he said, nothing about either farming or running a factory.
27. Memorandum by A.H. Ebtehaj, 26 Sept. 1986.
28. Memorandum by A.H. Ebtehaj, 14 Nov. 1986.
29. Interview with Azar Ebtehaj, 18 Nov. 1987. As the Ebtehajs had no cash to invest in their new enterprise, Mrs Ebtehaj sold her house in Takhte Jamshid Avenue, Tehran, to raise the necessary capital. She recollects that although their friends wanted to buy shares in the Bank, they were in many cases afraid to do so in case they got into trouble with the government and the Shah.
30. Memorandum by A.H. Ebtehaj, 14 Nov. 1986.
31. Despatch #198, U.S. Embassy Tehran to State Department, 24 Sept. 1959, USSD 888.00/9–2459.
32. Cook Interview, pp.718–20.
33. A photograph of Iranians' Bank appeared in *The Financial Times*, see Graham, *Iran: Illusion*, p.198 and Chapter 11, footnote 26; a gossip columnist in *Iran Tribune*, April 1974, referred to it as a 'very "classy" bank building'. The new headquarters' building was formally opened in Jan. 1973, see *Tehran Journal*, 9 Jan. 1973.
34. Interview with Azar Ebtehaj, 18 Nov. 1987. Private banks were normally helped to find their feet by the deposit of funds by the Bank Markazi and Bank Melli, as well as such organisations as NIOC.
35. R. Schott to F. Bostock, 9 April 1986. Robert Schott was political/ military officer at the U.S. Embassy Tehran from 1967 to 1970. He had also been in Iran in the 1950s. In 1970 he resigned from the U.S. Foreign Service, in frustration over the directions taken by U.S. policy in Iran, and joined Iranians' Bank as Ebtehaj's personal assistant. Hoveyda's account with Iranians' Bank was mentioned in *Tehran Journal*, 9 Jan. 1973.
36. Memorandum by A.H. Ebtehaj, 14 Nov. 1986; Interview with Azar Ebtehaj, 18 Nov. 1987; John Donald Wilson, *The Chase* (Boston, Mass, 1986), pp.231, 296.
37. Memorandum by A.H. Ebtehaj, 14 Nov. 1986.
38. Harold van B. Cleveland and Thomas F. Huertas, *Citibank, 1812–1970* (Cambridge, Mass, 1985), pp.263–5, 435 footnote 18. It was not possible for foreign banks to enter the Iranian market directly on any basis other than that of a minority shareholding. Apart from Iran, Citibank made three much larger investments in foreign banks in the 1960s. It bought a controlling interest of 50%, later reduced to 25%, in the Mercantile Bank of Canada in 1962; a 40% minority interest in the

REFERENCES

Banque Internationale pour l'Afrique Occidentale in 1965; and a similar 40% interest in National and Grindlays of the United Kingdom in 1968. The first two moves took Citibank into markets which it was unable to penetrate in any other way: the third enabled it to compete in an area – India – where it was finding difficulty gaining a deposit base.

39. The negotiations with Ebtehaj were undertaken by Peter Wodtke, Citibank's Middle Eastern representative at the time, based in Beirut: information on the negotiations came from him – Interview, 5 Feb. 1987; and from Ebtehaj – Memorandum of 14 Nov. 1986.
40. Memorandum of Conversation between A.H. Ebtehaj and U.S. Embassy economic and financial officials, 15 July 1968, USSD: in the Embassy's view, Citibank's aggressive style would 'put the Bank of America on its toes' – the Bank of America owned a 20% interest in the Foreign Trade Bank in Iran.
41. R. Schott to F. Bostock, 9 April 1986; Interview with P. Wodtke, 5 Feb. 1987; Interview with J. Kruthoffer, 10 Feb. 1987 (Kruthoffer ran Citibank's agency in Tehran for a period in the mid-1970s).
42. Roy Assersohn, *The Biggest Deal: Bankers, Politics, and the Hostages of Iran* (London, 1982), pp.50–1. Citibank's representative office in Tehran had grown very rapidly. In the early 1970s, it had a staff of 94, twice as many as some of Iran's leading investment banks and 20 times as many as the representative offices of other foreign banks. When examined by Bank Markazi officials, Citibank's documentation revealed that it had been operating a fully-fledged bank, taking deposits, making loans to the cream of Iran's banking customers – including members of the royal family – and providing a wide range of other banking services. The Shah initially ordered that its office should be closed down completely, but in the end, in a compromise solution, it got away with drastically reducing the size and scope of its operations.
43. Interview with Azar Ebtehaj, 10 Nov. 1987: the affair between Ebtehaj and Azar caused such a scandal because Ebtehaj, who had just returned to Iran from the United States, was known to be on the point of accepting a big job at the Shah's request (the Plan Organisation). Moreover, the Ebtehajs and Azar all moved in Court circles. Like Maryam, Azar was friendly with Princess Ashraf. Azar was in the process of obtaining a divorce from her second husband after a very short and unsuccessful marriage (her first husband, whom she had married when she was very young, having died leaving her with two small children). Both Ebtehaj and Azar were subjected to considerable pressure from their friends to refrain from such an 'unsuitable' match, Ebtehaj's age and lack of money being constantly referred to.
44. Interview with Azar Ebtehaj, 18 Nov. 1987; Interview with Peter Avery, 2 April 1986.
45. Cook Interview, pp.740–2.
46. J. Bharier, *Economic Development in Iran 1900–1970* (London, 1971), pp.253–6, 278–9.
47. In 1978 Hozhabr Yazdani was indicted for grand larceny by the Sharif-Emami government as part of an attempt – futile as it turned out – to placate the *mollas*.
48. Memorandum by A.H. Ebtehaj, 21 July 1986; Interview with J. Kruthoffer, 10 Feb. 1987.
49. Interview with J. Kruthoffer, ibid.
50. Memorandum by A.H. Ebtehaj, 21 July 1986.
51. Ibid; and Interview with Azar Ebtehaj, 18 Nov. 1987. Information on Ebtehaj's wish to purchase government bonds came also from P. Avery, Interview, 2 April 1986; and from R. Schott to F. Bostock, 9 April 1986.
52. Interview with J. Kruthoffer, 10 Feb. 1987.
53. A.H. Ebtehaj to Mrs Helen Lilienthal, 29 July 1987.
54. R. Schott to F. Bostock, 9 April 1986.
55. Memorandum by A.H. Ebtehaj, 13 Jan. 1987 – This was the second such protest: in Nov. 1978, a similar but shorter list had been published on which the name of

PLANNING AND POWER IN IRAN

Ebtehaj's wife appeared and Ebtehaj had at once telephoned the Governor of the Central Bank, reminding him of the facts of the case. He was assured that the list, which indeed included the Governor's own name, had nothing to do with the Central Bank or government.

CHAPTER NINE

1. Harvard Project: Farmanfarmaian Interview, Tape 4, p.3.
2. Shaul Bakhash, *The Reign of the Ayatollahs* (London, 1985), p.10. For perceptive insights about the often unwitting support given to the Shah's regime by such 'free-floating forces' as Ebtehaj, see J.A. Bill, *The Eagle and the Lion* (London, 1988), pp.354, 359.
3. Harvard Project: Farmanfarmaian Interview, Tape 4, p.5.
4. Ibid, Tape 4, pp.18–19.
5. Memorandum by A.H. Ebtehaj, 3 Nov. 1986.
6. Harvard Project: Farmanfarmaian Interview, Tape 2, p.22.
7. Robert E. Huyser, *Mission to Tehran* (London, 1986); Barry Rubin, *Paved With Good Intentions* (New York, 1980); Gary Sick, *All Fall Down* (New York, 1985).
8. R.K. Ramazani, 'Who Lost America? The Case of Iran', *The Middle East Journal*, 36, 1, 1982, p.17.

BIBLIOGRAPHY

A. Archives

Bank of England Archives, London
British Bank of the Middle East Archives, Hongkong Bank Group Archives, Hong Kong
Foreign Office Correspondence Series 371 and 248, Public Record Office, London
State Department Records, United States National Archives, Washington D.C.

B. Iranian Government and Banking Publications

Bank Markazi Iran Bulletins (Tehran)
  'Banking in Iran', Vol 1, No 1, 1962
  'The Economic Stabilization Program', Vol 1, No 5, 1963
  Mehdi, Samii, 'Some Observations on Problems of Banking in Iran', Vol 2, No 10, 1963
Bank Melli Iran Bulletins (Tehran). In particular,
  'Iran's Development Plan' and 'Iran's Seven Year Plan', No 83, 1946
  'The Seven Year Development Plan Bill', Nos 93–5, 1948
  'Seven Year Development Plan Act', No 98, 1949
  '$75 Million World Bank Loan to Iran Act, 1956', No 180, 1957
Iranian Embassy, *An Economic Survey of Iran* (London, 1957)
Ministry of Labour and Plan Organisation, *National Manpower Resources and Requirements Survey, Iran, 1958* (Tehran, 1959)
Plan Organisation, Division of Economic Affairs, *Review of the Second Seven Year Plan* (Tehran, 1960)
Plan Organisation, Public Relations Bureau, *Historical Review* (Tehran, undated: 1959?), based on a Report by A.H. Ebtehaj to the Iranian Legislature
Plan Organisation, *Second Seven Year Development Plan of Iran* (Tehran, 1956)

C. Foreign Government Publications

United States, Department of State, *Foreign Relations of the United States* (Washington, D.C.)

D. Other Primary Works

Development and Resources Corporation, New York, 'The Unified

Development of the Natural Resources of the Khuzestan Region', *Report to Plan Organization, Government of Iran* (Tehran, March 1959)

Ebtehaj, Abol Hassan, 'A Program For Economic Growth', Paper delivered at *International Industrial Conference* (Stanford Research Institute, San Francisco, September 1961)

Ebtehaj, Abol Hassan, 'It's Getting Late in Iran', Paper delivered at *International Industrial Conference* (Stanford Research Institute, San Francisco, September 1957) in James Daniel (ed), *Private Investment: The Key to International Industrial Development* (New York, 1958)

Farmanfarmaian, Khodadad, 'Formation and Development of the Economic Bureau 1957-1963', *Report to The Ford Foundation* (Tehran, May 1963)

Luce, Henry R., 'America's Unfinished Business', Chairman's Address to *International Industrial Conference* (Stanford Research Institute, San Francisco, September 1957) in James Daniel (ed), *Private Investment: The Key to International Industrial Development* (New York, 1958)

Overseas Consultants Inc., *Report on Seven Year Development Plan for the Plan Organisation of the Imperial Government of Iran* (New York, 1949), 5 Vols

E. Newspapers and Journals

Kayhan International
Iran Tribune
Tehran Journal
The Economist
The Economist Foreign Report
New York Times
Washington Post
Time Magazine

F. Oral History

B.B.C. Panorama, Interview by James Mossman (London, 6 Feb. 1961)

C.B.S. Report, 'Iran: Brittle Ally' (United States, 18 December 1959)

Christopher Cook, Oral Interviews of Abol Hassan Ebtehaj (London, 1985), 22 Tapes. These interviews have been supplemented by a series of Memoranda by A.H. Ebtehaj (London, 1986-87), elaborating on particular issues.

Ladjevardi, Habib, 'Interview of Dr Khodadad Farmanfarmaian', *Iranian Oral History Project* (Harvard University, Center for Middle Eastern Studies, November 1982). Copies of the Ladjevardi Interviews have been lodged with the Bodleian Library, Oxford.

Interviews with:
Peter Avery
Aqa Khan Bakhtiar

BIBLIOGRAPHY

Abol Hassan Ebtehaj
Dr Azar Ebtehaj
Dr Eprime Eshag
Dr Khodadad Farmanfarmaian
Dr Cyrus Ghani
Manouchehr Kazemi
Jan Kruthoffer
Dr Reza Moghaddam
Robert Schott
Peter Wodtke
Sir Denis Wright

G. *Secondary Sources*
This bibliography is intended as a guide to the most relevant literature to the themes pursued in this book. It does not list all the sources cited in the text, while it does list some literature which has not been cited but has been read for background information.

Abrahamian, Ervand, *Iran Between Two Revolutions* (Princeton, 1982)
Acheson, Dean, *Present at the Creation: My Years at the State Department* (New York, 1969)
Afkhami, Gholam R., *The Iranian Revolution: Thanatos on a National Scale* (Washington, 1985)
Afshar, Haleh (ed), *Iran: A Revolution in Turmoil* (London, 1985)
Agah, M., 'Some Aspects of Economic Development of Modern Iran' (D.Phil Thesis, Oxford, 1958)
Akhavi, Sharough, *Religion and Politics in Contemporary Iran* (New York, 1980)
Amirsadeghi, Hossein (ed), *Twentieth Century Iran* (London, 1977)
Amuzegar, Jahangir, *Iran: An Economic Profile* (Washington, 1977)
Amuzegar, Jahangir, *Technical Assistance in Theory and Practice: The Case of Iran* (New York, 1966)
Amuzegar, J. and Fekrat, M.A. *Iran: Economic Development Under Dualistic Conditions* (Chicago, 1971)
Assersohn, Roy, *The Biggest Deal: Bankers, Politics, and the Hostages of Iran* (London, 1982)
Avery, Peter, *Modern Iran* (London, 1965)
Bagley, F.R.C., 'A Bright Future after Oil: Dams and Agro-Industry in Khuzistan', *The Middle East Journal*, Vol 30, 1976
Bakhash, Shaul, *The Reign of the Ayatollahs* (New York, 1984)
Baldwin, George B., *Planning and Development in Iran* (Baltimore, 1967)
Banani, Amin, *The Modernization of Iran 1921–1941* (Stanford, Calif. 1961)
Bayne, E.A., *Persian Kingship in Transition* (New York, 1968)
Beck, P.J., 'The Anglo-Persian Oil Dispute 1932–3', *Journal of Contemporary History*, 1975

Bharier, Julian, *Economic Development in Iran 1900–1970* (London, 1971)
Bill, James A., *The Eagle and the Lion: The Tragedy of American Iranian Relations* (London, 1988).
Bill, James A., *The Politics of Iran: Groups, Classes and Modernization* (Columbus, Ohio, 1972)
Bill, James A. and Louis, Wm Roger, *Mussadiq, Iranian Nationalism, and Oil* (London, 1988)
Binder, Leonard, *Iran: Political Development in a Changing Society* (Berkeley, Calif. 1962)
Binder, Leonard, 'The Cabinet of Iran: A Case Study in Institutional Adaptation', *The Middle East Journal*, Vol 16, 1962
Bochenski, Felix and Diamond, William, 'TVAs in the Middle East', *The Middle East Journal*, Vol IV, 1950
Bonine, M. and Keddie, N.R. (eds), *Continuity and Change in Modern Iran* (Albany, N.Y., 1981)
Bostock, Frances and Jones, Geoffrey, 'British Business in Iran, 1860s–1970s', in Davenport-Hines, R. and Jones, G. (eds), *British Business in Asia Since 1860* (Cambridge, 1988)
Browne, E.G., *The Persian Revolution of 1905–1909* (London, 1910)
Carey, J.P.C. and Carey, A.G., 'Industrial Growth and Development Planning in Iran', *The Middle East Journal*, Vol 29, 1975
Carey, J.P.C. and Carey, A.G., 'Iranian Agriculture and its Development: 1952–1973', *International Journal of Middle East Studies*, Vol 7, 1976
Carey, J.P.C. and Carey, A.G., 'Turkish Industry and the Five Year Plans', *The Middle East Journal*, Vol 25, 1971
Chubin, Shahram and Sepehr, Zabih, *The Foreign Relations of Iran* (Berkeley, Calif. 1974)
Clapp, Gordon R., 'Iran: A TVA for the Khuzestan Region', *The Middle East Journal*, Vol II, 1957
Cottam, Richard W., *Nationalism in Iran* (Pittsburgh, 1964)
Daftary, Farhad, 'Development Planning in Iran: A Historical Survey', *Iranian Studies*, 1973
Diamond, William, 'Activities of the International Bank in the Middle East', *The Middle East Journal*, Vol III, 1949
Diba, Farhad, *Mossadegh: A Political Biography* (London, 1986)
Dunsterville, L.C., *The Adventures of Dunsterforce* (London, 1921)
Elwell-Sutton, L.P., *Modern Iran* (London, 1941)
Elwell-Sutton, L.P., 'Nationalism and Neutralism in Iran', *The Middle East Journal*, Vol 12, 1958
Elwell-Sutton, L.P., *Persian Oil: A Study in Power Politics* (London, 1955)
Farmanfarmaian, K., 'The Oil Industry and Native Enterprise in Iran', *Middle Eastern Affairs*, Vol VIII, 1957
Ferrier, R.W., *The History of the British Petroleum Company*, Vol 1, *The*

BIBLIOGRAPHY

Developing Years 1901–1932 (Cambridge, 1982)
Floor, Willem, *Industrialisation in Iran 1900–1941* (Centre for Middle Eastern and Islamic Studies, University of Durham, Occasional Papers Series No 23, 1984)
Forbis, W.H., *Fall of the Peacock Throne: The Story of Iran* (New York, 1980)
Franck, D.S. and Franck, P.G., 'The Middle East Economy in 1948', *The Middle East Journal*, Vol III, 1949
Franck, D.S. and Franck, P.G., 'The Middle East Economy in 1949', *The Middle East Journal*, Vol IV, 1950
Frye, Richard, *Iran* (London, 1954)
Ghani, Cyrus, *Iran and the West: A Critical Bibliography* (London, 1987)
Graham, Robert, *Iran: The Illusion of Power* (London, 1978)
Green, Jerrold, *Revolution in Iran: The Politics of Counter Mobilization* (New York, 1982)
Gupta, Raj Narain, *Iran: An Economic Study* (New Delhi, 1947)
Hakim, George, 'Point Four and the Middle East', *The Middle East Journal*, Vol IV, 1950
Halliday, Fred, *Iran: Dictatorship and Development* (Harmondsworth, Middlesex, 1979)
Halliday, Fred, *The Making of the Second Cold War* (London, 1986 edn)
Harris, Franklin S., 'The Beginnings of Point IV Work in Iran', *The Middle East Journal*, Vol VII, 1953
Higgins, B., *Economic Development* (London, 1959)
Hooglund, Eric J., *Land and Revolution in Iran 1960–1980* (Austin, Texas, 1982)
Hoveyda, Fereydoun, *The Fall of the Shah* (London, 1980)
Hull, Cordell, *The Memoirs of Cordell Hull* (London, 1948), Vol 2
Huyser, Robert E., *Mission to Tehran* (London, 1986)
Issawi, Charles, 'Iran's Economic Upsurge', *The Middle East Journal*, Vol 21, 1967
Issawi, Charles, *The Economic History of Iran 1800–1914* (Chicago, 1971)
Jabbari, A. and Olson, R. (eds), *Iran: Essays on the Making of a Revolution* (Lexington, 1981)
Jones, Geoffrey, *Banking and Empire in Iran* (Cambridge, 1986)
Jones, Geoffrey, *The State and the Emergence of the British Oil Industry* (London, 1981)
Kane, Joseph, *Development Banking: An Economic Appraisal* (Lexington, 1975)
Kapuscinski, Ryszard, *Shah of Shahs* (London, 1986 edn)
Katouzian, Homa, *The Political Economy of Modern Iran* (London, 1981)
Kazemzadeh, Firuz, *Russia and Britain in Persia: 1864–1914* (New Haven, 1968)
Keddie, Nikki R., *Religion, Politics and Society: Collected Essays* (London, 1980)
Keddie, Nikki R., *Roots of Revolution* (London, 1981)

Keddie, Nikki R., 'The Iranian Power Structure and Social Change 1800–1969: An Overview', *International Journal of Middle East Studies*, Vol 2, 1971

Khamenei, Anvar, *Forsat-e Bozorg As Dast Rafteh* (Great Opportunity Lost) (Tehran, 1984 edn)

King, John A., *Economic Development Projects and their Appraisal: Cases and Principles from the Experience of the World Bank* (Baltimore, 1967)

Ladjevardi, Habib, *Labor Unions and Autocracy in Iran* (Syracuse, N.Y., 1985)

Ladjevardi, Habib, 'The Origins of U.S. Support for an Autocratic Iran', *International Journal of Middle East Studies*, Vol 15, 1983

Lambton, Ann K.S., *Landlord and Peasant in Persia* (London, 1953)

Lambton, Ann K.S., 'Persia', *Journal of Royal Central Asian Society*, Vol 31, 1944

Lambton, Ann K.S., *Qajar Persia* (London, 1987)

Lambton, Ann K.S., *The Persian Land Reform 1962–1966* (Oxford, 1966)

Lenczowski, George (ed), *Iran Under the Pahlavis* (Stanford, Calif. 1978)

Lenczowski, George, *Russia and the West in Iran, 1918–1948* (Ithaca, N.Y., 1949)

Lenczowski, George, *The Middle East in World Affairs* (Ithaca, N.Y., 1980 edn)

Lilienthal, David E., *The Road to Change 1955–1959*, Vol IV of *The Journals of David E. Lilienthal* (New York, 1969)

Limbert, John W., *Iran: At War with History* (London, 1987)

Looney, Robert E., 'Origins of Pre-Revolutionary Iran's Development Strategy', *Middle Eastern Studies*, Vol 22, 1986

Looney, Robert E., *The Economic Development of Iran* (New York, 1973)

Looney, Robert E., 'The Impact of Oil Revenues on the Pre-Revolutionary Iranian Economy', *Middle Eastern Studies*, Vol 21, 1985

Lotz, J.D., 'Problems and Proposals', *The Middle East Journal*, Vol IV, 1950

Louis, William Roger, *Imperialism at Bay 1941–1945* (Oxford, 1977)

Louis, William Roger, *The British Empire in the Middle East 1945–1951* (Oxford, 1984)

McDaniel, R.A., *The Shuster Mission and the Persian Constitutional Revolution* (Minneapolis, 1974)

McGhee, George, *Envoy to the Middle World: Adventures in Diplomacy* (New York, 1983)

Maclachlan, K., 'Land Reform in Iran', in Fisher, W.B. (ed), *Cambridge History of Iran* (Cambridge, 1968), Vol 1

Makki, Hossein, *Tariqh-e Bist Saleh-e Iran* (Twenty-Year History of Iran) (Tehran, 1985 edn)

Mason, Edward S., *Foreign Aid and Foreign Policy* (New York, 1964)

Mason, Edward S. and Asher, Robert E., *The World Bank Since Bretton Woods and After* (Washington, 1973)

Michaelis, A., 'The Middle East Economy in 1950', *The Middle East*

Journal, Vol 5, 1951
Mikesell, Raymond F., 'Sterling Area Currencies of the Middle East', *The Middle East Journal*, Vol 2, 1948
Miklos, Jack C., *The Iranian Revolution and Modernization: Way Stations to Anarchy* (Washington, 1983)
Millspaugh, Arthur C., *Americans in Persia* (Washington, 1946)
Millspaugh, Arthur C., *The American Task in Persia* (London, 1925)
Mofid, Kamran, *Development Planning in Iran: from Monarchy to Islamic Republic* (Wisbech, Cambs., 1987)
Olsen, B. and Rasmussen, P.N., 'An Attempt at Planning in a Traditional State: Iran', in Hagen, E.E. (ed), *Planning Economic Development* (Holmewood, Illinois, 1963)
Pahlavi, Mohammad Reza Shah, *Answer to History* (New York, 1980)
Pahlavi, Mohammad Reza Shah, *Mission For My Country* (New York, 1961)
Parsons, Sir Anthony, *The Pride and the Fall* (London, 1984)
Payer, Cheryl, *The World Bank: A Critical Analysis* (New York, 1982)
Pesaran, M.H., 'The System of Dependent Capitalism in Pre- and Post-Revolutionary Iran', *International Journal of Middle East Studies*, Vol 14, 1982
Phelps Grant, C., 'Iran: Test of Relations Between Great and Small Nations', *Foreign Policy Report* (New York), Vol XX, 1945
Ramazani, Rouhollah K., 'Iran and the United States: An Experiment in Enduring Friendship', *The Middle East Journal*, Vol 30, 1976
Ramazani, Rouhollah K., *Iran's Foreign Policy 1941–1973* (Charlottesville, 1975)
Ramazani, Rouhollah K., *The Foreign Policy of Iran 1500–1941* (Charlottesville, 1966)
Ramazani, Rouhollah K., 'Who Lost America? The Case of Iran', *The Middle East Journal*, Volume 36, 1982
Razavi, Hossein and Vakil, Firouz, *The Political Environment of Economic Planning in Iran, 1971–1983* (Boulder, Colorado, 1984)
Roosevelt, Kermit, *Countercoup: The Struggle for Control of Iran* (New York, 1981)
Rubin, Barry, *Paved With Good Intentions* (New York, 1980)
Saikal, Amin, *The Rise and Fall of the Shah* (Princeton, 1980)
Shafaq, S.R., 'The Iranian Seven Year Development Plan', *The Middle East Journal*, Vol IV, 1950
Sick, Gary, *All Fall Down – America's Tragic Encounter with Iran* (New York, 1985)
Singer, Hans, *International Development: Growth and Change* (New York, 1964)
Skrine, Sir Clarmont, *World War in Iran* (London, 1962)
Sullivan, William H., *Mission to Iran* (New York, 1981)
Thorpe, J.A., 'The Mission of Arthur C. Millspaugh to Iran, 1943-45' (PhD Thesis, University of Wisconsin, 1973)

Warne, William E., *Mission for Peace* (New York, 1956)
Waterston, A., *Development Planning: Lessons of Experience* (London, 1966)
Wilber, Donald N., *Riza Shah Pahlavi: The Resurrection and Reconstruction of Iran 1878–1944* (New York, 1975)
Woodhouse, C.M., *Something Ventured* (London, 1983)
Wright, Denis, *The English Amongst the Persians* (London, 1977)
Wright, Denis, *The Persians Amongst the English* (London, 1985)
Yar-Shater, E. (ed), *Iran Faces the Seventies* (New York, 1971)
Zabir, Sepehr, *The Mossadegh Era* (Chicago, 1982)
Zonis, Marvin, *The Political Elite of Iran* (Princeton, 1971)

INDEX

Ahmad Shah Qajar, 11
Acheson, Dean, 93
Agricultural Bank, 27, 31
Ala, Hossein, 30–1, 32, 34, 82–3, 88, 89, 94, 98, 102, 105, 106–7, 118, 155–6, 192, 201n11, 218n29
Alam, Assadollah, 171
Algeria, 171–2
Alsop, Stewart, 51, 92
Amini, Dr Ali, 95, 220n3, 221n4
Amuzegar, Jahangir, 162
Anglo-Iranian Oil Company (formerly Anglo-Persian Oil Company, subsequently British Petroleum), 19, 20, 23–4, 52, 54, 63, 65, 66, 68, 69, 70, 71, 81, 95, 96, 100, 102, 108, 111, 211n78
Anglo-Russian Convention (1907), 12, 148
Arouzi, Alireza, x, 180, 183
Arouzi, Elahé, 180
Ashraf, Princess, 35, 219n41, 223n43
and the affair of the fur coat, 218n34
Asian Development Bank, 172
Avery, Peter, x, 147, 220n68
Azerbaijan, province of, 38, 55, 75, 76, 84, 104, 138
Azmoudeh, Dr Morteza, 83

Bader, Mahmoud, 81
Bakhtiari, Amir Hossein Ilkhan, 35
Bank of England, 50, 56, 62, 66, 73, 79, 80
Bank Markazi Iran (Central Bank), 180, 184–5, 223n55
Bank Melli Iran (National Bank)
 Ebtehaj at, 1, 4, 5, 27–8, 30–1, 34–49, 50–1, 53, 55, 57, 62, 66, 68, 71–2, 73, 77–84, 89–90, 94, 96, 99, 100, 102–6, 109, 142, 159, 191, 192, 194, 197
 foundation of, and initial scandals, 22–3, 32–4
 and Iranians' Bank, 176–7
 and Plan Organisation in the 1950s, 131, 143, 155
Bank Rahni Iran (State Mortgage Bank), 27, 31–2, 37, 38, 39, 40, 46, 105
Binger, Walter, 121–2, 213n34
Black, Eugene, x, 62, 84, 120, 121, 129, 130–1, 135, 165, 177, 178–9, 214n58
Bolton, George, 62
Bretton Woods Conference and Agreement (1944), 4, 44, 58–9, 61, 64
Britain, 14, 31, 51, 63–8, 93–4, 101, 103, 185
 Anglo-Iranian financial relations, 57, 63–5; Financial Agreement (1942), 47, 52–7, 63–4; Memorandum of Understanding (1947), 66–7, 68, 102 3
 British business interests in Iran, 12, 19–20, 23, 50, 66, 70, 101
 British imperialism in Iran, 1, 12, 16, 28–9, 47, 50, 52–5, 107, 148–9, 197
 British 'racism', 23 4, 72
 see also Foreign Office, British
Bullard, Sir Reader, 54, 55, 78
 'never liked Iran', 204n11

Canada, 32, 46
Casey, Richard, 55
CENTO (Central Treaty Organisation), 170
central banking, 32–3, 48, 72
Chase Manhattan Bank, The (Chase Bank before 1955), 106, 129, 177, 178–9
China, 11, 68, 88
CIA (Central Intelligence Agency) and its predecessor, Office of Strategic Services, 49, 107
Citibank (formerly First National City Bank), 179–80, 182–5, 222n38, 223n42
Clapp, Gordon, 135, 136–7, 163
clergy, Islamic (*mollas*), 2, 22, 46, 112, 168, 185, 191
Cobbold, C.F. (later, Lord), 62, 79–80
Cold War, 50, 80
Commonwealth Bank of Australia, 72
Commonwealth Development Corporation, 84

233

Constitutional Revolution (Iranian) 1905–09, 2, 3, 13
corruption, 1, 6, 7, 12, 23, 28, 33, 48, 96–7, 103, 117, 123, 124, 147, 150, 151, 158, 163, 169, 185, 194, 196, 198
Costanzo, Al, 179, 182–3
Cripps, Sir Stafford, 67, 79–80

D'Arcy, William Knox, 12, 19
Davar, Ali Akbar, 23, 27, 30, 34, 192
suicide of, 30
Dehlavi, Ismail, 78
Development and Resources Corporation (D & R), 131, 135, 137, 141, 142, 143, 151–2, 163, 165, 167
Development Plans
First (1949–55), 63, 81, 88, 91, 94, 96, 98–9, 100, 101, 103, 104, 111–13, 125, 193, 194, 195, 196
Second (1955–62), 111, 113, 118, 123, 124, 125–8, 130–3, 138, 143, 149, 163, 194, 195, 196, 213–14n47
Third (1962–67), 5, 123, 127, 128, 138, 142, 173
Fourth (1968–73), 5, 138
Dez Dam, 130–1, 133, 138
Dulles, Allen, 107
Dunn, G.F., 94
'Dunsterforce', 17
Dunsterville, Major General L.C., 16–17

Eady, Sir Wilfred, 67
Ebrahim, Ebtehaj ol-Molk (father of Ebtehaj), 11, 13, 14
influence on Ebtehaj, 24, 192
murdered, 18
Ebtehaj, Abol Hassan
career, childhood and early years, 11–18; service with Imperial Bank, 19–23; government service, 27–32; as Governor of Bank Melli, 32ff; benefits from patronage, 34, 192; opposes Millspaugh, 43–5; role in Anglo–Iranian Financial Agreement (1942), 53–7; attends Bretton Woods Conference, 58–61; challenges Imperial Bank of Iran, 70ff; dismissal from Bank Melli (1950), 80, 82–4, 104, 105, 109, 208n41; Ambassador to France, 105–6; at IMF, 106–8; appointed Head of Plan Organisation (1954), 110; service at Plan Organisation, 111ff; defies Prime Minister's tank, 118, 192; obtains non-specific

World Bank loan, 129; resignation (1959), 147, 156–7, 168, 197; delivers controversial San Francisco talk, 93, 159–62; gaoled by Shah's government, 7, 147, 162–7, 219n53; Americans ask him to become Prime Minister (1963), 169–70, 220–1n4; establishes a bank and insurance company, 159, 168, 176ff; surprised by Islamic Revolution, 185
character and beliefs, 192–3; conviction that he is always right, 82, 125, 193; ego, 45, 49, 150; honesty and incorruptibility, 1, 6, 28, 37, 38–9, 41–2, 44, 68, 117, 123–4, 147, 148, 166; impatience, 38, 51, 125; inability to compromise, 34–5, 140, 148, 219n43; lacks political ambitions and skills, 37, 49, 82, 117–18, 125, 140, 193; 'megalomaniac', 73, 79; nationalism, 4–5, 16, 20, 24, 43, 50, 81, 149, 191; 'one of the most intelligent people in Iran', 66–7; sense of urgency, 115, 116, 131, 194–5
family and personal life, 11, 13–16, 22, 180–1, 187, 223n43
policies, belief in economic growth, 6, 92–3, 97, 127–8, 160; 'foreign stooge', 4, 6, 141, 148–9, 150; opposes military spending, 154, 156–7, 161–2, 169–70, 172, 197–8; pioneers economic planning, 5, 87–91, 99–100, 194; planning beliefs and philosophy, 88, 92–3, 97, 156, 159, 191, 193–5, 208–9n14; proponent of multilateral aid, 107, 148, 159–62, 171; views on land reform and worker profit sharing, 173–5
relations with Mohammad Reza Shah, 35–7, 51, 80, 117–18, 119–20, 151, 153, 156–8, 159, 170–2, 175–6, 184, 186, 192–3
significance in Iranian history, 4–5; as Iran's first technocrat, 5, 28, 48, 148; possible alternative path, 198
Ebtehaj, Dr Azarnoosh, ix, 162, 165, 167, 180–1, 184, 185, 217–18n29, 218n34, 219n43, 222n26, 222n29, 223n43, 223n55
makes Ebtehaj's life in gaol bearable, 219n53
'shrewd, ambitious and beautiful',

INDEX

181
Ebtehaj, Davar, 181, 183
Ebtehaj, Gholam Hossein, 14–15, 17, 18
Ebtehaj, Maryam, see Nabavi, Maryam
Ebtehaj, Shahrsad, 180
Economist, The, 50, 165
Egypt, 11, 57, 58, 59, 88, 135
Eisenhower, President, 107
Eqbal, Dr Manouchehr, 120, 153, 155
Eshag, Dr Eprime, x, 41
Exchange Control Commission, 46, 67, 74
  see also Iran, exchange controls
Export–Import (EXIM) Bank, 119, 128, 215n61
Exter, John, 179

Farmanfarmaian, Dr Khodadad, ix, 92, 97, 115, 116, 118, 122, 128, 142, 153, 157, 192, 196
Farzin, Mohammad Ali, 31
Fateh, Mustapha, 24
Fatemeh Khanoum (mother of Ebtehaj), 11, 13, 18
Fathallah Akbar Khan, Sepahdar Azam, 13, 18
Financial Agreement, Anglo-Iranian, see Britain, Anglo Iranian financial relations
Firouz, Mozaffar, 35
Food and Agriculture Organisation (FAO), United Nations, 133, 135, 136
Ford Foundation, 122
Foreign Office, British, 5, 20, 22, 56, 65, 70, 76–7, 79
  see also Britain, imperialism in Iran
France, 14, 88, 105–6

Garner, Robert, 63, 101
George Fry and Associates, 175
Germany and Germans, 14–15, 16, 17, 29, 31, 33, 87
Gerschenkron, Alexander, 93
Ghods–Nakhai, Hossein, 170–1
Gibson, Dr Weldon, x, 165, 220n61
Gilan, province of, 13, 15, 16–17
Greece, 69
Gudarzi, Dr Manouchehr, 124, 142
Gulbenkian, Sarkis, 105

Harvard University
Harvard Advisory Group, 122, 143
Hammarskjöld, Dag, 166
Hedayat, Khosrow, 158, 217n12

Hoffman, Paul, 170
Hoveyda, Amir Abbas, 172, 178, 184, 222n35
Hull, Cordell, 61–2

Iliff, W.A.B., 54–6, 76
Imperial Bank of Iran (Imperial Bank of Persia until 1935, British Bank of Iran and the Midddle East 1949–52, British Bank of the Middle East since 1952)
  challenged by Ebtehaj after 1942, 6, 43, 48, 70–80, 82, 102–3
  Ebtehaj's employment with them, 11, 19, 22–5, 27–8, 30, 37
  origins and business, 19–20, 32–3, 53, 55, 191
India, 16, 59, 63, 88, 96, 136, 194, 195
Indo–European Telegraph Department, 19
Indo–European Telegraph Company, 19
Industrial and Mining Bank, 96, 103
Industrial and Mining Development Bank of Iran (IMDBI), 42, 140, 178
Industrial Credit Bank, 140, 179
International Bank for Reconstruction and Development, see World Bank
International Development Association, 107
International Development Society, 170–1
International Industrial Conference, San Francisco, 159–62, 169, 170
International Monetary Fund (IMF), 37, 59, 61, 62, 68, 79, 93, 98, 100–1, 106, 107, 108, 109, 120, 127, 135, 143, 144, 149, 162, 170, 171, 177, 179, 214n48
Iran
  alleged 'anti-planning' culture, 7, 142, 144, 193, 196
  currency, note issue and inflation, 46–8, 50, 51, 52–7, 63–4, 71, 74, 76, 80, 96, 102–3, 105
  economic, political and social conditions in, 1–4, 11, 28–9, 127, 168–9, 191, 194, 196–7, 214n48
  exchange controls, 46, 52, 53, 74, 77–8
  foreign exchange, 48, 52, 57, 64–5, 68, 71–2, 74, 75, 77, 79–80, 81, 103, 155, 194
  government a 'soggy mess', 97, 111, 194
  military expenditure, 153, 156, 157,

235

161, 169, 172–3, 191, 197, 220n3
  occupied by Allies (1941), 52–3, 74, 148, 194
  westernisation in, 2, 6, 22, 192, 195, 198, 199n14
Iran America International Insurance Company, 180–2, 185, 187
Iranians' Bank, 159, 165, 176, 177–9, 180–1, 182–4, 187, 219n43
Irano-Soviet Treaty (1921), 170
Iraq, 19, 59, 157
'Godless regime', 191
Islam, 2, 4, 181, 191
Islamic Revolution in Iran (1978–79), vii, 1, 2, 3, 6, 7, 8, 147, 148, 175, 182, 184, 185, 197

Jangalis, 16–18, 20
Japan, 1, 11, 12, 87, 98, 198

Karaj Dam, 118–9
Kayhan International, 166
Kennedy Administration, 165–6, 169, 174, 197, 220–1n4
Kennet, Lord, 73, 79
Keynes, John Maynard, 59, 61
Kheradjou, Abol Qassem, 42
Khomeini, Ayatollah Ruhollah, 168, 185, 198
  forced into exile, 218n36
  'in the pay of the British', 148
  similar character to Ebtehaj, 192
Khosrovi, General Amir, 31, 34
Khuzestan Development Services, 137
Khuzestan, province of
  regional development programme, 5, 123, 130–1, 133, 135, 136–8, 140, 141, 142, 143, 150, 151–2, 195
  sugar cane project, 133, 138, 151–2
Khuzestan Water and Power Authority (KWPA), 137
Kuchek Khan, Mirza, 16

land reform, 168, 173–5, 222n22
Lazard Frères, 135, 140
Lilienthal, David, 135, 136, 137, 150, 163
Lindenblatt, Dr Kurt, 33–4
Lippmann, Walter, 165
London School of Economics, 41
Loombe, Claude, 73, 79
Lotz, John, 98
Luce, Henry, 160, 165

McCloy, John J., 62, 129
McGhee, George, 165, 169

Majles, 13, 16, 29, 35, 42–5, 47, 54, 56, 76, 82, 92, 98, 99, 103, 104, 108, 113, 117, 118, 120, 121, 125, 126, 129, 130, 132, 152, 155, 156, 157, 163
Mason, Edward S., 122
Memorandum of Understanding, Anglo-Iranian, *see* Britain, Anglo-Iranian financial relations
Meyer, André, 140
Middle East (Cairo) Financial Conference (1944), 44, 45, 57, 59
Middle East Supply Centre, 57
military expenditure, *see* Iran, military expenditure
Millspaugh, Dr Arthur, 33, 37–8, 39, 42, 43–5, 57, 59, 61, 166
  accuses, and is accused by, Ebtehaj of being unbalanced, 45
  'in a mental hospital', 203n48
Mohammad Ali Shah Qajar, 11
Mohammad Reza Shah Pahlavi
  and Ebtehaj, 1, 7, 34–5, 37, 51, 75, 80, 82, 84, 105, 108–10, 117–21, 126, 130, 135–6, 140, 142, 147–8, 151–7, 158, 163, 167, 170–1, 175, 184, 192–3
  character, dictatorial, 4, 172, 191; drive for power, 158; 'inherent weakness', 185; megalomania, 193; mistresses, 155; paranoia, 172
  military aggrandisement, 92, 101–2, 153, 169, 172–3, 191, 197, 220n3
  policies, 1, 6, 29, 68; corruption, 7, 151, 197; divide and rule tactics, 158, 197–8, 218n36; excesses, 187, 198; grandiose and fatal ambitions, 127–8, 198; White Revolution, 168, 174
  relations with United States, 7, 61–2, 69, 84, 102, 108, 147, 149, 157, 159, 169, 197; restored to power with CIA help (1953), 107
mollas, see clergy, Islamic
Morrison Knudsen and Company Limited, 94–5, 98, 119
Mossadeq, Dr Mohammad, 3, 4, 48, 54, 68, 70, 104–8, 123, 148, 149, 153, 193, 194, 197
Moyne, Lord, 57
Mozaffar al-Din Shah Qajar, 11, 12
Murrow, Edward, 159, 165

Nabavi, Maryam, 22, 117–18, 180, 181
Nabavi, Taghi (Muazzez al-Dowleh), 22
Naficy, Dr Hassan Mosharef, 95–6, 98, 99, 100, 209n29
Naser al-Din Shah Qajar, 11, 12, 77, 87
Nasr, Dr Taghi, 83, 84, 207–8n40

INDEX

Nassiri, General, 182
National Iranian Oil Company (NIOC), 107, 108, 109, 178
New York Herald Tribune, 92
New York Times, 1, 165
New Zealand, 32
Nixon Administration
  uncritical support for the Shah, 197

oil, in Iran
  industry, 3, 12, 19, 50, 109, 130, 168
  nationalisation of, 67, 70, 80, 104–5, 108, 111, 193
  revenues from, 3–4, 7, 63, 64–5, 102, 109, 113, 122, 140, 180; at a standstill (1951–54), 104, 111, 128, 193; diverted to military spending, 159, 169, 172; main source of foreign exchange, 52; used by Ebtehaj for development, 116, 128, 131, 132, 143, 149, 151, 153, 156, 160, 191, 197–8
Ottoman Bank, 72
Ottoman Empire, *see* Turkey
Overseas Consultants Incorporated (OCI), 98–9, 103, 104, 107, 112

Pahlavi dynasty, 1, 4, 8, 22, 148, 198
  see also Mohammad Reza Shah *and* Reza Shah
Pahlavi Foundation, 169, 176, 181
Pakistan, 106
Payne, Leslie, 79
Plan Organisation, 1, 5, 6, 7, 28, 35, 42, 48, 92, 100, 147, 152–3, 155, 159, 163, 166, 168, 176
  after Ebtehaj, 150, 158, 173
  Ebtehaj's resignation from, 37, 147, 156–7, 168, 170, 176, 197
  Economic Bureau of, 116, 122, 123, 125, 130, 141
  independence of, 96–7, 99, 109–10, 113, 115–17, 126, 143–4, 154, 157–8, 193–4
  initial problems, 103–4, 111–14
  policies under Ebtehaj, 118–26, 128ff, 174–5, 191, 192, 194
  Technical Bureau of, 116, 120–2, 123
  see also Development plans
Point Four (United States Overseas Mission: USOM) programme, 112, 123, 136, 142
  'anti-Ebtehaj', 150
Prud'homme, Hector, 120–2, 137

Qajar dynasty, 11–13, 148

  see also Ahmad Shah, Mohammad Ali Shah, Mozaffar al-Din Shah *and* Naser al-Din Shah
Qavam, Ahmad, 32, 34–5, 39, 51, 90, 92, 94, 192

Radford, Admiral Arthur, 153–4, 157
Razavi, Hossein and Vakil, Firouz, 5
Razmara, General Haji Ali, 82–4, 103–5
regional development, *see* Khuzestan, regional development programme, *and* Seistan, regional development
Reuter, Baron Julius de, 12
Reza Shah Pahlavi, 1–5, 22–4, 27–35, 50, 52–3, 87–9, 191, 195
  abdication of, 29
  modernisation and industrialisation programme, 1, 2, 3, 22–3, 28–9, 30–1, 52, 87, 195
Rockefeller, David, 178
Roosevelt, Kermit, 107
Roosevelt, President, 59, 61, 62
Russia, *see* Soviet Union

Saed, Mohammad, 100
Samii, Mehdi, x, 41–2
SAVAK (Iranian state security), 168, 182, 219n43
Sepahdar Azam, *see* Fathallah Akbar Khan, Sepahdar Azam
Seistan, province of
  regional development, 138
Shiraz fertiliser plant, 154–5, 157, 158, 218n30
Siepmann, Henry, 73
social improvement programme (Second Plan), 131–2, 196
Soviet Union (Russia before 1917)
  banks in Iran, 20
  criticises Shah, 157
  Ebtehaj wants to involve in multilateral aid agency, 162
  economic planning in, 87–8, 96
  imperialism and political ambitions in Iran, 1, 12, 14–18, 29, 38, 50, 55, 75, 90, 92, 101, 148, 160, 170
  offers financial assistance to Iran (1950s), 129
Soviet-Iranian Financial Agreement (1943), 56
Stalin, Josef, 61, 87, 88
State Department, United States, 5, 7, 59, 61, 81, 102, 165, 169
  see also United States, foreign policy in Iran

Sterling Area, 52
Stevenson, Adlai, 165–6
Stone and Webster, 98–9

Tabatabai, Sayyed Zia al-Din, 35
Tehran Conference (1943), 61
Tehran Journal, 150
Teimurtash, Abdol Hossein, 23
  murdered by Reza Shah, 33
Tennessee Valley Authority (TVA), 135, 136, 137
Thornburg, Max W., 98, 104
Times, The, 50
tobacco protest, 12
Tripartite Treaty (1942), 90
Truman Administration, 112
  reluctance to aid Iranian 'rat–hole', 69
Tudeh Party, 41, 82, 106
Turkey (and Ottoman Empire), 14–15, 16, 17, 59, 69, 88, 96, 194

United States of America, 6, 8, 32, 57–9, 64, 98, 136, 140, 174, 192, 194
  and Ebtehaj, 5, 51–2, 102, 106, 147–9, 159, 165–6, 169–70, 187, 220–1n4; hostility towards in 1950s, 150, 157; role in dismissal from Bank Melli, 84, 197, 208n41
  attitude to Iranian military spending, 7–8, 152–3, 157, 166
  Development and Loan Fund (DLF), 129, 130, 140, 143
  economic and military aid to Iran, 102–3, 107, 112, 113, 122–3, 128–9, 148, 152, 161, 167
  foreign policy in Iran, 3, 7, 29, 61–2, 68–9, 81–2, 93–4, 101–2, 107, 147, 148–9, 157, 169, 177; 'could have prevented Islamic Revolution', 185; criticised by Ebtehaj, 7, 161–3, 172–3, 186; 'misguided and mischievous', 197

McCarthyism, 107
U.S.–Iranian Financial Agreement (1943), 56
UNFAO, *see* Food and Agriculture Organisation (FAO)
UNICEF, 138
UNO, Economic and Social Committee, 91
USOM, *see* Point Four

Walter, Vivian, 78–9
Washington Post, 165, 167
westernisation, *see* Iran, westernisation in
White, Harry Dexter, 59
White Revolution, 168, 173–5
  see also land reform, *and* worker participation in industry
women, liberation of in Iran, 22, 168
worker participation in industry, 173, 174–5
World Bank, 51–2, 62–3, 68, 84, 93–4, 96, 98, 106–7, 111, 115–16, 123, 128, 135, 140, 144, 148, 150, 153, 155, 162, 170–2, 177–8, 205n40
  established, 59
  Iran's large loan request in late 1940s turned down, 100–2
  non-specific loan to Iran 1957, 84, 122, 129–31, 152–3, 214n57
  recruiting agent for Plan Organisation, 120–2
World Wars
  First, 3, 14, 15, 16, 23, 70, 148
  Second, 3, 5, 29, 38, 45, 47, 52, 55, 58–9, 72, 74, 87, 102, 133, 148, 168

Yazdani, Hozhabr, 182–3
  indicted for grand larceny, 223n47

Zahedi, General Fazlollah, 108, 109–10, 117–18, 120
Zand, Ebrahim, 84